Language, Nation and Power

Language, Nation and Power

An Introduction

Robert McColl Millar
University of Aberdeen

First published in 2005 by
PALGRAVE MACMILLAN
Houndmills, Basingstoke, Hampshire RG21 6XS and
175 Fifth Avenue, New York, N.Y. 10010
Companies and representatives throughout the world.

PALGRAVE MACMILLAN is the global academic imprint of the Palgrave Macmillan division of St. Martin's Press, LLC and of Palgrave Macmillan Ltd. Macmillan® is a registered trademark in the United States, United Kingdom and other countries. Palgrave is a registered trademark in the European Union and other countries.

ISBN-13: 978–1–4039–3971–5   hardcover
ISBN-10: 1–4039–3971–3   hardcover
ISBN-13: 978–1–4039–3972–2   paperback
ISBN-10: 1–4039–3972–1   paperback

This book is printed on paper suitable for recycling and made from fully managed and sustained forest sources.

A catalogue record for this book is available from the British Library.

Library of Congress Cataloging-in-Publication Data

Millar, Robert McColl, 1966–
    Language, nation, and power : an introduction / Robert McColl Millar.
        p. cm.
    Includes bibliographical references and index.
    ISBN 1–4039–3971–3 (cloth) – ISBN 1–4039–3972–1 (pbk.)
        1. Language and languages – Political aspects. 2. Standard language.
    3. Language planning. 4. Nationalism. I. Title.

P119.3.M55 2005
306.44'9—dc22   2005043357

10 9 8 7 6 5 4 3 2 1
14 13 12 11 10 09 08 07 06 05

Printed and bound in Great Britain by
Antony Rowe Ltd, Chippenham and Eastbourne

Contents

List of Maps and Figures

Maps

Figures

Acknowledgements

This book would have been impossible without the help, support and encouragement of a great many people, some of whom inspired me without realizing. I want in particular to mention my colleagues at Aberdeen – Barbara Fennell, Carmen Llamas, Derrick McClure, Seumas Simpson and Dom Watt – for many interesting conversations on these and related topics. Other colleagues from elsewhere, most notably Steven Barbour and Jeremy Smith, have also helped me on my way. I am especially grateful to Sue Wright, whose comments on an earlier draft of this book were both generous and helpful. Many students have also helped me view the topics under discussion from different (national and personal) points of view, particularly Marjan Amini, Susana Calvo, Pilar Escobias, Isabel Fässler, Mari Imamura, Barbara Loester, Madelaine King, Sandra McRae, Sheena Middleton, Maria Perez, Iordana Tsiona and Jacqui Weeks. They might not all agree with everything which is said here, but my gratitude is great nonetheless.

My family have, as ever, provided me with much support, as well as a bidialectal (bilingual?) home to grow up in. My family-in-law have been endlessly hospitable, and have provided me with a model of how societal multilingualism works. Fernand and Josianne Wagner have given me much help with accessing central European materials. Finally, my beloved wife Sandra has put up with obsessive questioning about her linguistic behaviour and attitudes, let me bounce ideas off her at the most inopportune moments, helped me with translations and read a number of drafts of this work. This book is dedicated to her.

Preface

Language is arguably the most human attribute we possess. Without language we would be unable to transmit complex concepts and learned responses across time. Our knowledge and experience would die with us. The complexity of human society and its historical development would be impossible without this facility. With literacy, the ability to transmit ideas and experience across space and time is increased and enhanced. In the office where I am writing this, there are books published in a wide range of places about a considerable array of subjects. The oldest book I have in my possession was published well over 150 years ago. Although I know (or at least have met) a number of the authors represented on my shelves, I am unlikely ever to meet most of them. Yet in some strange way I am connected to them through my having read what they wrote.

Yet language also acts as a means of dividing us. We are all faced occasionally with a situation where we do not understand the language in which significant events are taking place. For most of us, this is deeply frustrating, perhaps even humiliating. Sometimes those who understand the other language may be using that language to cut us out of active participation; generally, however, thoughtlessness or genuine inability on both sides explains what is happening.

In a deeper sense, however, language can be used as a means of excluding people politically, economically or even historically. There are considerable inequalities between languages. At present, I, as a native speaker of English, will immediately have access to greater resources of knowledge, and, no matter how poor I might be, economic and political power, than will a speaker of a major African language such as Hausa. Speaking of the nineteenth century, Mugglestone (1995: 70) has observed that '[l]anguage is an instrument of communication as well as ex-communication'.

This book, *Language, Nation and Power*, explores the ways in which language divides and unites us. It examines the means by which language impinges upon our identity as individuals, as members of a particular ethnic or national group, and as citizens of a given polity. The historical and social perspective to the use of language is particularly emphasized, paying attention to the nature and process of language planning and standardization. Essentially, this can be analysed as the interface between society, culture, history and language.

The nine chapters which follow discuss a range of interlocking themes. The first discusses the ways in which different varieties of language may interact within a society, and what this might tell us about the society itself. After this the concepts of *nations* and *nationality* are introduced, paying particular attention to the means by which language is used in their construction. Chapter 3 analyses a number of different ways of categorizing language varieties. What do we actually mean by words such as *language* or *dialect*? Chapters 4–7 can be seen as a unit, interpreting the nature and processes of language standardization and planning. Chapters 4 and 5 discuss and exemplify standardization, whilst the different forms and experiences of language planning and language planners are presented in Chapters 6 and 7. Chapter 8 gives more in-depth analysis to a number of rather different situations where language has been used for the purposes of nation-building. In Chapter 9, future prospects for the relationship between language, nationality and power will be discussed and a recapitulation of the argument of the book is provided.

1
An Introduction: *Diglossia* and its Aftermath

1.1 Fergusonian *diglossia*

Switzerland is one of the most developed countries in the world, with an affluent and highly educated population, speaking a variety of languages. The largest linguistic community is made up of German speakers. As with many mountainous polities, German-speaking Switzerland is divided into a range of different dialect groups, none of which is at all close to standard High German.

If the Swiss dialects were part of the English (or French) language community, it is likely that these language varieties would be spoken in their most *dense* forms (McClure 1979) only among people who had had the least access to education and its concomitant social mobility, or at least associated themselves strongly with a specific place and its value-system. The German-speaking world has generally been tolerant of the use of dialect in a range of linguistic domains by people from a range of backgrounds, however. This is particularly the case in Switzerland, where the level of linguistic distance to and from the standard (perceived as external both to the local district and the country as a whole) is especially great. Almost everyone who comes from a particular valley will speak essentially the same dialect. There is little or no social obligation to use the external standard in everyday life. Indeed, use of the standard in certain circumstances might even be considered offensive. If you were having a meal with friends from your neighbourhood in a local restaurant, for instance, it would be considered strange if you chose not to speak the local dialect (Weber 1984).

But there are occasions where the use of dialect would not be acceptable. A politician from your district, who would normally use the dialect you speak in everyday conversation, would be far less likely to do so in the formal circumstances of the cantonal assembly or the national parliament. Most of your community would agree that this split is perfectly natural. Any attempt to alter these habits might be considered threatening and radical; it would certainly take a considerable effort on the part of the speech community (the linguistic community of which you consider yourself, and are considered, to form a part) to change the status quo.

Ferguson (1972 (1959)) defined such contexts as diglossia, suggesting that, on these occasions, a High variety (H) and a Low one (L) exist, 'with each having a definite role to play' (1972 (1959): 233). In his work, he distinguished this from both the alternate use of standard and dialect, and also from those situations where two separate languages were used 'each with a clearly defined role' (1972 (1959): 233).

As we will see, there are problems with both of these distinctions. In the first place, Ferguson's examples are largely those of a particular regional variety (in other words a dialect) with a diglossic relationship with a standard (whether local to that area or from elsewhere). He may have been thinking of the situation in parts of the English-speaking world, where, due to language attitudes, only some people are likely to speak the local dialect, rather than the near-universal use of two contrasted varieties he put forward. We will return to this point in our discussion of the views of Fishman.

Ferguson used the following situations to illustrate his views:

High	Low
Qur'anic Arabic	Vernacular Arabic
Katharevousa Greek	Dhimotiki Greek
Standard High German	Swiss German
Standard French	Haitian Creole

Some of the terms for language varieties used here are problematical. For instance, as we will see in Chapter 5, his distinction between *Katharevousa* and *Dhimotiki* as the High and Low varieties of Greek represents an elision, since the terms are normally associated with competing standard varieties, rather than mutually exclusive use by the same person of a High and a Low variety. Nevertheless, his definition of diglossia appears to hold water.

The first feature which he distinguished for diglossia was *function*. Either a High or Low variety is acceptable depending upon the purpose of the use of language, as illustrated in this table:

Situation	H	L
Sermon in church or mosque	X	
Instructions to servants, workmen, clerks		X
Personal Letter		X
Speech in parliament, political speech	X	
University lecture	X	
Conversation with family, friends, colleagues		X
News broadcasts	X	
Radio 'soap opera'		X
Newspaper editorial, news story, caption on picture	X	
Caption on political cartoon		X
Poetry	X	
Folk literature		X

The absolute nature of these distinctions is questionable. Some preachers, for instance, might use a 'folksy' tone in order to get their point across, employing the low variety to make them appear closer to the people. Poetry may not always be the sole concern of the High variety, as the work of poets of the calibre of Mistral (for Occitan), Hugh McDiarmid (for Scots) or Derek Walcott (for Caribbean patois) demonstrates. With each of these exceptions, however, there are pertinent reasons why these disparaged varieties are considered fit vehicles for the expression of 'high' ideas, mainly associated with the histories and cultures of the areas in question.

The second characteristic feature of diglossia is *prestige*. Fasold (1987: 36) suggests that '[h]igh regard for H and its appropriateness for elevated functions outranks intelligibility as a criterion for the choice of dialect in these situations'. Someone may have limited ability in H, but still regard it as a more fitting and prestigious variety. In Norway, when the language of scripture and liturgy moved away from Danish towards more Norwegian varieties in the course of the nineteenth and early twentieth centuries (as discussed in Chapter 7), many of the strongest protests came from people from the least Danicized areas, since, despite the problematical intelligibility of Danish, its prestige and appropriateness for such functions was unquestionable.

A central reason for this prestige is, in Ferguson's view, the possession of a *literary heritage*. Many language varieties may not have this. It is quite natural that speakers will take pride in the perceived antiquity of their language, even if they have never read any elements of the literary heritage themselves. The possession of a literary heritage can also be used by the educational system to reinforce ideas of appropriateness and prestige. Naturally, modern print technologies have meant that a standard variety of a language may be the only one reproduced over wide areas within a language community; it is certainly difficult to have 'high' literature published in any other variety. At least two of the 'exceptions' to these 'rules' on the use of High varieties for 'high' literature discussed earlier possess a considerable literary heritage themselves. More features associated with this apparent discrepancy will be discussed in Chapters 3 and 4.

The fourth feature of the diglossic relationship is the way someone acquires a particular variety. As a general rule, most people who live in a society, which has diglossia, learn L as a young child within their family. Conversely, H is generally acquired by 'artificial' means: native speakers learn the variety consciously, at school or in equivalent institutions, such as centres of religious teaching. Most people speak L; on the other hand, the 'artificial' nature of the learning of H may make an individual's command of that variety less than perfect, particularly when he or she has, through lack of formal education, little active experience with H, or L and H are particularly divergent from each other. Nevertheless, many speakers will believe that their perfect command of L in some way demonstrates the 'perfection' of H.

Part of this 'perfection' comes from the *standardized* nature of H, discussed in greater depth in Chapters 4 and 5. All languages vary across space. Thus, someone living five hundred years ago in northern England would have spoken a strikingly different dialect from someone from the south of England. Over time, however, certain varieties which form part of this *dialect continuum* assume prestige across wider expanses. More than one written form of a language might have existed; over time, only one remains. In general, it is treated as if it were the 'best', most 'perfect', variety. No matter how you speak, this will be the way you have been taught to read and write. It is also the only fully available means of communication outside your immediate area. All other varieties of the language are not regularized in this way: although you may speak a variety of this type more fluently, you will still consider this standardized variety to be superior.

Ferguson's fifth criterion is *stability*. As we have already seen, most members of diglossic communities tend to accept, mainly unconsciously, the status quo. Feelings of prestige for the High variety, and of homeliness for the Low, cannot be easily dismissed. Inevitably, there will be some 'seepage down' of usage from H to L; the opposite does occur, but is unusual. For instance, educated speakers of Arabic may well pepper their colloquial usage with turns of phrase which derive from the classical variant. In those contexts where H would generally be expected, low usages would usually be avoided as being inappropriate, perhaps even *wrong*.

Nevertheless, diglossia can collapse. For instance, in late antique Western Europe the diglossic relationship between Classical Latin and the various regional forms which would develop into the Romance languages broke down. The economic and political crisis and collapse which we term the 'decline and fall of the Roman Empire' was a central cause, evinced in a precipitate decline in levels of literacy. New forms of diglossia would eventually develop for the daughters of Latin; there would also be a vestigial diglossia between Romance and Latin fostered by the Church. Yet even under these circumstances, this would have been limited by low literacy as well as the Church's desire for comprehension.

Part of this difference can be seen in the different *grammar* to be found for H and L. For instance, standard High German employs four cases with nouns, pronouns and adjectives, as well as two simple indicative tenses with the verb; Swiss German employs three cases and one simple indicative tense. These differences – which tend to show H as being more grammatically complex than L – demonstrate that non-standardized varieties exhibit change more quickly than standardized, since they are not subject to the conservative power of print. Native speakers, however, despite regularly making grammatical errors with H, will still consider H more 'correct' than the 'corrupt' L.

Ferguson's final categories refer to the use of the *lexicon* and *phonology*. Although from basically the same origin, many High and Low varieties do not employ the same words for certain items. In Katharevousa Greek, *inos* means 'wine', while Dhimotiki uses *krasi*. In everyday language, *inos* is used when asking for wine from a waiter, or offering it to a guest, while *krasi* is what you drink. Greater politeness is necessary when wine is requested or offered than when it is made or consumed. The first word derives from the Hellenic past, while the other is contemporary.

In Swiss German, in relation to standard High German, there is also a range of lexical differences, some (such as the use of *Velo*, rather than *Fahrrad*, for 'bicycle') due to the influence of the other languages of Switzerland, others from local usages. As striking are the phonological differences. Many Swiss German speakers would, in those situations where the Low variety is most acceptable, use the pronunciation /xint/ whereas, in the High contexts, they would say /kint/ for High German

Kind, 'child'; again, High German *Zeit* 'time' would be pronounced as /tsait/ in High contexts, but as /tsi:t/ in Low. Of course, most Swiss German speakers speak with a Swiss accent, but this goes far beyond this. The same phonological system is employed in different patterns depending upon the context.

This is, of course, common for speakers of divergent dialects. I use two pronunciations for the English word *house*: /həus/ and /hus/. These are largely socially conditioned, since I would not often use the latter in formal contexts, whilst it would be more likely in situations where I feel comfortable. This is similar to diglossia – indeed Scots could in the past have been seen as being L to English H – but not entirely the same. Because of the influence English has exerted over Scots (of which more in Chapter 5), English variants will occur in informal situations; conversely, because Scots has a considerable literary heritage and is associated with my country and culture, I do use apparently Low variants in High contexts. Swiss German is different, since a near-absolute distinction is made between the use of the two phonological systems: this is the essence of diglossia.

1.2   Broad diglossia

One of Ferguson's central contentions was that diglossia could only truly be present in a situation where varieties of the same language were spoken. This view was challenged by Fishman (1967). Fasold (1987: 53) describes Fishman's view as an example of *broad diglossia*. While Fishman agrees with Ferguson's general points about diglossia, he claims that the phenomenon *can* exist not only where classical (or standardized) and vernacular varieties of the same language are spoken, but also that different languages can serve different purposes within the same community. He suggests a dynamic relationship for diglossia with bilingualism. Fasold suggests (1987: 41) how different types of language use of this type could be laid out schematically:

		Diglossia	
		+	–
Bilingualism	+	1. Both diglossia and bilingualism	2. Bilingualism without diglossia
	–	3. Diglossia without bilingualism	4. Neither diglossia nor bilingualism

The first division, those contexts where bilingualism and diglossia interact, can be illustrated, as Fasold does, by the linguistic situation in (urban) Paraguay, where every local would agree that the High variety is Spanish, associated with formal and elevated contexts, as well as with external communication. Almost everyone would have some command of this language. On the other hand, a local language, Guaraní, is a major symbol of national identity, no matter your origin. It is almost unthinkable for a Paraguayan not to be able to speak this language. Nevertheless, Guaraní does not have the social cachet of Spanish. In fact, it fulfils the roles suggested by Ferguson for the Low partner in diglossia.

The second division suggested is one where bilingualism is present but not diglossia. Many Aberdonians are of South Asian origin. Many will maintain a language associated with their ethnic origin. The relationship between this language and the local vernacular, along with Standard English, is not diglossic, however, since, in the larger society of Aberdeen, and also within the minority community itself, no associations based on the social appropriateness of a language variety can be made.

The third distinction is where diglossia, but not bilingualism, exists. This might appear nonsensical, since it is difficult to imagine how a polity with two or more speech communities with little or no knowledge of each other's languages could be effectively run. It is possible, however. In a traditional Agrarian Literate culture, as discussed in Chapter 2, where the ruling class considers itself to be separate in behaviour, culture and language from the majority of the population, there will be little attempt on their part to learn the language of the ruled. There would, of course, have to be professional interpreters, or even, as in imperial China, a mandarin class of scholar civil servants who interpreted (and enforced) imperial edicts, composed within a conservative literary tradition, to the great mass of peasants (Grieder 1981: chapter 1; Smith 1994: chapters 3 and 4; Hsü 2000: chapter 3).[1] Interestingly, this absolute distinction may be played out in views on prestige and appropriateness even by the ruled. Social rules may be so rigid that certain situations which demand the use of H would actually be barred to most inhabitants, as was the situation in pre-Revolutionary Russia, where the ruling classes were often native speakers of French or German (no matter their ethnic origin) with little ability in the native language of the polity (Fasold 1987: 41). The same situation was probably in England after the Norman Conquest of 1066; it is reminiscent of the linguistic ecologies of many colonial and post-colonial states.

Fishman's fourth category is where only one variety is present. Whether this is possible is questionable: it would demand a highly egalitarian society, along the lines of those suggested for rural Madagascar by Keenan and Ochs (Ochs 1973). Societies of this type would have to be both anarchist (in the sense of having no rulers, leaders or elite class), and be small-scale, to exist. Since most of us live in societies which are structurally complex and organized hierarchically, it is difficult to imagine such a situation ever becoming terribly widespread.

1.3   Is diglossia universal?

Are all situations where there is variation in language depending upon social situation inherently diglossic? Let us consider the English-speaking world. Certain forms of language *are* more prestigious in certain contexts than are others. To equate this with Ferguson's diglossia is questionable, however. There is too much inter-penetration of usage between different levels to speak in these terms. On the margins of the English-speaking world this may still be possible – it was the case in Scotland until recently. Elsewhere, literacy, and the subtle (and less than subtle) homogenization in language associated with acquiring literacy have made true diglossia a thing of the past, however. That does not mean that social roles and contexts are not represented by language; but the contextual variation, which almost all English speakers exhibit, is more a matter of the use of different registers rather than true diglossia. Other societies which have a long tradition of language standardization and elitism, coupled with mass literacy, such as the French-speaking world, will also have gone beyond diglossia (Schiffman 1996: chapter 4).

This leads us to a central theme of this book. The last two or three centuries have produced unprecedented change in the relationship between language use and the twin concepts of power and nation. Who controls and guides opinion and decision-making? What does citizenship mean in an increasingly globalized environment? Where does language fall in all of this: what are its functions; how is it changed by its associations? What are the effects of changes in language function and status for speakers of both prestigious and disparaged language varieties? It is to these topics that this book is dedicated.

2
Nation and Language

2.1 Introduction

Like many Scots, I find defining my nationality difficult. If I look at my passport, I see that I am a British subject, resident in the United Kingdom of Great Britain and Northern Ireland, part of the European Union. From a legal point of view, this is correct. Nowhere on my passport does it mention what I consider my nationality: Scottish. Whilst I am European, it is not an identity I think about regularly. Although I am not offended if someone calls me 'British', it is not a term I would use myself.

Matters are different for my parents. Although both of them are prickly in defending their Scottishness, they are much more comfortable in defining themselves as 'British'. This may be due to a sense of shared purpose during the War; partly what they learned in school about 'Britishness' and progressive imperialism; partially the mid-twentieth century left-wing distrust of 'nationalism', which in terms of the British Labour Party tended to see the standing political structure of a unitary state governed from Westminster as progressive and natural.

My experience is not unusual. This chapter will suggest that concepts of *nationality* and *nationalism* are variable, and that identity and loyalty can change over relatively brief periods. It is in the interest of a particular nationalism to portray the national and cultural identity it represents as unchanging. But much of what makes up national identity is a construct; as with many other political constructs, it can change and be reinterpreted.

I do not mean to imply that nationalism is not a potent force for good and ill, and that the loyalties people feel towards their nations are not intense. At the heart of nationalism, or, more correctly, a sense of large-scale group identity, are often shared historical, cultural and, most

9

importantly from our point of view, *linguistic* features. How this sense of *belonging* has been interpreted and employed has changed through history, however.

2.2   Interpretations of *nationality*

In 2002, the Queen's Golden Jubilee was celebrated. What I found interesting (and unsettling) was that a country which prides itself on its representative institutions deriving from the revolutionary seventeenth century, where individuals are referred to as *citizens*, suddenly reverted to one where 'subjects' gave 'loyal and humble addresses' to their 'sovereign lady'. A large part of this was show; yet it also demonstrated an often forgotten facet of the United Kingdom: constitutionally, the Queen is not merely head of state, but rather someone inherently different from all other inhabitants of the polity, as representative of a dynasty who, from time immemorial, have possessed the right to rule.[1]

In 2003, England won the Rugby World Cup. This achievement was greeted with delight in England. Celebration was rather more muted in other parts of the United Kingdom, however. Because England is the strongest nation, politically and demographically, within the union, the broadcast media were dominated by this news. Intriguingly, many English people found it difficult to distinguish between 'England' and 'Britain' under these circumstances. Many no doubt considered the terms synonyms (this is a commonplace both in England and outside the British Isles); others may have associated 'England' with right-wing extremism, preferring 'Britain' as more ideologically neutral. Many, I suspect, found using 'England' unambiguously empowering in their quest for national identity.

The conflict between these two experiences demonstrates the tension between national identity constructed from the political system under which we live, including who rules us, and the impression of shared culture and, to some extent, language.

Before the eighteenth century, most polities were united not through this shared connection, whether that be of culture, ethnicity or language, but rather through their rulers: the *dynastic* state. A striking example of this is the territories formerly ruled by the Habsburg family. Map 1 shows what was then the Austro-Hungarian Empire and the surrounding countries in 1911.

A great deal has changed in the last hundred years. Almost all of central Europe was included in one polity. This is jarring, since today a number of states are found in this area: Austria, the Czech Republic,

Map 1   Austro-Hungarian Empire – 1911

Slovakia, Hungary, Poland, the Ukraine, Romania, Italy, Slovenia, Croatia, Bosnia-Herzegovina and Serbia-Montenegro are all at least partly constructed upon the territory of this country. As well as the German-speakers, Czechs, Italians, Slovenes, Slovaks, Magyars, Poles, Croats, Serbs, Bosnian Moslems and Romanians, who make up the majority or dominant ethnic-linguistic communities in these polities, there are also communities which do not have (at least at present) national status: for instance the Hutzul in the Carpathian mountains, or the Roma and Sinti tribes which are found throughout the area. There is still a small minority of people of Jewish background living within this area; at the time this map represents, this population was considerably larger.

Significantly, these linguistic-cultural-ethnic groups were not confined to the states associated with them today. Most of the modern countries had German-speaking inhabitants – both recent settlers and long-term colonists; many had Polish or Hungarian speakers; Yiddish was spoken by minorities in most areas. Many cities shown on this map had more than one name. The city of Zagreb was known to many subjects of the Habsburgs as *Agram*. Bratislava, the present capital of Slovakia, was (and is) also *Preßburg* to German speakers and *Pozsony* to Magyar. Most poignant is the city called *Lemberg* on this map, which, between the World Wars, became the Polish city of *L'wow* and, in the post-War period, became the Soviet (later Ukrainian) city of *L'viv*. A flavour of this complexity can be found in Rindler Schjerve (2003).

How did such a multilingual and multi-ethnic country come into being? Largely due to the apparently bottomless hunger for position and land, more often acquired through marriage than by warfare, of the Habsburg family (Wheatcroft 1995a). The state only existed because a single family dominated. It could continue to exist only by discouraging the development of national sentiment among the subject peoples. This became increasingly difficult as nationalism came to be the norm, and power was increasingly seen as deriving from the will of the people. By 1918 it had become impossible.

2.3 The concept of nation in history

It is very human to believe that your family, or ethnic group, is in some way more venerable than other such groups. Most nationalist movements assume that their nation is ancient. For instance, the generally accepted national anthem of Scotland refers to the Battle of Bannockburn (1314) as the defining moment of our nationhood; similar claims are made in the national anthem of Slovakia, among others. In combative forms of nationalism (there are few nationalisms which have not gone through such a stage), this antiquity is often contrasted with the 'newness' of neighbouring states. For instance, German nationalist (and, in particular, Nazi) ideology held, as discussed by, among others, Oergel (1998) and Lambert (1998) that their Slav neighbours had no 'civilization', no 'culture', before the 'civilizing mission' of the Germans in the Baltic region in the medieval period. As with many forms of ethnocentrism, such views were used to explain and excuse the inequalities of power and wealth experienced in those areas of central Europe dominated by German speakers.

For states which cannot claim an ancient origin, an important episode in the past takes on a unifying function. For instance, in the United States of America, Thanksgiving, and the lyrics to 'The Star Spangled Banner', highlights the view of the nation as a place of special providence, of a coming out from some kind of 'bondage' into a new dispensation forged by sacrifice, a point to which we will return in Chapter 8.

A new beginning for a country with venerable roots can also be fore-grounded. For instance, the French national anthem refers to the formation of the revolutionary French nation and army during the defence of the new republic from its reactionary internal and external enemies. It is interesting to note, however, that 'La Marseillaise' actually includes lyrics which could be interpreted as harking back to a golden age for the nation before the advent of a 'foreign'/ barbarian ruling class:

> Aux armes citoyens!
> Formez vos bataillons,
> Marchons, marchons!
> Qu'un sang impur
> Abreuve nos sillons.

> To arms, citizens!
> Form up your battalions:
> let us march, let us march!
> that their impure
> blood should water our fields.

Naturally, the notion of 'belonging' (or *not* belonging, for that matter) is ancient; it is an innate element in any human's identity. But the idea that, prior to the modern age, this belonging was associated with a particular political (rather than cultural) unit is dubious. For instance, a bound peasant of 850 CE, living in Essex, would have been unlikely to define himself as 'English', or even 'East Saxon'. He would probably have defined himself in terms of his relationships: to superiors, whether civil or ecclesiastic; to his family; to the manor where he lived – most importantly, as a Christian. To have a concept of nationality, there must either have been a defining event in a country's history (for instance, the Hussite revolution in what is now the Czech Republic, or the resistance against China in Vietnam), or of a shared, and literate, sense of citizenship.

Greenfield (1992: 9–15) proposes a taxonomy of how the concept of *nation* developed, suggesting that its original Roman definition of 'foreign nation' gradually began to assume the idea of an elite in the Middle Ages, whether this be due to intellectual prowess or the right of property and descent. Thus, well into the modern period, the Polish and Hungarian nations, for instance, defined themselves in terms of their membership of the noble estate, rather than their ability to speak either Polish or Magyar. Indeed, most Polish or Magyar speakers would not have been considered members of their 'nation'.

We can therefore argue that, until the early modern period, the *nation* was only seen as part, sometimes even a small part, of the population of a state. Why is it then that, by the nineteenth century, the inhabitants of most states which followed the European model would have considered at least the dominant ethnic group, and possibly the whole population, as citizens of a nation?

Anderson (1991) suggested that modern nations are 'imagined communities'. In order to function, there must be an awareness from all those who consider themselves to be members of that community that they share much in common with people whom they have never met (or are ever likely to meet). This consciousness (which Anderson would equate with nationalism) is extremely potent: something for which people die.

Anderson explains this 'imagining' of a community as being part of the ongoing secularization of the western world. Whereas, as we have seen, Europeans of the middle ages defined themselves largely by their adherence to a particular religious tradition (this, as we will see in Chapter 7, persisted in the Ottoman Empire), the unity of Christendom was rocked in the sixteenth and seventeenth centuries by religious dissent and the challenge by new sciences to a fundamental view of the faith. Simultaneously, print capitalism, the ability to mass-produce ideas and concepts, along with increasing literacy, began to induce a world view which replaced religious loyalties. This was connected both to the rise of the middle classes as an economic and political force and the decline of Latin as the lingua franca of European culture. As Anderson points out, the ability to read a newspaper article dealing with events somewhere else within the polity in which you lived (or outside) developed the awareness of shared experience and identity.

At the same time, the revolutionary developments of the late eighteenth century, most notably in France and the United States, led both to the concept of the nation as a revolutionary instrument and also to a means by which the existing powers attempted to shore up their rule by 'playing the patriotic card' – particularly prevalent in autocracies such as Tsarist Russia, as we will see in Chapter 8. But the latter viewpoint attacked the foundations of the dynastic state: the idea that someone had the right to rule a territory because of who his ancestors were. Anderson (1991: 85) gives an apposite example of this. The Hohenzollern family possessed Prussia because of their position as landholders. They ruled over people who spoke a variety of German dialects and also others who spoke Slavonic or Baltic dialects. Some of their subjects were Protestants; others were Catholics; not an insubstantial number were Jews. To a king such as Frederick the Great (1740–1786), the primary concern was to maintain and expand his rule. Frederick himself would probably not have considered himself a German – he was Prussia. Indeed, his spoken and written German was rusty; he preferred the use of French in practically all contexts. His collateral descendant in the position of King of Prussia, Kaiser Wilhelm II (1859–1941; reigned as Emperor and King, 1888–1918) considered himself to be 'No. 1 German': his position as Emperor had been assigned to him because he represented the nation. But, if the nation considered him to be unworthy, he could be removed: something which would have been unthinkable for a dynast.

Essential to this change is the fact that, as the nineteenth century advanced, more countries in western Europe and the Americas had, at least, representative governments, and possibly even democracy (if only for white males). Whilst democratic governments can often be as doctrinaire in their view of the language use of their citizens as authoritarian, the idea that *all* matters can be debated by *all* the people's representatives means that, at least theoretically, the rights of both majority and minorities within the national community have to be respected. Even if the late nineteenth century represents the apogee of the spread of liberal nationalism and middle class representative government, the more authoritarian regimes which began to spread in the early twentieth century, with a few partial exceptions, such as the Horthý 'regency' in Hungary, paid at least lip service to the idea that they represented 'the people'.

Gellner (1983) derives many of the same conclusions from slightly different precepts. The development of free market capitalism in the course of the eighteenth century led to greater opportunity to move within the social system than had been the case in the previous Agrarian Literate social system. Instead of the 'horizontal integration' of social estates (like the Hungarian nation already discussed), there would be 'vertical integration', where a member of the nobility (while that estate endured) would have had more in common with a peasant from his own community than with a member of the same estate from another polity.

No matter its source, however, nationalism became the presiding ideology of the nineteenth century. Its repercussions have continued to the present day. Its presence as an abiding feature in people's lives is one of the givens of this book. Yet its results are by no means straightforward. How do we define ourselves as a nation? What makes us unique in ourselves, and different from other peoples or nations?

On a number of occasions, what *nationality* meant became highly controversial.[2] For instance, a 'thorn in the side' for the Habsburg monarchy in the nineteenth century was the growing self-confidence of nationalists within the Kingdom of Hungary, as shown on Map 1. In 1848, Hungary constituted itself as a truly separate state with, at most, vestigial connections to the Habsburg centre. If Hungary had been, as it is today, an overwhelmingly Magyar ethnic state, this would not have been problematical. At the time, however, Hungary included within its borders large parts of what are now Croatia, Serbia, Romania and Slovakia, as well as the present Austrian province of Burgenland. Within these boundaries there were large numbers of speakers of Serbo-Croat, Romanian, Slovak and German. In many places, these linguistic minorities were in the majority, although there were always significant minorities of ethnic Magyars, often within the socially powerful classes.

The Hungarian ruling class (which derived from a variety of different ethnic sources), had assumed a Magyar identity in the name of the people of the whole of the crown lands of St. Stephen (in other words, Hungary in terms of conquest and possession rather than ethnicity). As reaction triumphed, these Magyar patriots were genuinely surprised that their fellow 'Hungarians' should have allied themselves with the conquering Austrian and Russian allies in the face of what, to the minorities, would have seemed enforced Magyarization.

This suppression of Magyar nationalism was only temporary, however. In the aftermath of its defeat at Sadowa in 1866, the Habsburg monarchy had to accept a compromise whereby Hungary became self-governing, connected to Vienna only in foreign and military matters. In theory, Hungary became a rather elitist democracy along the lines of Britain or the United States at the time, although its nationalist policies became increasingly rightist from the 1890s on (Kovács 1994). In effect, however (with the partial exception of Croatia) one of the nationalities of the kingdom, barely in a majority, was set up defining itself as the nation, culturally and linguistically.

The literature on this matter is fraught with problems. Even now, when nearly a century has elapsed since the collapse of the kingdom, with its replacement by 'national' states, what happened before 1919 is hotly disputed. I have on my desk a number of books published by a group named Romanian Historical Studies which, if taken as sole witness, would create a very dark portrait of Hungarian tyranny, as titles such as *Hungary's Struggle to Annihilate its National Minorities* (Pâclişanu 1985 (1941)) suggest. Beside them is another book, published by a Hungarian exile group, which sets out to debunk the 'Daco-Roman myth' of Transylvania (Du Nay *et al.* 1997). Ideological considerations notwithstanding, the situation was unpleasant enough for minorities. Due to problems with the national minorities, in particular the Romanians in

Transylvania, the central Hungarian authorities had made their position plain by the 1890s: in what was the mainstream nationalist ideology of the time, there was only one nation in Hungary – the Magyar nation. This did not mean that other cultural and linguistic groupings were ignored. The assumption was that these groupings were an intrinsic part of the Magyar nation. There was no such thing as a Romanian in Hungary; rather Hungary contained members of the Magyar nation who at present spoke Romanian. Any suggestion that this difference extended beyond this was, at times, vigorously suppressed by the authorities.

Even at its most reactionary, other languages were not illegal in Hungary; but their presence and influence was constitutionally circumscribed. Almost all teaching in state schools was in Magyar (and dealt with a curriculum which viewed the history of the region from a purely Magyar perspective); any use of the local language was permitted merely as part of a transition process to the 'national' language and culture. In the bureaucracy, supplicants were permitted to use their language; there was no guarantee that a speaker of that language would be available, however. Above the most menial level, all state employees had to have native command of Magyar; there was no obligation (save for those taking part in military service in the combined Habsburg armed forces, where German was the vehicular language) to know or learn any other language but Magyar. Since Magyar is not Indo-European, while the minority languages are, the barriers to learning were, in any event, considerable on both sides. Many members of these minorities *did* learn Magyar; most became part of an underclass, excluded from the decision-making process by their culture and language, however. Naturally, the evolving educated middle classes of these minorities would have baulked at this overt discrimination, particularly since, by the end of the nineteenth century, a number of these communities, most notably the Romanian, had national 'homelands' outside the Hungarian realm.

The problem with this situation and many others, first in Europe and then the world, was that many of the ideas on nationhood, and its equation with language and ethnicity, were developed before, during and, especially, immediately after the Napoleonic Wars in a Germany beginning to unite in defiance of a common enemy. Writers such as Fichte and Herder considered the German nation to be German because of its German language and culture. Despite their occasional claims for exclusivity, this concept could be extended to other nations. But whilst Germany is quite homogenous linguistically (if not culturally), this is difficult to apply elsewhere.

Moreover, the idea of membership of a nation was not, and is not, as universal as these Germans thought. Even if Germany had suffered centuries of weakness and disunity, there was still a latent sense of nationhood. This could not be said for many ethnic groups. In the aftermath of the revolutions of 1848, Engels suggested a distinction between *historic* and *non-historic* nations. The former possessed a 'national' history based on common membership of a polity, shared cultural values, as well as a (written) language; the latter had few (or none) of these advantages. Although, as discussed by Bauer (1924), Engels intended the distinction to be pejorative, the former *did* have distinct advantages over the latter in their chances of achieving and maintaining autonomy.

A case in point is Slovakia. Before 1918–1919, no country of that name had ever existed. After the Magyar invasions of the eighth to ninth centuries, the west Slav population east of the River Morava and the Little Carpathians became a peasantry, exploited by the Hungarian noble nation, some of whom were ethnic 'Slovaks'. Although there were stirrings of nationalist feeling in the nineteenth century, 'Upper Hungary' remained an integral part of that nation, with a mixed population. The Slovak element of the new Czechoslovakia was therefore at a disadvantage in comparison to their partners from the historic Czech nation. The rapid assumption of 'ancient' Slovak symbols and traditions, as well as the twentieth century tension between the two nations, should be interpreted in light of this. A significant element in this expression of nationhood is the codified and standardized form of the Slovak language which, from the nineteenth century on, has been engineered to be as little like Czech as possible.

Language can be used as a means of uniting people within a nation, therefore, but can also cause problems when a variety of populations, speaking different languages, and (probably) possessing different cultures, are included within a single polity. In an absolutist, horizontally ordered system, where religion is seen as a key element in identity, it is possible to ignore the languages of the people, because the people are not involved in government. This is not true in modern nations because, no matter how tyrannical or unrepresentative a regime might be, it would claim that it rules by the will of 'the people' (however defined). What language(s) the people speak matters.

2.4   Societal multilingualism

It is a rare country indeed where only varieties of one language are spoken. Even when a territory is ethnically homogenous, as in the case of Iceland, historical developments have led to contact between Icelandic speakers and speakers of other languages (particularly Danish and English) within the national territory. Most nations will contain smaller or larger ethnic groups, some of which are *autochthonous*, having lived in that territory for a considerable period, while other groups may have migrated into the territory rather more recently.

But it often actually suits a nation-state to ignore its multilingualism, for economic, social or, regularly, political and ideological reasons. It is easier (and cheaper) to teach (and govern) a population in one language. One language may be of higher prestige than any other spoken in that territory, so that a hegemonic assumption of superiority might be made. Since at least the French Revolution, there have been times on all continents (although the view is particularly prevalent in Europe) when the general view in a country was that a 'true patriot' should speak the *national* language; suspicion falls on those who spoke both this language and another, or spoke different languages altogether. Yet it should be stressed that societal multilingualism is the norm – monolingualism is unusual.

Individual members of any society need not be multilingual, naturally. It would be a mistake, however, to consider monolingualism as the norm at an individual level. For instance, reports from Laos suggest that the national language, Lao (itself arguably a form of Thai), is known widely among people who speak aboriginal mountain languages; there is also some multilingualism among speakers of Lao (and other Tai) dialects, although, given the power differences that exist between the different communities, this multilingualism is not so prevalent (Izikowitz 1969).

In the following sections we will consider reasons why states may become multilingual, as well as discussing those occasions – increasingly common in Europe in particular – where non-hegemonic autochthonous (native to a territory for a considerable period) languages, in particular, have ceased being spoken, thus making a nation move towards monolingualism.

2.4.1   Reasons for societal multilingualism

In his excellent, although now somewhat dated, *The Sociolinguistics of Society* (1987), Fasold puts forward four reasons for societal multilingualism:

2.4.1.1   *Migration*

Fasold (1987: 9–10) in the main concentrates on recent migration. Almost any city (or, indeed, town) in the 'developed' world is likely to have communities of speakers of languages other than the autochthonous ones. For instance, Aberdeen has noticeable minorities from a variety of different linguistic backgrounds, particularly south and east Asia.

Nevertheless, immigration of this type is not at all exceptional; in any historical era it has been a common human trait to migrate, for a variety of reasons. As Bartlett (1993) points out, the eastern parts of present and pre-1919 Germany serve as an example of this. East of the River Elbe, almost all old settlements have Slavonic or Baltic names, the language of the majority when literacy first began to spread in the area. This is not the place to trace the history of the medieval German *Drang nach Osten*, 'push to the east', a combination of crusade and trading venture; nonetheless, it was a form of migration. German speakers *did* move into the area. It is more difficult to trace the extent to which these immigrants were the ancestors of later German speakers. It would be rather unlikely if this were always the case. Rather than speaking of a critical mass of immigrants overwhelming the locals physically, it is better to think of the process as a combination of numbers and technological attractiveness, if not superiority. Where you had the latter, but not the former, eventually the balance of linguistic power would shift to the local language; elsewhere, where both influences were present, as established for Wrocław/ Breslau by Davies and Moorhouse (2002), the balance of power shifted in favour of German. Yet the multilingual nature of these territories remained a reality until the modern era; indeed, in provinces such as Silesia and West and East Prussia, the official use of German in the Prussian, and then German, state masked the presence of a large and often aggrieved minority of speakers of another language (and often of a different religious confession).

Multilingualism due to migration may only attain permanence when migration is both major in terms of numbers of speakers, and the migrants are of considerable prestige. Recently, a combination of these features has caused considerable problems between speakers of south Asian languages and natives in Fiji, as discussed by Mamak (1978). In the Baltic republics, native speakers of Russian are (in the view of the locals) dangerously close to numerical dominance (Smith 1994). A further reason for the survival of an immigrant language is ghettoization, whether this be self-ghettoization, as seen in the survival of Yiddish among some ultra-Orthodox Jews in New York City, or one engineered by outside forces, as seen among speakers of the same language in Tsarist Russia.

2.4.1.2 Imperialism

The presence of speakers of European languages on all continents can be associated almost completely with imperialism, or at least – as has been the case with the influence of American English – profound cultural and economic influence. Even where territorial or economic conquest has not been the expressed aim, as in the activities of missionaries, there has often been a transfer of language use associated with the transfer of value systems. In some places, such as Australia, this has led to a near-monolingual situation (at least until the arrival of non-Anglophone immigrants); in some places, such as South Africa, it led to conflict between two imperialist languages (Dutch and English);[3] in the majority of situations, however, the long-term effect of imperialism was the presence of an alien language of high prestige as the language of an elite. In the Philippines, a creole elite has ruled since imperial times, using first Spanish and then English, over the majority, who can speak neither (Anderson 1991, 1998). When a newly liberated country attempts to use a language other than that of the imperialists, it faces an uphill struggle. In some places, such as Tanzania (as discussed in Chapter 8), this was mainly successful; in others, such as India, it was largely not. In the case of India or Nigeria, this failure can be ascribed to the presence of many different (and populous) language communities within the same area, and, as suggested by Schiffman (1996), entrenched views on language use.

2.4.1.3 Federation

With federation, those areas where a single linguistic group dominates (or has dominated in the past) should be distinguished from those where a genuine federation has been accomplished through the conglomeration of previously existing polities. Examples of the former include the United States of America (initially dominated by English speakers) and Brazil (initially conquered by the Portuguese). These rarely bring about long-term linguistic pluralism.

The second category can be illustrated by Switzerland or Canada. In these countries, sizeable populations, speaking different languages, chose to federate. It will be interesting to see whether evolving federations, such as the European Union, will develop towards a multilingual society, or whether a small multilingual elite will translate between largely monolingual populations.

A third category might also be suggested – 'marriages of convenience', the most obvious examples of which being Belgium and, for some 75 years, Czechoslovakia (although the latter was even more problematical, since the dominant languages were close relatives of each other), as well as Nigeria. The social and political problems caused by multilingualism are most visible in federations of this type.

2.4.1.4   *Border areas*

Fasold (1987: 12) amply illustrates this category by his discussion of the south-western regions of the United States. Elsewhere, an interesting example can be found in the county of Cerdanya/Cerdaña/Cerdagne in the Pyrenees, where the Spanish (Catalonian)/French frontier cuts through a previously monolingual Catalan valley. The linguistic fall-out of the two states/three languages reality of the last three hundred years has led to strikingly different situations north and south of the political border (Sahlins 1989). In contemporary Europe in particular it is unusual for this multilingual border identity to be represented officially, exceptions being Luxembourg, and some of the German-speaking areas of Belgium.

2.4.2   Societal monolingualism

If multilingualism is the norm, how can a polity be largely (if not completely) monolingual? If we move beyond those nations which were founded on previously almost or completely uninhabited islands – some of the Polynesian islands – the answer must be: through conscious human intervention.

2.4.2.1   *By shifting frontiers and 'ethnic cleansing'*[4]

The early kingdom of Poland was a fairly loose conglomeration of western Slav tribes centred on the Vistula valley. Other peoples may have been in the area: certainly, Germanic tribes had passed through this part of central Europe. Various Aryan and Turkic tribes were also present. As the medieval kingdom developed, it acquired peoples from a variety of ethnic and linguistic sources. From the west and south came German-, Czech- and Magyar-speakers. As we have seen, some of the western areas of the kingdom became so dominated by German-speakers that they ceased to be 'Polish' in any meaningful sense. The kingdom spread east into the debateable lands where an Orthodox east Slav agglomeration had previously flourished. In the aftermath of the Mongol invasions, and union between the Poland and Lithuania from 1396 on, the *Rzeczpospolita's* boundaries reached almost to the Black Sea. Within its borders would have been, in the seventeenth century, Catholic Polish, Czech, Lithuanian, German and Magyar speakers, Protestant German, Magyar (and a few Polish) speakers, Orthodox east Slavs and Romanian speakers, Yiddish-speaking Jews, Turkic-speaking Karaim (a heterodox Jewish sect) and Moslems of Turkic language. Within this conglomeration, religion counted more than language or ethnicity in determining identity. Thus, Catholic peasants living beside Orthodox peasants,

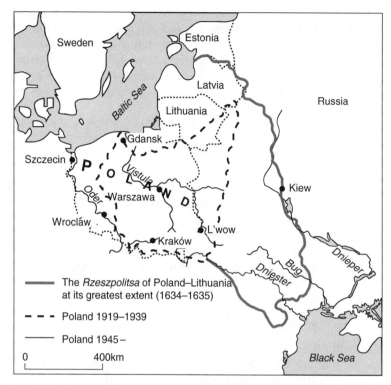

Map 2 The historical borders of Poland

speaking essentially the same dialect, would have considered themselves to be speaking 'Polish', while the latter would not. Throughout the Commonwealth, the nobility (and later the urban bourgeoisie) would have spoken Polish, and identified themselves as Poles.

Something of this multiethnic and multilingual identity survived the eclipse of Polish power during the eighteenth century, culminating in the disappearance of the country as an entity in 1795. In those areas of historical Poland which were dominated by Tsarist Russia, Poles maintained their privileged position in a multilingual community. In the Poland which was re-established after the First World War, Poles made up the majority of urban inhabitants and the landowners, while the peasantry was largely east Slav and Orthodox in the east of the country. In the west, there was a significant German-speaking minority. Throughout the country there were Jewish speakers of Yiddish, Polish and other languages. Polish speakers made up a bare majority.

The after-effects of the Second World War – the wholescale slaughter of European Jewry, a mass movement of Poles from what had become Soviet Ukraine and Belorussia, and a concomitant movement of German-speakers from the lands east of the River Odra – led to the foundation after 1945 of a Polish state which was both highly homogenous in language and ethnicity, and also situated within similar frontiers to the original Polish land.

Although this is a particularly extreme example of historical processes of ethnic and linguistic heterogenization and homogenization at work, the developments involved are not unusual. In both the recent and more distant past, a number of polities have attempted to change frontiers (or had their frontiers changed) to make their populations as homogenous as possible; some have moved beyond expulsion and mass conversion towards attempts at genocide of one kind or another. Beyond the Nazi example, the modern era has witnessed the 'ethnic cleansing' of large parts of both the Balkans and Anatolia. The 'patchwork quilt' of ethnicities and languages which made up the Ottoman Empire has been replaced by states where linguistic and cultural conformity is to a greater or lesser extent enforced.

2.4.2.2 By official egalitarian policy

As we will discuss in Chapter 5, in the late middle ages France was a dynastic state which united a range of territories of different laws and languages together under the rule of one person. In the north of France, *Francien*, the dialect of the Ile-de-France, did have a certain cachet, but other dialects also had written forms alongside their spoken forms. The King of France and Navarre also had subjects who spoke other Romance languages, such as Occitan and Gascon, Germanic languages, such as German and Dutch, as well as Breton and Basque. Conversely, many French speakers did not live in France. This is very different from the contemporary situation. All of these other languages continue to be spoken in France (although few are healthy), along with languages such as Corsican and Catalan, whose speakers were added during the expansion of the country in the seventeenth and eighteenth centuries, and speakers of many languages from the present, and former, French Empire. Until very recently, however, these languages' public presence was highly limited. France is a highly centralized state where possession of, and ability in, the 'correct' form of French is considered to be the chief marker of 'Frenchness'. Even those who are bidialectal, or bilingual, are considered to be in some way *unrepublican* by many of their fellow citizens.

France is perhaps an extreme case of this tendency; particularly striking given the country's democratic heritage. Yet similar tendencies are by no means uncommon; especially since France has proved such a blueprint for societal change since the Revolution. There are very few countries where members of the intelligentsia have not claimed that the nationwide use of a single variety (never mind language) would be egalitarian. For instance, the early twentieth-century Marxist Gramsci (Crowley 1996: 42–3) argued for the enforcement of a prescriptive form of 'Italian'. He believed that the plethora of dialects in Italy aided forces who wished to discourage solidarity between workers from different geographical backgrounds. Many intellectuals would claim that removing the ability to critique someone's language use from a sociolinguistic perspective would render a society ethnicity blind.

The problem with such a view, however, is that it ignores the question of *whose* language variety should be employed as the chosen marker of social egalitarianism. Given the nature of standardization, as we will see in Chapters 4 and 5, it is very unusual for this variety to be anything other than the language of the ruling class. Therefore, for many, the retention of local varieties and languages may well be seen as egalitarian in comparison to the hegemonic forces promoting uniformity in *their* linguistic image.

2.4.2.3 By 'benevolent neglect'

The United Kingdom has never had an official language policy (with the exception of action against Welsh in Wales since it was officially united with England in 1536); nor does the state as a whole have an official language. The country may never have needed to make declarations of this type, since Standard English has been dominant for so long. Since the late middle ages, the other languages of the British Isles have all been in retreat in the face of Standard English.

But although there have been attempts on occasion actually to attack the use of these languages, largely from an elitist point of view, points to which we will return on a number of occasions in this book, the decline of languages other than English has been most precipitate when there has been least aggression towards them.

As we will see in Chapter 5, from the early modern period on, much of the educational, ecclesiastical and, to some extent, governmental establishment in what became the United Kingdom has generally believed that the territory in question would be better served by the universal use of Standard English (often with a particular accent). Unlike France, however, this belief was never put fully into practice, again with the exception of Welsh in Wales. Certainly, those who spoke a Celtic language were placed at a considerable disadvantage within the English-speaking state, unless they had native skills in English; doubtless, on occasion, children were punished at school for speaking their native language. By the same token, varieties of English and Scots which did not conform to the received idea of progress were also stigmatized. But it would normally be impossible to talk in terms of active persecution of minority language use.

In fact, the chief enemies of the lesser-used languages were economic forces, rather than political or philosophical ideology (with the possible exception of the *improvement* movement of the late eighteenth century (Millar 2003)). Because of earlier developments, the areas where the Celtic languages were spoken became peripheral. For many who lived in these areas, the only hope of 'getting on' was to conform to the language and mores of the majority culture. This culture did not so much enforce this adherence as expect it as its due.

Similar tendencies can be seen in a number of different territories in the recent past. The languages of immigrants to the United States, for instance, have rarely been actively attacked by the English-speaking establishment as languages, with the exception of those, such as German during and after the First World War and Japanese during the Second World War (and, perhaps, in the present day, Arabic) which were seen as the language of enemies. Yet economic forces, and the expectation and desire to conform to the norms of this new society, have acted against these languages and their transfer to new generations, a point to which we will return in Chapter 8. Here, as in the case of France, civic nationalism leads to monolingualism.

2.4.2.4   By catastrophe, whether engineered or natural

The situation has been much worse for speakers of native languages of the Americas. While immigrants could look extraterritorially towards speakers of their language, this was not the case for the natives of the area which became the United States. A combination of 'crossing over' to the hegemonic culture for personal gain (or sometimes through hopelessness), catastrophic illness and the loss of native species, demoralization, forced migration and the enforced separation on occasion of children from parents, war and overwhelming economic power differences, has caused large-scale language death. Even for those who have maintained their ancestral languages the difficulties in gaining any foothold in the educational apparatus or the broadcast media beyond the most local level are manifest and great. In a country which rightly prides itself on the equality of all citizens, and where the overwhelming majority are native speakers of *the* hegemonic language, it is almost impossible for other voices to be heard without some accusation or other of positive discrimination. The problem is, that, as discussed in Section 2.4.2.3, without some meaningful and positive help, those native languages which remain will be swept away. It is true that Congress passed the Native American Languages Act (1990). As Schiffman (1996: 263–4) points out, however, 'now that Native American languages are … practically extinct, and pose no threat to anyone anywhere, we can grant them special status.'

This is much more starkly the case with similar situations elsewhere in the world. In Australia in the past, and Amazonia at present, the state of many native languages is catastrophic. Economic changes, devastating illnesses (sometimes artificially engineered by white settlers in order to clear the land), splitting up of families and losses of native habitat, have led, or are leading rapidly, to language shift. Similar developments can be predicted for large sections of Africa, where medical conditions such as AIDS, and the presence of debt and social insecurity, have led to population flux and movement.

2.4.2.5 Discussion

At the heart of the spread of monolingualism lie power differentials. Those who have more power (whether economic or political, or both) are able – whether consciously or not – to impose their language on those with less power (or, in a democratic age, less access to the centre of power). Those with less power may also move towards the use of the majority language by compulsion or, as regularly, by a sense of demoralization about their native languages and cultures. Societal multilingualism may have been the norm, but societal monolingualism may well be more normal in the future. Nevertheless, minority language use continues, perhaps even increases.

Although the nationalist equation of nation and language has not been abandoned by most polities, this goal is inherently a vanishing point. Even the most powerful nation states are part of a global economy in which, for better and worse, the English language is a primary lingua franca. At the same time, the same global economic system has encouraged the movement of people to more affluent areas: there will always be urban communities who do not speak the national language as their native language. Finally, the increasing federalization of areas such as Europe has meant that the languages of regions may begin to assume more importance as an expression of cultural identity, particularly as fear of homogenization grows.

2.5   *Nationism* and *Nationalism*

How does a nation decide on a national language, therefore? What factors underlie it? Fishman (1968, 1973) proposed a distinction between *nationalism* and *nationism*. Nationalism represents a belief in an ethnic, cultural and linguistic connection within a grouping, and their belief both in their right and ability to govern themselves. Other critics term this *ethnic nationalism*. Nationism, on the other hand, is an attempt to form a collective identity from a disparate group of people. Nationist symbols might concentrate on the unity in diversity of the people involved and a shared recent history. Other critics term this *civic nationalism*.

From a linguistic point of view, nationalism demands the dominant ethnic group's language as the official language; nationism, on the other hand, looks for a language whose use causes the least offence to the greatest number of citizens, as well as having a large number of speakers, whether native or not, within the polity.

It should be stressed that these two features often coexist in the language policy of any polity. The use of the French language in France has nationalist *and* nationist elements: it *does* represent the dominant Paris-based cultural group, but is also the language most readily understood by the majority of citizens. In India, on the other hand, Hindi is the nationalist language at the federal level, while the language of former imperialism, English, has the nationist function of assuaging the fears of Hindi language hegemony felt by speakers of Dravidian languages.

The Grand Duchy of Luxembourg provides a particularly striking example of the tensions felt between nationism and nationalism within a Europe which has been home to the modern nationalist impulse for over two hundred years. Around two-thirds of the population speak *Lëtzebuergesch*, 'Luxembourgish', a Middle German dialect with profound influence from French, as their native language. For historical reasons, however, the official language is French. Although it has no actual official function, German has a position of some importance within the country. Either of these two languages could suit the nationist function, primarily because of their international prestige. At first glance, German would make more sense as a choice for this function since it is a close relative of the local dialects; for historical reasons this is unacceptable, however.

Until recently, Luxembourgish had no official status. Conversely, the fact that it was the native language of the majority made knowledge of it a central part of the identity of a native Luxembourger, thereby fulfilling the nationalist function. This classic diglossic (if not *triglossic*) state was altered in 1984, when Luxembourgish became the national language.

It is normally impossible to achieve Luxembourg citizenship without knowledge of this language. Since this period, teaching of the national language has increased in schools; production of both literary and non-literary prose has grown (Berg 1993). A standard spoken variety appears to be developing (Gilles 1998). As we will see in Chapter 3, these functional domains are those most associated with the achievement of full language status.

Nevertheless, the importance of French within the country must be recognized. In part, this is because the combination under the same 'roof' of Germanic and Romance languages, once so common along the linguistic frontier, is now a special feature associated with Luxembourg and Switzerland (Millar 2004a): it makes Luxembourg Luxembourg. At a more pragmatic level, the international status of French is useful to the Grand Duchy, since a country with only around 400,000 inhabitants, reliant on commerce, needs a major language as its 'window to the world'. This level of happy compromise is not possible in other places, however.

As we will see again in Chapter 8, language planning in post-imperial contexts is particularly challenging. In Europe it can be assumed that, at the very least, a large part of the population of a country speaks a single language and has a shared cultural heritage (even if, in origin, such uniformity was often not present, and the contemporary state has been achieved through authoritarian nation-building on the part of the ruling class); this is not the case elsewhere, however. Especially striking are those occasions where boundaries have been drawn according to the wishes of the imperial powers rather than due to the ethnic and cultural considerations which informed their own nation building. Thus the present Republic of Cameroon has, in the last hundred years, been a unitary German colony, been divided into a French and a British protectorate, reunited as a federal republic, divided into 'French' and 'English' sections, before finally becoming a unitary republic in the 1970s. The country is home to a wide range of peoples from different ethnic and linguistic backgrounds (Eyongetah Mbuagbaw *et al.* 1987). A nationalist solution to the post-colonial nation-building is not possible, since this would almost inevitably lead to civil war: particularly obvious to near-neighbours of Nigeria, which suffered just such a war in the 1960s. The nationist use of a European language is also problematical because of the presence of two major world languages, which perceive each other as rivals, in the same unitary territory. Moreover, the French and British imperial authorities had somewhat different views on language use, with the British being a little more tolerant of native languages and creoles than the French. Under the protectorates, each authority developed an educational system which emphasized the unique nature of British or French culture and language whilst denigrating, whether overtly or not, the other.

The result of this has been a compromise, with both languages having equal status and separate educational systems. This solution pleases no one, but at least no one can be said to be either winner or loser. Bilingualism costs, however, even for affluent societies like Belgium or Canada; it is dubious whether it can be sustained in a less affluent society like Cameroon. Moreover, the bilingualism of 'European' and European-settled first-wave nationalist nations, like Belgium or Canada, is based upon large numbers of speakers of both the languages; this is rarely the case in post-colonial contexts. Thus, in avoiding the civil strife which would have almost inevitably followed a nationalist solution to the language problem, countries like Cameroon have instead perpetuated the power of an elite group, who speak the language of the former colonizers, acting as interpreters for the great mass, who are practically denied access to power (Koenig *et al.* 1983; Wolf 2001).

2.6 Conclusion

As we will see again in Chapter 8, language lies at the heart of the construction of many nations. It appears a convenient and incontrovertible means of establishing difference; a means which cannot be called into question as can some other cultural artefacts. As this book will demonstrate, however, it is not always easy to define what we mean by an independent language, a point to which we will return in the next chapter. Moreover, while language itself is a facility which all of us have from birth, even if we learn only one mother tongue, the languages which we learn to read and write are standardized, and to a high degree planned: they bear the mark of conscious human intervention. This book will also discuss the ways in which these processes are carried out, by whom, and for what reason. At the centre of this is the desire to increase or maintain power and influence for one group and its language. Competition between languages represents competition between groups.

Bearing this in mind, the next chapter will discuss the methods – social, historical, cultural and linguistic – by which scholars have attempted to delineate what distinctions there are between a language and other language varieties. As much of this book will demonstrate, many of these criteria are based essentially upon political and national grounds, and are liable to change over time.

3
Language and Dialect

3.1 Introduction

Most of us believe we know what we mean by language. For many, the idea is approached primarily from the experience of learning a foreign language: a set of problems and tasks associated with the acquisition of lexis, phonology and syntax; the end product being (we hope) the ability to communicate in this new code. Awareness of this distinctive system proves to us that we are learning another language.

Yet is this the case? A speaker of English will not be able to understand German without first learning the language; even a small amount of exposure to either language would prompt the recognition that they are related. This is not possible for a native speaker of English even after lengthy exposure to, for instance, Finnish. Does this make German less of a language than Finnish?

The problem becomes exacerbated when we talk of dialect. Different people interpret the word differently. I am often told, particularly in German-speaking countries, that my dialect of English is difficult to follow when I am actually speaking Standard English with a Scottish accent. The popular use of the term is obviously at odds with the scientific.

Yet what do linguists mean by dialect? Dutch is much closer to German than is English. Somebody from Amsterdam cannot understand someone from Munich if both are speaking their native dialects or their standard national language. But there is considerable mutual comprehension on both sides of the German/Dutch frontier. Where does 'German' begin and 'Dutch' stop? Is Dutch a dialect of German?

In Scandinavia, considerable mutual comprehension exists between Danish, Norwegian and Swedish. Native speakers of one do not learn another as I learned French, for instance. Rather, schoolchildren are exposed to writing in that language, and any potentially confusing differences are explained. Nor are these distinctions always associated with frontiers. Some eastern Norwegian varieties are more like Swedish than they are like some western dialects. Obviously the linguistic situation in Scandinavia is more complex than the political situation implies. Are Swedish, Norwegian and Danish dialects of the same language, or separate, closely related, languages?

Conversely, it is customary to speak of the dialects of Chinese (Kratochvíl 1968: 13–9). Yet a southern 'dialect', such as Cantonese, is considerably less comprehensible to a speaker of the northern dialect Mandarin than Icelandic is to a German. But because of the common logographic script, the two are considered dialects.

Similar, but distinct, is the case of Sardu, the Romance variety native to Sardinia. There is little mutual comprehension between Sardu and any Italian dialect. Yet Standard Italian is the bureaucratic and business language on the island. There is a written (although not codified) form of Sardu, but most Sardinians are literate in Italian only. Since Sardinia is relatively poor, the language of the 'mainland' is attractive to potential migrants (Parry 1998). Therefore, Sardinian dialects are considered to have the same relationship with Standard Italian as have the dialects of Piedmont, which *are* mutually intelligible to a degree with the standard. Is Sardu a language or a dialect?

This problem has both linguistic and sociolinguistic elements. It is also one in which, as we will see, the historical, cultural and social development of a region must be borne in mind. How can we best represent these elements?

3.2   An algebraic view: Ferguson

Ferguson (1966) puts forward a model for the comparison of relationships, within a nation, between languages. It offers an opportunity for the definition of language in relation to its status and function. He suggests 'a condensed, algebraic formula ...[of] the sociolinguistic profile of a nation' (Ferguson 1966: 309).

He defines three sub-categories of language which may be spoken within a nation: *major languages* (Lmaj), *minor languages* (Lmin) and *languages of special status* (Lspec) (Ferguson 1966: 310). A major language within any given country will have:

> one or more of the following characteristics:
> (a) It is spoken as a native language by more than 25% of the population or by more than 1,000,000 people. Example: Quechua in

Bolivia, where roughly a third of the population speaks Quechua, but Spanish is the only official language and the language of education.
(b) It is an official language of the nation. Example: Irish in Eire, where only 3% of the population speak Irish natively, but it is an official language.
(c) It is the language of education of over 50% of the secondary school graduates of the nation. Example: English in Ethiopia, where only a negligible percentage of the population speaks English natively and Amharic is the official language, but English is the medium of instruction in most of the secondary schools and higher education in the country.

A minor language has:

one or more of the following characteristics:
(a) It is spoken as a native language by no more than 25% of the population and by either more than 5% or more than 100,000 people. Example: Basque in Spain.
(b) It is used as a medium of instruction above the first years of primary school, having textbooks other than primers published in it. Example: Dagbane in Ghana.

Special status is applied to a language (Ferguson 1966: 310–11) in

one of the following ways:
(a) It is widely used for religious purposes. Example: Pali in Ceylon, where it is the language of the Buddhist scriptures and is widely studied by monks and scholars.
(b) It is widely used for literary purposes. Example: 'Classical' Chinese in Taiwan, used for some forms of modern literature and studied for the classics of older Chinese literature.
(c) It is widely taught as a subject in secondary schools. Example: French in Spain, where most secondary school students [in the early 1960s] study French as a foreign language.
(d) It is used by a substantial number of people as a lingua franca within the country. Example: Pidgin English in Liberia, used for inter-tribal communication along main transportation routes.
(e) It functions as a major language for an age-sector of the population. Example: Japanese in Taiwan, where most educated people in the age-group 35–55 [in the early 1960s] were educated in Japanese and still use it for a variety of purposes.

At this stage of his argument, '[a] formula of this kind ... hardly offers enough information to be of real value for comparative purposes ...'. It is impossible to tell whether there are any functional and administrative distinctions between major languages found in the same polity, as, for instance, in Belgium or Switzerland. Such a formula is naturally simplistic and impossible to cross-reference.

To counter this problem, Ferguson revises Stewart's (1962) typology for multilingualism. Ferguson (1966: 311–12) suggests five types of language:

Vernacular (V): The unstandardized native language of a speech community.

Standard (S): A Vernacular which has been standardized.

Classical (C): A Standard which has died out as a native language.

Pidgin (P): A hybrid language which combined the lexical stock of one language with the grammatical structure of another language or group of languages.[1]

Creole (K): A Pidgin which has become the native language of a speech community.

Ferguson recognizes that 'the line between V[ernacular] and S[tandard] is sometimes difficult to draw'.

This extension of the formula appears more informative; again, without background knowledge, meaningful comparisons between different varieties are difficult. As Ferguson admits (1966: 312), '[t]he added information about the "types" is less important, however, than information about the functions of the respective languages in the life of the nation.' He uses a revised version of Stewart's work again, therefore, to ascribe social function to a variety:

g: Used primarily for communication within a particular speech community, marking it as an identifiable group in the nation.

o: Used for official purposes: either designated by law as official or used for general governmental, educational, and military purposes at the national level.

w: Used as a lingua franca or language of wider communication within the nation. (Stewart did not establish a distinction between national lingua francas and languages used for international communication; see *i* later.)

e: Used for educational purposes above the first years of primary school, having subject matter textbooks published in it. (More careful specification of e than Stewart indicated proved desirable. Cf. the definition of 'minor' languages above.)

r: Widely used for religious purposes.

s: Widely studied as a subject in schools.[2]

Accordingly, the formula for Spain in the early 1960s would read:

$$5L = 2Lmaj (So, Sg) + 1Lmin (Vg) + 2Lspec (Crs, Ss)$$

This could be interpreted as: 'In the early 1960s, Spain had two major languages, both standardized, one of which (Castilian) was official, while the other (Catalan) served for group communication purposes. One minor language (Basque), existing only as a vernacular, was used for group communication purposes. Two languages of special status were also present. One (Latin) was a classical language, used for religious purposes and taught in schools, while the other (French) was a standard language and taught in schools.'

This is clearer. The two major languages are distinguished by function, as are the languages of special status. But why should such distinctions exist in a particular nation? The formula cannot tell us. If it is to be used to compare nations, this is not a primary concern. If, however, we are particularly interested in the social and historical relationships between language varieties, the 'algebraic' description of a nation's languages and their functions can only give an incomplete answer.

Ferguson's model also allows diglossia to be distinguished (1966: 312):

If a language exists in two varieties in the kind of functional comple-mentation called diglossia ... , this is shown by a colon with C[lassical] or S[tandard] on the left and V[ernacular] or K[reole] on the right. Thus, for example, in Morocco Arabic is represented by C: Vorw, where the lower case 'function' letters refer in part to the C[lassical] variety and in part to the V[ernacular] variety, in accordance with the characteristics of diglossia,

as well as those situations where (Ferguson 1966: 313) 'the total number of speakers of a group of languages might be quite high even though the speakers for any one of them might be well below the minimum for minor languages'. This situation is particularly prevalent in regions where European-style nationalism has only recently been adopted. To counter this imbalance, he proposes the use of a superscript $<^+>$ alongside the number of languages counted for the nation in question, and the use of $<\{\ \}>$ surrounding a capital letter which 'is usually V[ernacular], but may be S[tandard] or unspecified L[anguage] when appropriate'. Ethiopia in the early 1960s could be represented by:

$$5^+ \text{Lmin (Sei, 4Vg, \{V\})}^3$$

According to this formula, Ethiopia had more than five minor languages, one of which is a standardized language, acting as both an educational tool and as a means towards wider communication internationally, four vernaculars, which are used for group communication, and an unspecified number of vernaculars, each of which has a relatively insignificant numbers of speakers, but, when added together, make up a considerable number of speakers.

3.2.1 Discussion

Ferguson's 'algebraic' model appears to be a concise means of comparing and contrasting the linguistic situation of different countries. More importantly, it seems to offer a means of distinguishing different language and dialect types. It is relatively straightforward to learn and apply. Yet many of its virtues are also failings. Ferguson admits (1966: 314) that the summaries he provides for the formulae 'are more directly informative and even perhaps more usefully comparable from country to country, which would suggest the need to review or replace the kind of formula used here'.

Moreover, his formulae do not include information on matters such as population, gross domestic product, date of the present nation's foundation, or per capita earnings. It *is* informative to see Belgium being compared with the Philippines; the comparison is not as straightforward as Ferguson suggests, however. Belgium *is* a relatively recent nation (1830); its two main language communities have, however, a long history of native literacy. Both are also spoken outside the national frontiers; one of these languages is a major vehicle of international communication. The Philippines' tortuous road to independence began at the end of the nineteenth century. Its main languages of literacy were importations of an alien ruling class (Anderson 1998). Belgium, on the other hand, was ruled by other European powers before the equation of nation and language had been fully established. This does not even consider the manifest inequalities in population, wealth, and other factors which distinguish the countries.

Another problem which is not recognized is where similar linguistic usages are treated as if they were separate from each other. Thus, there would be no way of telling that, in the former Czechoslovakia, the two official and standardized languages – Czech and Slovak – were mutually intelligible, and that there are cultural and historical, rather than linguistic, reasons, why this distinction should be made. Another example of this phenomenon is Norway. That country was, until very recently, ethnically and culturally homogenous. Using Ferguson's model, Norway's formula might be:

$$1L = Lmaj$$

This suggests that Norway has only one language. Yet this does not give proper emphasis to the tensions between *Bokmål* and *Nynorsk*, the two standard varieties of Norwegian (as discussed in Chapter 7); nor does it recognize Sámi, the Finno-Ugric language spoken in the north of the country, which has relatively few speakers, but is of some importance historically and culturally, or Finnish, the language of a number of inhabitants of the border zone between Norway and Finland. English also has some importance as an educational language. A more comprehensive formula might be:

$$5L = 2Lmaj \ (Sow, So) + 2Lmin \ (S:Vg, Sg) + 1Lspec \ (Ssi)$$

Yet this does not recognize the diversity of the 'dialects' of Sámi; nor does it explain the relationship between 'official' and 'language of wider communication' which the two major languages have (Bokmål, being historically close to Danish, and bearing phonological similarities to Swedish, could be seen as an almost ideal Scandinavian lingua franca; Nynorsk does not suit this task so well).

Perhaps the greatest flaw of Ferguson's model is his use of the term *algebraic*. Certainly his formulae look like those used in algebra; but can they truly be said to represent a mathematical problem and implied outcome? In algebra, there is only one possible solution for any given problem; the variables are inhabitants of a purely mathematical universe which has little in the way of connection with the 'real world'. Ferguson's model is different: it stands or falls on our understanding of the way that societies function linguistically. Even this is not possible, since the formulae do not present historical or cultural background. The terms *standard* or *vernacular* are not explained.

Further, an algebraic problem implies the possibility of a solution. It seems unlikely that this is the intention of (or, in fact, possible for) Ferguson's formulae. All societies with 2 Lmaj will not have *exactly* the same social or linguistic relationship as all others. Bearing this in mind, the *absolute* value of variables in mathematics is not suitable, even as a metaphor, for the relationship between language varieties within any society.

3.3   Another view of similar material: Stewart

Stewart (1968) provides a more pragmatically useful model for describing the means by which language varieties interact. Unlike Ferguson's model, there is no suggestion of an algebraic 'solution'. Instead, he describes three means of specification: *language types, language functions* and *degree of use*.

In a radically different way from Ferguson, Stewart suggests (1968: 533) that

> it is important to take account of the fact that linguistic systems may differ, not only in their structures, but also in their histories, their relationships to other linguistic systems, the extent to which they have acquired codified norms of usage, and in the manner of their transmission from generation to generation. Such social and technical characteristics can have an effect on the role which a particular linguistic system may assume in the linguistic makeup of a multilingual polity, so that linguistic systems characterized by different configurations of such attributes will tend to fall into different categories of intrinsic social value, insofar as their use in a particular polity is concerned.

The categories which analyses of this type present are termed *language types*: 'the classification of linguistic systems into language types can be made on the basis of the presence vs. the absence of four attributes' (Stewart 1968: 534).

The first of these is *standardization*: 'the codification and acceptance, within the community of users, of a formal set of norms defining "correct" usage'. Different forms of standardization exist: *monocentric*, with 'a single set of universally accepted norms' and *polycentric*, 'where different sets of norms exist simultaneously'. The former can be illustrated by French or Dutch; the latter by English, Portuguese, Moldavian/Romanian and Hindi/Urdu – found in a number of competing norms based upon political, ethnic and religious allegiance. Political separation is not the only source for polycentric usage: cultural and historical developments may also come into play, as was the case with Serbo-Croat in Yugoslavia.

Where a standardization of the polycentric type has occurred in more than one country, *multimodal standardization* can take place. This can be either *endonormative*, when the norm is based upon native models, or *exonormative*, where it is based on foreign models. A genuinely endonor-mative standard, diverging considerably from other standard forms of the same language, is something of a rarity. Stewart may be thinking of an autonomous standard such as Standard American English (in com-parison with the Standard English of England); certainly, the level of autonomy in the United States is considerably greater than that found in Australia or New Zealand. But, as we will see in Chapter 5, all forms of Standard English stem from basically the same source, essentially stan-dardized before the English (later British) imperial expansion began, with the possible partial exceptions of Irish Standard English and, in particular, Scottish Standard English (discussed in Chapter 8). Even in the case of Serbo-Croat, where different alphabets were used depending upon the historical religious community to which a speaker belonged, the dialect upon which the standard was based, while Serbian in origin, bore many similarities to the (Croatian) dialect of Dubrovnik (Greenberg 2004: 25–6). What has happened to Croatian since the independence of Croatia in 1991 might be described in endonormative terms, although both language planners and speakers would deny such a conclusion. In this sense the model which Kloss put forward (discussed in section 3.4.3) gives more 'room for manoeuvre'.

Exonormative standards appear common where the standard language has been imported from another country, often due to imperialism (Stewart 1968: 537). Jamaicans learn essentially the Standard written English of England; Virgin Islanders the Standard written English of the United States, even though natives of both speak varieties of English Caribbean creoles. Indeed, it might be argued that the move towards an autonomous national standard is often a matter of historical devel-opment, rather than any large-scale, once-for-all, breach.

The second category Stewart recognizes (1968: 537) is *autonomy*: 'a linguistic system will be autonomous in terms of any other linguistic system with which it is not historically related'. Thus, even at the height of Norman power and of the prestige of French culture and language in medieval England, no one would ever have suggested that French and English were part of the same linguistic system. As Stewart recognizes, the problem comes when two close relatives stand side by side. When do these become separate, but close, languages? When are they dialects of the same language? Stewart (1968: 535) makes the point that the term language is not absolute, but rather is liable to different interpretation and considerable change over time (Stewart 1968: 535, footnote 9):

> A linguistic system will be *heteronomous* in terms of another, historically related, one, when the former functions in the linguistic community

as a dependent variety of the latter, and is consequently subject to 'correction' in its direction, i.e. is subject to regular readjustment so that it will come to resemble the other more closely.

This is particularly useful when discussing formerly autonomous linguistic systems such as Scots (one of the native vernaculars of Scotland) or Occitan (the native vernacular of southern France).

The third specification is *historicity*: '[w]hat gives a language historicity is its association with some national or ethnic tradition' (Stewart 1968: 536). In general, this sense of past will give the linguistic system a sense of 'normalcy': the language has always been of this type, with perfectly natural 'rules'.

One factor which Stewart only hints at is that many European languages – often, although not always, the languages of imperialism – have advantages over many other languages in terms of historicity, simply because their history is a written one. In a world where the written word is paramount, these languages are inevitably considered more important than those with only a patchy written history, or none at all, even if their oral testimony is considerable.

The final specification which Stewart identifies is *vitality*, the 'use of the linguistic system by an unisolated community of native speakers' (1968: 536). As we will see in Chapter 7, it is precisely this lack of speakers in any particular place which has helped create the perilous state of contemporary Irish.

Stewart then presents his typology of language types. Like Ferguson, he provides means by which these distinctions can be shown, first in abbreviated, and then in tabular, form. Standard languages (S) are defined no further than in terms of 'the official languages of Europe' (1968: 536). In the case of multimodal standardization, the symbol S should be modified by a numeral representing the number of norms. Thus, Standard German could be represented as

S_3,

since there are slightly divergent norms in Germany, Austria and Switzerland. Where the divergent norms have specific names (rather than 'Austrian German'), these names are given parenthetically (1968: 537), again making his system more informative than Ferguson's. The situation for Serbo-Croat (at the time he was writing) was

S_2 (Serbian; Croatian).

Exonormative standardization is marked by a subscript $<x>$ following S, with the source for the standard expressed in parenthesis (Stewart 1968: 537). Thus the standard form of English employed in recently independent former British colonies would be

S_x (British norm),

whilst territories with close connections to the United States, such as Liberia, would be described as

S_x (American norm).

Classical languages (C) are recognized as less numerous than standards, but 'often play a very important role in a society in which they are used' (1968: 537–8). As well as Latin and Sanskrit, he makes a distinction (1968: 538) between the C which is classical or literary Arabic in those territories conquered permanently in the Muslim expansion following the death of the Prophet Mohammed, and Maltese, where Catholic religious tradition and (southern) European culture, coupled with close connections with Britain, have made it necessary for a standard form of the local Maghrebi Arabic dialect to be produced (elsewhere in the Arabic-speaking world, as Abd-el-Jawad (1992) reports, classical Qur'anic Arabic is the only acceptable standard, even when this diverges to the point of incomprehension from the local variety).

A language type Stewart does not share with Ferguson is the category *artificial* (A), which he associates with languages like Esperanto. A language's artificiality could also be seen in its function. Certain pidgin, or near-pidgin, languages, such as Lingua Franca or Chinook Jargon, have been used as trade languages across wide areas; their existence as living languages was only supported by the trade and cultural conditions then current. When trade changed, or other languages became dominant in the area, the languages quickly withered.

Vernacular (V) languages are defined by Stewart (1968: 538) as

first or native languages. ... Due to their lack of formalized lexicons and grammars, V[ernacular]s are generally accorded less prestige than either S[tandard language]s or C[lassical language]s. However, a V[ernacular] may become an S[tandard] through the codification and acceptance of its grammar and lexicon, cf. the case of Tagalog in the Philippines.

Unlike Ferguson, Stewart proposes a separate category: *dialect* (D) (1968: 538). Most dialects need not be discussed independently of the standard or vernacular of which they are generally believed to form a part. But two categories of dialect are of some importance to his typology, however. In the first place, he notes (1968: 538–9) that

> a particular D[ialect] may enjoy special status in a national situation (e.g., it may be associated with a special function, or used by a special group and perhaps have a special name).

As examples of this he cites Swiss German and Neapolitan in Italy. Another example might be Algerian Arabic, which in the Maghreb and France has associations with a particular culture and with styles of music popular even among those who do not understand the lyrics. Also worth considering is Macedonian, which could be considered a variety of Bulgarian, but is treated as an independent language for historical and political reasons, and has been developed to emphasize this (Friedman 1993).

The second category are languages which 'may be isolated politically from what would normally be [their] superordinate system' (1968: 539). These include the French varieties spoken in the North-East of the United States, and the English variety of the Leeward Islands of the Netherlands Antilles. On both these occasions, the varieties are divorced from the standard norm of their language. As Stewart says, '[i]n these and similar cases, it will generally be useful to specify such D[ialect]s in a sociolinguistic profile of the nation' (1968: 539). We will discuss these and similar concerns further when we come to the work of Kloss. Stewart has gone far beyond Ferguson in seeing language types as open to categorization beyond a particular state or region. His final two categories are *creoles* (K) and *pidgins* (P).

In order to combine his analysis of specifications and language types, Stewart presents a table (1968: 537):

Attributes				Type	Symbol
1	2	3	4		
+	+	+	+	Standard	S
+	+	+	−	Classical	C
+	+	−	−	Artificial	A
−	+	+	+	Vernacular	V
−	−	+	+	Dialect	D
−	−	−	+	Creole	K
−	−	−	−	Pidgin	P

where 1 = standardization, 2 = autonomy, 3 = historicity and 4 = vitality.

He then attempts a specification of language function. Many of the abbreviations will be familiar from our discussion of Ferguson's adaptation of Stewart's 1962 essay; nevertheless, they are sufficiently different to encourage discussion and exemplification. Stewart (1968: 540–1) recognizes ten basic forms of language function:

His first category is *official* (o), which he defines (1968: 540) as a 'legally appropriate language for all politically and culturally representative purposes on a nationwide basis. In many cases, the o[fficial] function of the language is specified constitutionally'.

Unlike Ferguson, Stewart suggests the category *provincial* (p) for those languages which 'function as a provincial or regional official language'. This category would be a useful means of describing the situation of Catalan or Basque in Spain today.

A language of *wider communication* (w) is 'a linguistic system (other than one which already has an o[fficial] or p[rovincial] function) predominating as a medium of communication across language boundaries within the nation' (Stewart 1968: 540).

International (i) is defined (1968: 540) as 'a linguistic system (other than one which already has an o[fficial] or p[rovincial] function) [acting] as a major medium of communication which is international in scope, e.g., for diplomatic relations, foreign trade, tourism, etc.'

Another function which Stewart does not share with Ferguson is that of *capital* (c), which he defines (1968: 540) as 'a linguistic system (other than one which already has an o[fficial] or p[rovincial] function) as the primary medium of communication in the vicinity of the national capital'. In the former British colonies and mandates in east Africa, where English was strongly foregrounded in official terms, Kiswahili, although not spoken by a majority of the residents, was of considerable importance in cities such as Mombassa or Nairobi, even among people from elsewhere (including people of European origin), of which more in Chapter 8.

Stewart's sixth category is *group* (g), which he would describe (1968: 540) as 'the normal medium of communication among the members of a single cultural or ethnic group, such as a tribe, settled group of foreign migrants, etc.'

His last four categories (1968: 542–3) are 'highly restricted functions … marginal to the patterns of communication within the polity', although, as we will see, this statement is only true in the most general of senses. *Educational* (e) is 'a language (other than one which already has an o[fficial] or p[rovincial] function) [acting] as a medium of primary or secondary education, either regionally or nationally' (1968: 540).

School subject (s) is defined (1968: 541) as a 'language (other than one which already has an o[fficial] or p[rovincial] function) ... commonly taught as a subject in secondary and/or higher education'. *Literary* (l) implies (1968: 541) a language 'used primarily for literary or scholarly purposes'. Finally, *religious* (r) refers to a language used 'primarily in connection with the ritual of a particular religion' (1968: 541).

Some languages associated with these types could be used to question the idea of 'marginality'. For instance, German has only quasi-official status in Luxembourg. Nor is it associated with any one group within the population, or with wider communication within the nation (where French would be used, if the use of Luxembourgish is inappropriate for linguistic or social reasons). It is, however, a language of international communication, as well as a close relative of the national language, and is used in schools from an early age in order to facilitate this international use.

More marginal, but still important, are the literary uses of languages which are not widely spoken (or spoken at all). Historically, Old Church Slavonic was the literary language among Orthodox Slavs, even when their language had diverged considerably from the classical form. Despite the low levels of (historical) literacy in a country such as Russia, it is impossible to ignore the influence which Old Church Slavonic has had on, for instance, word formation in Russian (in comparison with Belarusian or Ukrainian, where the Catholic, rather more Western, influences of Polish are stronger (Mayo 1993: 938–9; Shevelov 1993: 990–1)). Nevertheless, Stewart's point holds if we confine ourselves to a discussion of the day-to-day linguistic reality of a place. Latin, for instance, had considerable importance among Catholics; it was not – except under unusual circumstances – the language of choice in their everyday communication.

Again unlike Ferguson, Stewart recognizes (1968: 541) that certain functions normally include others within them, and in particular that 'the o[fficial] function generally includes uses which are otherwise classified as w[ider communication], i[nternational], c[apital], e[ducational], and s[chool] functions'. A distinction can therefore be made between different functions, depending both on place and context, even when the specific language type does not differ. This complexity matches the complexity of relationship between language varieties in the 'real world'. Thus Catalan is no less of a standardized language because it acts as a group language in Roussillon in France, unlike in Catalonia itself, where it has a provincial function.

Stewart also recognizes (1968: 541) the need to represent a diglossic situation with the symbol *d*. He also suggests (1968: 541–2) that the relationship between 'High' (H) and 'Low' (L) varieties should be explained in any description. Thus the situation in Haiti would be described (1968: 542):

French So (d: L = Creole)
Creole K (d: H = French),

where the relationship between the two varieties in the same place is explicit. Again, this is a considerable advance on Ferguson's model.

3.3.1 Discussion

Stewart's model, in its attempts to transmit in a coherent manner the ways in which social function can affect the status of a given language variety within a given society, has many advantages over Ferguson's position. Yet it also falls down in its attempts to compare unlike with unlike. What both Ferguson's and Stewart's models lack is a sense of comparative historicity. The model to which we will now turn attempts to inject this factor into its discussion.

3.4   Terminological-functional approaches: Kloss

In distinction to approaches based primarily on comparison by means of a commonly agreed set of abbreviations portrayed in what appear to be – although actually normally are not – mathematical formulae, a competing set of traditions exists where a language variety is described by the use of a range of terms which expand upon those already existing – *language, dialect, vernacular*, and so on – to achieve greater accuracy in description. In this framework, comparison is not achieved through the placing together of similar (or apparently similar) formulae, but instead by implication, with each term (and the ideas which underlie them) being associated with particular linguistic and social situations. This implicitness is problematical when it comes to comparison at macro level, particularly when different scholars (sometimes even the same scholars) use a term in different ways. It does allow a considerable level of cross-linguistic, instead of transnational, comparison, however. Rather than assumptions being made about the linguistic nature of a given language variety, whilst the great part of the analysis is given over to its societal status, as with both Stewart and Ferguson's models, this can be expressed explicitly and compared with other similar – and dissimilar – environments.

A number of scholars of considerable perspicacity, such as Meillet (1928), Sommerfelt (1938) and Haugen (1972, 1966), have employed these terminological approaches. It is in the work of Heinz Kloss, however, that they reach their full potential.[4]

3.4.1   Kloss

Kloss' breakthrough is the recognition that contemporary (particularly European) languages can be defined as such according to two criteria. The first of these refers to those languages he terms *Abstand* (languages believed by speakers to be distinct because of inherent linguistic distance),[5] which he describes (1967: 29) as representing 'a linguistic unit which a linguist would have to call a language even if not a single word had ever been written in it'. An Abstand language in its most 'perfect' sense would be one like Basque, which has no living relatives and is therefore incapable of being thought of as a dialect of another language.

More capable of misinterpretation is Kloss' other term: *Ausbau* language (a language by development). Kloss (1978: 10–11) emphasizes that *development* should be distinguished from *evolution*, a point to which we will return in Chapter 4. Essentially, an Ausbau language is one which develops through language planning: 'Terms such as reshaping or remoulding or elaboration, by focusing on deliberate language planning, help us to avoid a misunderstanding that the term development might lead to, namely that "Ausbau" might come about by that slow, almost imperceptible growth that we are wont to call natural' (Kloss 1967: 29).

To illustrate this distinction, Kloss provides the following illustration (Figure 3.1) where three languages, each made up of two close but distinct dialects, are compared.

There is an absolute linguistic distinction between languages X and Z. The material which they contain is inherently different; no one could claim that they were close relatives of each other: this is an Abstand relationship. More problematical is the relationship between languages X and Y. Whilst different from each other, the four dialects involved are similar enough for the relationship between the two languages to be obvious; even, probably, to non-linguists. An Ausbau development must be

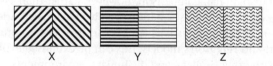

Figure 3.1   Ausbau and Abstand relationships
Source: Kloss 1967: 30.

assumed to explain the distinction between them. As Kloss puts it (1967: 30): 'The concept of ausbau language is primarily a sociological one.'

A number of languages are defined as languages both by Abstand and Ausbau criteria (Kloss 1967: 30). Thus French is intrinsically linguistically different from Italian, for instance; by the same token, French has also assumed a linguistic identity because of its association with a range of different uses within the French state, and elsewhere in *Francophonie*, a point to which we will return in Chapter 5. Kloss suggests, however, that

> a great many other tongues fall into that category ('languages') merely by virtue of their being ausbau languages. If one asked whether a given language would be accorded that designation if its speakers had adopted a closely related standard language as their chief medium of literary expression, one would probably be surprised at how many would have to be classified as mere dialects (or clusters of dialects).

The examples which he gives of the processes and implications of this development include (Kloss 1967: 30) the

> assumption that if the Icelandic language had been adopted by all speakers of Faeroese dialects, the Irish language by all speakers of Scots Gaelic dialects, the Catalan language by all speakers of the Occitan (or Provencal) dialects, the Portuguese language by all speakers of Gallego (Galician), the Danish language by all speakers of Swedish dialects, that under these circumstances nobody would dream today of claiming that the clusters of Faeroese, Gaelic, Gallego, Occitan, Slovak and Swedish dialects, respectively, because of their intrinsic distance, constitute independent linguistic units to be listed separately in language files all over the world.

As Kloss himself admits, this absolute polar relationship between Abstand and Ausbau is not possible in real world situations. He recognizes the potential for a grey area between his concepts and the *polycentric* standard languages suggested by Stewart. In order to distinguish between these concepts, he sets up four internally coherent and distinctive states of relationship between language varieties.

The first of these, which he illustrates, is what he terms (Kloss 1967: 31) 'the normal situation' (see Figure 3.2). Using the example of Breton he analyses this (1967: 31) as 'a standard based on some of the spoken speech [sic] forms and neither subdivided into two major variants nor exposed to the competition of another standard based on other Breton dialects'.

Figure 3.2   The 'normal situation': standard and dialects
Source: Kloss 1967: 31.

Kloss then turns to a discussion of polycentric standard languages, 'those instances where we have two variants of the same standard, based on the same dialect or a near-identical dialect' (1967: 31), which he illustrates (1967: 32) thus, using the (then) example of Serbo-Croat (see Figure 3.3).

Kloss' third illustration (1967: 32) is of two languages which have developed by means of Ausbau, but which are not distinctive in terms of linguistic distance (Figure 3.4).

The category is illustrated by Czech and Slovak, two languages whose distinctiveness can be described almost entirely in historical, sociological and sociolinguistic terms, not in linguistic ones. Other examples which he mentions (1967: 31) of this phenomenon include Danish and Swedish and Bulgarian and Macedonian. As we will see in Chapter 4, Ausbau implies language planning towards a standardized form. The actual processes he proposes will be discussed in greater depth then.

Kloss' final illustration of these distinctions is of 'two written standards based on clusters of dialects, and considered to be languages by virtue of their intrinsic distance' (1967: 31), in other words, due to an Abstand relationship (see Figure 3.5).

The fact that he uses the German and Dutch languages to illustrate this phenomenon will be discussed in the following.

One of the central innovative points in Kloss' model is that

> The relation between the polycentric standard language (as typified by Serbo- Croatian) and the ausbau language (as typified by Slovak in its relation to Czech) is not a static but a dynamic one. (Kloss 1967: 33)

Figure 3.3   Polycentric standard languages

Figure 3.4   Ausbau languages

Figure 3.5   Abstand languages
Source: Kloss 1967: 32.

He suggests that a polycentric standard language may move towards a monocentric one, as seems to be the case with modern Norwegian, as we will discuss in Chapter 5. He also focuses (Kloss 1967: 33) upon the Soviet Union, where the policy was

> to widen the rift between domestic standard languages and their kin tongues abroad so that it is quite possible that some day Moldavian will be more than just a variant of standard Roumanian.

In fact, this particular process is unlikely to happen; largely, again, because of political events. A more apposite example for the post-Soviet period is the drift from a polycentric standard language to Ausbau for Croat (in relation to Serb) and the development of 'Bosniak' as a potentially separate south Slav variant.

An opposing tendency is visible in another dynamic development which Kloss proposed: *near-dialectalization*. In the Ausbau process, inevitably, there will be winners and losers; this is particularly true for those languages which share many features in common. Kloss would claim (1967: 35) that near-dialectalization pertains in situations such as the relationship between Standard High German and Low German and Italian and Sardinian, among others. He illustrates (1967: 35) this relationship as in Figure 3.6.

The close linguistic relationship between the two originally separate languages is represented by similar use of line; only one of the spoken groupings can be said to have an immediate relationship with the standard, however.

A number of Kloss' comments on this matter are perhaps better served in a discussion of the stable nature, or otherwise, of diglossia.

Figure 3.6 Near-dialectalization

Nevertheless, he provides a useful distinction between near-dialectalized languages, such as Occitan and Low German, which were of considerable importance both within their own speech communities, and elsewhere, and which suffered from a downgrading of their non-literary use in favour of their use in *belles lettres*, in comparison with a language, such as Sardinian or Haitian Creole, which

> cannot boast of a prestigious past nor of a present-day literary output of significant caliber (while after all one of the neo-Occitan writers won the Nobel prize – Frédéric Mistral). But neither do they seem to be menaced by extinction and that perhaps precisely because of the high degree of illiteracy and overall backwardness among their speakers.

Thus the relationship between survival of a language and the level of literacy in this language is a causal one; this causal relationship may not be what would be expected, however, particularly when a prestigious related language is available to a literate populace.

There are, however, a number of similarities between these two groupings. Kloss observes (1967: 36) that

> [e]xcept for a small minority among the elite ... the speakers of these languages are willing to put up with their present status. They feel and think and speak about these languages in terms of dialects of the victorious tongues rather than in terms of autonomous systems. To some extent these two features – acceptance of the social status of the mother tongue and underrating of its linguistic status – may be interdependent.

Although, as we will see, Kloss does not classify Scots in this category, his observation has a bitter truth to it. It saddens me to hear speakers of Scots – Scots so 'dense' (McClure 1979), that it would not be intelligible to a monolingual English speaker – referring to their language as 'slang'. Yet that is their privilege; such a view has been created, as will be seen in Chapter 8 in particular, not only by an Anglicized political elite, but also by a cadre of language activists whose use of Scots distances them from the usage and experience of native speakers.[6]

Kloss would claim (1967: 35) that a distinction exists between these near-dialectalized languages and 'fully dialectalized vernaculars'. The distinction is between a *language* which has gone through the Ausbau process, and a *vernacular*, which might even be Abstand from the standard language of the territory concerned, but which does not have a fully developed literary form. He suggests (1967: 35) that

> [i]f e.g. Slovakia would replace standard Slovak by standard Czech then it would be correct to call Slovak 'dialectalized'. This is what happened in Scotland after the speakers of the ausbau language called Scots (or Lallans) adopted English as their sole medium for serious literature.

No doubt many Scots would object to the comment on serious literature! More worrying for our purposes is his apparent collation of two separate language states. As we will see in Chapter 5, Scots has gone through an Ausbau stage in its development, whereas a number of other languages (such as, at least until recently, Rusyn in Slovakia (Magocski 1996)) have never attained a fully literate language status. Surely the two stages cannot be conflated? I have generally applauded Kloss for his 'dynamic' concept of language as an entity. On this occasion, he seems to fall into the trap of seeing language states as static.

Kloss himself appreciated some parts of this problem, and attempted to define distinctions between near-dialectalization and dialectalization. For instance, in a work co-authored with Haarmann (Kloss and Haarmann 1984), the terms *controversial* languages, or *quasi-independent* languages (*Einzelsprachen* in German) are suggested.[7] They define these in the following categories:

1. Speech varieties, held by the champions of co-equality to be independent languages, but held by others to be mere sub-varieties of some other prestigious language.
2. Speech varieties, held by some to designate separate languages, which ought to be included in language lists .... An opposing view however holds them to be generic or cover terms designating a kind of 'confederation' of closely related but independent tongues. (Kloss and Haarman 1984: 21)

The potential distinction between *language* and *tongue* should be noted. In the succeeding pages (Kloss and Haarmann 1984: 22–3), they give an exhaustive list of such 'languages' in Europe and (former) Soviet Asia associated with category 1 and also some (1984: 24) – not all, it would seem – of the 'federations' suggested. On all occasions, a reason for the belief in separateness is given, ranging from 'folk sentiment' in the case of Alsatian (German) or Flemish, through Ausbau in the case of Karelian (a Finnic variety spoken in the Russian Federation), to Abstand in the case of Istro-Romanian (the eastern Romance dialect spoken in Croatia and

Slovenia). Scots stands out on this occasion, nevertheless, because of the definition 'former Ausbau, Abstand', in a similar manner to Occitan and Low German. All three of these languages are separate from the others in this list in a number of ways; not least the number of speakers which they are assumed to have; more importantly, perhaps, because of their former status.

Some elements of this problem are dealt with in the terms *kin tongue* and *Halbsprache* 'half language', which Kloss proposed on a number of occasions. He suggests (Kloss 1984) the former term as appropriate to Scots (although the same arguments could be made for Low German and Occitan). He makes the point that

> [t]o belong to the 'inner circle', i.e. to be speakers of a kin tongue, does not imply a complete mutual intelligibility but a partial one or, at the very least, a mutual recognizability, making interlingual communication rather easy. (Kloss 1984: 74)

This 'ease' has knock-on sociolinguistic effects which do not help the 'lesser' of the kin tongues to maintain its linguistic or societal integrity. This can lead to certain attitudes on the part of speakers of the 'major' kin tongue, including a reduction in 'the willingness to grant basic lingual rights to the weaker tongue or group' (1984: 74). Perhaps more important is the fact that '[d]ue to all-too-facile interlingual communication the borderline between the two languages may get blurred and, in the long run, intermediate new speech varieties may come into being' (Kloss 1984: 74), which are not well thought-of in the 'lesser' kin tongue community and, in particular, among language activists. One of the central ironies of this position is that these intermediate varieties lead to even less weight being given to the idea of Abstand.

The second term – Halbsprache – also informs this debate somewhat. Kloss sets up (1976: 313) a continuum, at one end of which stands a *Normaldialekt* 'normal dialect', at the other an Ausbau language. In between, there are language types which are 'indeed less developed than an *Ausbau* language, but more developed than a *Normaldialekt*'.[8]

Kloss notes (1976: 314) that the term Halbsprache, which he has used in these contexts to describe forms of language such as Luxembourgish, Scots and Pennsylvania German, is not without its problems; not least the identification of *half* with less than generous measure. There are also problems with the alternative term *Ausbaudialekt*, 'Ausbau dialect', since this might give too much stress to the *dialect* part of the equation; particularly, we can assume, when Abstand is present, as is the case with Scots. Yet the distinction holds. In his definition of a Normaldialekt,

Kloss states (1976: 315) that

> [a] *Normaldialekt* in Germany in reality has been confined in terms of
> use in writing to *belles lettres* and in the broadcast media to entertain-
> ment (humour and lighter drama); it is more or less excluded from
> (for example) the press, school, church, film, political congresses, with
> the exception of local councils.[9]

This is in marked contrast to the situation with a Halbsprache, or Ausbau
dialect. He presents a schematization (1976: 316; my translation) which
explains the distinctions between such a linguistic situation and a
full-blown Ausbau language:[10]

Area of Application	Application possible for an Ausbau dialect ('Halbsprache')	Application practically only possible for an Ausbau language ('Vollsprache')
1. Church	Preaching, mainly 'low' services, and under special circumstances	Sunday morning services; liturgy
2. Parliament	Discussions, especially casual ones, and in local councils	Officially published proceedings; announcements from the governing body
3. Broadcast media	Some plays; simpler news broadcasts;'folksy' instruction and information programmes for, for example, farmers	Cultural and scientific instruction and information
4. Writing (except for those literary endeavours associated with Normaldialekt, e.g. humour and light verse)	Advanced literature (especially novels and 'serious' plays). Some 'folksy' non literary prose, such as brochures dealing with the culture of the 'home' area	The greater part of 'serious' literature; almost all non-literary prose
5. Print media	Some non-humorous periodicals or sections of periodicals, at times literary, biographical and religious in nature	The great majority of periodicals; all newspapers
6. School	Primers and other school books for beginners	The great part of all school materials
7. Film	Entertaining and 'light' films, including those to do with action	The great part of production, including films of some importance culturally

Like all schematizations, this table is more true in certain contexts for a given language than it is for others. For instance, Luxembourgish fares rather better in terms of the news media than Scots, although this was not always the case, as Donaldson (1986) shows; the same is true for use in church (although there are exceptions to this in Scotland, including a considerable amount of – often unconscious – Scots used in preaching). No doubt these advantages are due to the complete independence which Luxembourg enjoys and its (perceived) loyalty to the Catholic Church in distinction historically to Protestant Prussia across the border. Scots, on the other hand, fares better in literature and film, television and radio. It has a long literary pedigree; more important – particularly in a discussion of the media – is the matter of economies of scale: Scotland has more than ten times the population Luxembourg has. Nevertheless, the pattern suggested holds true; it might even apply to all 'lesser-used languages'.

In the list of *controversial* languages discussed above, a number of tongues – including, for instance, West Frisian – were defined by Kloss and Haarmann as lacking an 'overarching standard', what Kloss calls (1976: 317) a *dachlose Außenmundart*, 'external dialect without an over-arching standard/ roofless dialect'. As he points out (1976: 317–18), most contemporary dialects have an 'overarching standard', a standard representation of a language of which the dialects are considered a part (even a 'substandard' part). For historical or political reasons, these particular dialects do not share this fate. Because they are not directly under the aegis of the standard language most closely related to them, they may be influenced by another standard language which may be a more distant relative, as is the case with Corsican (in origin an Italian dialect, which has come under considerable influence from French), as discussed by Jaffe (1999), or Rusyn in Slovakia (in origin a Ukrainian dialect, spoken on the 'wrong' side of the Carpathian mountains), or a distant relative, if at all, as is the case with Croatian in Austria, Walloon in Luxembourg or the (former) German Empire, or Alsatian in France.

Having said that, there does seem to be a tendency towards dialects of this type taking on the nature of an Ausbau language: as might have happened with Moldavian, if the Soviet Union had survived (Kloss 1976: 318). If a long historical perspective is taken, Scots could be seen as just such a development: the dialect of 'English' which inhabited a political and cultural space different from all others on the Island of Britain.

One question which Kloss does not really address is the reason why processes of this type happen in some places at certain times, but not in other places at other times. For instance, the Swedish spoken by native speakers in Finland is often highly distinctive in comparison with the Swedish of Sweden; so distinctive at times as to cause intelligibility problems. Yet few would suggest that it is a separate Ausbau development, in marked contrast to, for instance, Corsican. Can a case be made for the results of developments of this type being different depending on the levels of literacy in different communities at the time when political, and cultural, separation took place?

3.4.2 Reservations about Kloss' model

The model established by Kloss and his successors is without doubt the most satisfactory; particularly so when read in tandem with the views of Stewart. The sense of a dynamic, and developmental, approach to the nature of what we mean by language energizes and informs our understanding. That does not mean that we can be blind to some of the model's failings, however.

In the first place, there is a danger of over-inflation in terms of terminology. We can see this in some of the examples in the above: the distinction between a near-dialectalized language and a Halbsprache is not – at least to me – entirely clear. Some of Kloss' successors – in particular Muljačić – could be accused of adding too many terms to too few contexts. It is not necessary to invent a term for every 'unusual' language state; otherwise, it is likely that we will not be able to distinguish patterns shared by different situations.

Moreover, despite his model's inherent dynamism, a sense of historicity is not fully developed (indeed, Kloss himself encourages this view by confining his comments in his magnum opus (Kloss 1978) largely to the period after 1800). Of course his model would encourage us to think of these states as being anything but static, but more examples of historical development would be helpful. A discussion leading us through the period from the middle ages on, in which some languages went through a successful Ausbau, some not, would be particularly illuminating: why, for example, would one language (for instance, English) be successful and dominate, whilst another (for instance, Scots) had its Ausbau at best retarded, if not actually reversed?

A further problem may lie in his definition of Abstand. His primary example of this state is German as against Dutch. As has already been pointed out, there is little, if any, mutual intelligibility possible between the standard varieties of these languages; yet in the relatively recent past (and, to some extent, still on the national and linguistic borders), it could be argued that Dutch and German are merely two Ausbau developments (along, perhaps, with Luxembourgish and, to some extent, Swiss German) of a range of 'Germans' which potentially existed as separate 'languages'. If, as was perfectly possible, Low German had maintained its status, it might have been possible to think of it as a dialect of Dutch, or vice versa, or even of a situation not dissimilar to that which existed for Serbo-Croat developing.

The time-depth involved in the development of Abstand between German and Dutch is not great in comparison with, for instance, German and Polish, where there is certainly a relationship, but one so ancient as to be essentially meaningless. Even more apposite would be the example of Swedish and Finnish, where they come into contact in Sweden and Finland. There *may* be an ancient relationship between the Indo-European and Uralic languages; speakers of the one language are faced with structures in the other which are utterly foreign to them, however. It would have to be suggested, therefore, that Abstand may well be as much of a continuum as is Ausbau; but while the latter's development is based to a very large extent on conscious, social, processes, the former's development is based upon largely unconscious, linguistic, processes.

3.5   Conclusion

Max Weinreich is reported to have said that 'a language is a dialect with an army and a navy'. It is possible to see what he meant by this: many languages could have been perceived as dialects of a larger language if the historical development of particular societies had been different; by the same token, there are a number of language varieties considered dialects which, if the history of the territories involved had been even slightly different, might now be perceived as languages. This is not the full story, of course. There are a number of speech varieties in the world which, by their very linguistic distance from other language varieties, would have to be treated as languages, even if nothing was ever written in them. Equally true, however, is the observation that, without a developed written state, and a presence in various types of media, it is relatively straightforward for even the most benign government to ignore a language's existence. Ignored or denigrated languages tend not to thrive. It is to these developments that the next chapter will turn.

From this viewpoint, Kloss' primary breakthrough is his description of Abstand and, in particular, Ausbau characteristics. He saw the concept *language* as being, in a developmental sense, a dynamic one, based upon a given language variety's presence in a range of (largely written) domains.

Thus, even the Abstand status of a language variety does not guarantee it an Ausbau status. Much of the nature of the Ausbau process will be discussed in the following chapter. As I have suggested, a single criticism which could be levelled at Kloss' work as a whole is that it conceptually lacks a full sense of historicity; this should not be taken as being damning for the terminological and conceptual basis of his work, however.

4
Language Standardization: Process

4.1 Introduction

When introducing the central analytical skills required in linguistics to first year University students, I often attempt the following experiment. I show them these examples:

1. Hands my wash I.
2. I have went to University.
3. I'm awfully annoyed with that boys.
4. I'll can see him tomorrow.

I then ask them to put their hands up for each of the examples if they think they are 'wrong'. I generally receive an overwhelming 'incorrect' response for all four examples. I then ask them to put up their hands if they use the phrase themselves.

This is where the experiment gets interesting. Naturally, no one puts up his or her hand for example 1. When I ask the same question for example 2, I rarely get many hands (18-year-olds, who make up the majority of the student population in the course in question, are not usually keen to draw attention to themselves, especially when there is a danger that they may be 'wrong'). Then I put up my hand to acknowledge that I, on occasion, use *I have went*. Slowly hands rise around the lecture theatre. There are never as many people admitting to using this 'wrong' expression as probably do so in reality, however.

I then move on to example 3. Again I ask for a show of hands. I will normally get a few hands raised. On this occasion, I do not put up my own hand, because I would not use this particular expression. I then ask everyone from the North-East of Scotland, the Black Isle and Caithness (the non-Gaelic areas of the North of Scotland) to raise their hands. Given Aberdeen's location, quite a few hands go up. I then ask the question about use again. More hands remain up than previously: some students have worked out that the use of the singular form with a plural noun is a marker of regional origin and identity.

We then come to the final example. I raise my hand. I am normally very surprised if any hands join me. I then ask whether any students come from the west of Scotland, the northern counties of Ireland, or the Appalachian mountains. Some hands will rise. I ask about usage; again, a few hands will stay up.

Students will – I hope – learn from this that there are different interpretations possible for what is 'correct' and 'incorrect' in a language. Example 1 is just plain wrong for any variety of English. Element order of that type would render any clause beyond the most simple utterly opaque to a native speaker. Example 2, on the other hand, is not 'wrong' in the same way. Almost all (if not all) students would understand the expression; native speakers from all over the English-speaking world would produce such a phrase, even when they consider it 'wrong' (or perhaps even 'ugly' or 'ignorant'). This is a different situation to that found for examples 3 and 4. Both the examples – the plural use of *that* and the double modal construction – are associated only with some dialects, not all. In that sense, example 2 is *non-standard*, while examples 3 and 4 are *dialectal* (although the boundary between the two categories is fluid). With all three examples, students who produce these usages natively have somehow imbibed the idea that what they are doing is 'wrong'. For this state of affairs to exist, some perception of *standard* use must be present. In order for this experiment to work for any language, that language must have gone through a planning process which included (as most of them do) notions of a specific standard.

Why do I do this? In the first place, I am encouraging bonding between students, most of whom have only arrived at University a week or so before. Second, I want them to start thinking about language as a matter which impacts upon their identity both as individuals, and as members of a community.

Because of education and upbringing, most of us do not question the idea of language planning, or rather its ultimate result, a standard form of a language. This is particularly the case if we come from a country which participated in the first wave of mass literacy in the nineteenth century. Years of exposure to, and training in, the standard make its use seem absolutely natural, even if we speak a strikingly different dialect.

As we will see, however, the process is fraught with both opportunity and danger, for the individual and the language.

4.2 The Ausbau process as part of standardization

In Chapter 3, the term Ausbau was used to refer to those varieties which are considered languages, separate from other equivalent systems, because of linguistic 'development'. Kloss would claim that, in all technologically advanced societies, a language, to be considered a *language*, must have passed through a development stage. What, therefore, is meant by 'development'? Kloss suggests (1967: 33) that, in the process of development in standardization, the written form as a planned process takes primacy. A particularly interesting corollary to this is what happens to lesser-used languages in a highly literate environment, where all speakers write in another variety, a point to which we will return in our discussion of attempts at the standardization of Scots in Chapters 5 and 8.

The processes by which an Ausbau language develops are defined by Kloss by means of the following diagram, which illustrates the use of the language variety in a range of non-literary prose contexts. The higher the arrow reaches, the more 'developed' a language is, as shown in Figure 4.1.

Folk ('volkstümlich') implies non-literary prose, dealing with humour or local values of importance. It would make no claims to being in competition with 'serious' writing. When this stage is represented in the broadcast media, it tends to be in drama, often with comic characteristics. If used at all in schools, it would be in a fairly limited capacity at a low level. *Elevated* prose would be found in 'serious' journalism; children would have materials, as well as be educated, in this variety until the

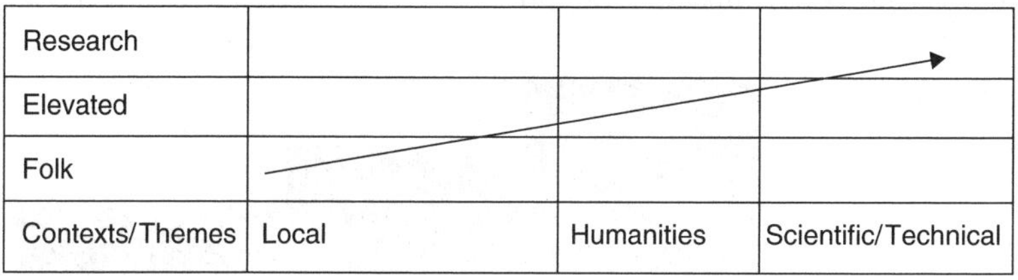

Research			
Elevated			
Folk			
Contexts/Themes	Local	Humanities	Scientific/Technical

Figure 4.1 Non-literary prose and *Ausbau*
Source: Kloss 1978: 304; my translation.

highest levels of school. It would be used in the broadcast media for news and current affairs programmes, although this might be at a local level. *Research* implies that the language is used in prose intended for an audience educated to university level. It would be found in research reports and scholarly articles. In the broadcast media it would be used as a language of authority in debate.

Local implies the use of the language variety when discussing local matters dealing with fauna, flora, local history and culture. *Humanities* implies themes discussing matters not necessarily associated with local concerns. Thus a variety might be used for a history of the world, or for literary criticism of the work of an internationally recognized author. *Scientific/Technical* implies themes associated with science and technology. The fact that non-literary prose is foregrounded is crucial to Kloss' argument. It is quite easy for a language variety to be boxed into a literary corner, as can be seen with Scots and Occitan.

There is, moreover, a linear and logical progression between different stages. No language variety could be used in *Folk* contexts only, but discuss *Scientific/Technical* themes, for instance. The main dividing line for language varieties developing towards Ausbau can be illustrated as Figure 4.2.

An emerging Ausbau variety can be used in *Folk* contexts when discussing matters of local interest, topics relating to matters in the humanities (the work of a local author would be a good example) or for scientific or technical matters, so long as this relates to highly practical and local issues, such as, for instance, gardening, farming or home improvements. The same variety is likely to be used to discuss *elevated* themes in relation to local matters (such as a discussion of local history intended for a well-informed but not specialist audience), and also for the humanities (when discussing, for instance, the music of a given composer in writing intended for the same general audience). At this level, the developing variety is unlikely to be used to discuss scientific or technical matters. In *Research*-based contexts, it is likely that it will only

Research			
Elevated			
Folk			
Contexts/Themes	Local	Humanities	Scientific/Technical

Figure 4.2   The Ausbau process and domain use
Source: Kloss 1976: 308–9; my translation.

be used when addressing local issues. In other words, the developing variety is increasingly unlikely to be used as we move from the local to the general, from an orientation in the humanities to an orientation in the sciences or technology.

Given the ways in which a number of world languages dominate in the domain of science in particular, it is difficult even for well-established languages to compete. For instance, it is possible to study humanities and science/technological subjects in Welsh at high school level in a range of locales in Wales. It is also possible to study these subjects in Welsh up to and beyond first degree level at a few institutions of higher education. The problem lies in resources, however. With only some million speakers, it is practically impossible to expect the production of, for instance, many scholarly monographs in Welsh on a subject such as inorganic chemistry. At this level, even a well-established minority language must bow to the inevitable dominance of a small number of world languages in certain fields. To an even greater extent, it might even be counter-productive for a language going through the process of Ausbau to try, since it is very likely that any language with which it competes will have a significantly longer history of being used to describe a range of themes. Even to native speakers of the developing variety, it may seem more apposite to use the fully developed variety when writing about certain topics. This is one of the central issues wrestled with by planners of Luxembourgish in relation to French.

As we saw in Chapter 3, Kloss' model has much to recommend it: language is not an absolute state, but rather dependent upon notions of a given variety's 'development' in relation to other varieties. The 'conquest' of functional domains is at its heart. Those situations which are not associated with literature, but rather with 'functional', informative, prose (*Sachprosa* in German), are central to Ausbau. At the heart of this view are both corpus and status planning, although this is not something which Kloss discusses in any great depth. We will return to this point in the following chapters.

It is difficult (if not impossible) to quarrel with this view. There are a number of points left out, however. The first is perhaps the most striking: what linguistic (rather than sociological) features does an Ausbau standard have which other dialects of the same language do not? Answers to this question are certainly *implied* by Kloss; the problem is rarely touched upon, however. Another question is also raised, but not answered: what are the historical, societal and cultural factors which encourage the development of an Ausbau variety, often at the expense of another pre-existing standard?

4.3   A historical model

Joseph (1987) puts forward a number of unidirectional propositions on the nature of the standardization process. He suggests that there is a tendency in all literate speech communities towards the choice of a particular variety as a 'more equal' representative of their language:

> Gradually the dominant dialect may change from first among equals to first among unequals. It may even give its name to the regional dialect as a whole, a process for which I have borrowed the rhetorical term SYNECDOCHE ... . Once a dialect had achieved this level of dominance, it is a short step for people both within and outside the region to consider it to be the dialect proper, with the dialects of other communities relegated to the status of variants or subdialects. (Joseph 1987: 2)

To become a true standard, this *synecdochic* dialect must be codified and written in a consistent manner. It must also be used in conjunction (and as an equal partner) with other standardized languages both inside and outside its speech community. Anticipating our discussions on language planning, the model deals with corpus planning, status planning and acquisition planning.

Why should a standardization process take place? Joseph suggests four basic motives for the process. The first he identifies as power and social hierarchy. As he points out,

> The interaction of power, language, and reflections on language, inextricably bound up with one another in human history, largely defines language standardization. The rise of one community's dialect as synecdochic within a linguistically fragmented region is both a manifestation of that community's power and a base for expanding it. A few users of the standard language accede to positions of authority which permit them to direct the future course of standardization. Individuals learn standard languages in order to increase their personal standing. And 'eloquence' in the use of language almost universally functions as a mantle of power. (Joseph 1987: 43)

In a sense, therefore, linguistic power begets linguistic power.

Beyond this largely speech-community internal force, Joseph distinguishes three inter-related factors, some of which at least act *upon* the speech community rather than from *within* it. The first of these is *imperialism.* Imperial aggressors have both the means and the ability to impose their language in their chosen form over those they have conquered. The second factor is *nationalism*. Nationalism has the propensity to encourage the iconic status of one particular variety of a language at the expense of all others, encouraging the view that it represents a 'truer' form (Joseph 1987: 46). Finally, he distinguishes *internationalism* as an ideological motivation for standardization. The need for relatively problem-free inter-cultural communication has led to the establishment of norms upon languages, the development of artificial languages and even the 'globalization' of English. All of these both demand and justify standardization in the minds of their proponents.

Joseph recognizes that, before a language variety can begin to move towards standardization, a number of features of the language situation as it then stands have to be worked through by native speakers. He postulates (Joseph 1987: 49) that all undeveloped varieties are subordinate to a dominant language in a state of superposition:

> Superposition is the coexistence of two or more languages of significantly different prestige within a single-speech community. In the great majority of cases of language standardization, the simple presence of a superposed system is more crucial in and of itself to the arising standard's course of development than is any detail of the nature of the relationship between the superposed 'high' system (hereafter H) and the more widely used 'low' (L) which is undergoing the standardization.

In essence, a primary motivation behind standardization is what might be termed *language envy*. The presence of an already standardized language which is foreign to a speech community may encourage members of that speech community to claim some of the cultural domain and learn some of the linguistic lessons which this high variety offers.

This leads to Joseph's third motivation: *acculturation.* Joseph (1987: 51) posits an avant-garde among the L community:

> The standardization of L begins when persons within its community of speakers become aware of the prestige difference between H and L – or if not of the prestige difference *per se*, then of some of the particular sources of H's prestige – enough so that these persons are motivated to learn to perform in H beyond whatever rudimentary communicative functions are demanded of them by the H community.

The prestigious associations which caused this shift may have repercussions which mean that more and more of the L community switch over to a variety of H. A particularly pertinent example of this is Scots during the seventeenth century, as will be discussed in Chapter 5.

What Joseph concentrates on, however, are those occasions where, for whatever social or historical reason, this initial shift towards the H variety by the linguistic avant-garde is matched by an eventual focus upon bringing the L variety into line with the prestigious features of the H variety (Joseph 1987: 53).

The combination of *eloquence* and *power* transforms a dialect among dialects into a standard(ized) language. Any L variety which achieves this transfer has accomplished two things: in the first place, it has overcome low linguistic esteem (often masking low ethnic esteem) felt towards it even by its own speakers, a point to which we will return in our discussion of Afrikaans in Chapter 6. It has also established itself in the rhetorical domains normally associated with H through the acquisition of its 'eloquence'. A new H has therefore been established. The rest of this chapter, and all of Chapter 5, will discuss the means by which this process can come about.

It could be argued that the synecdochic dialect, believed both by its speakers, and speakers of other dialects within the continuum, to be the *best* form of the language, is already a *standard*, since it has assumed a highly prestigious position. Joseph claims that it is at this stage that the acculturative process really begins, however – where the original H variety is replaced by another H, emerging from the vernacular dialects, but distinct from them. He would classify this stage as that of an *emerging standard*. At this point, Joseph makes a distinction between *circumstantial* and *engineered* forms of standardization (Joseph 1987: 60–2). The former represents those occasions where a standard form of a language is established through human agency, but without anything approaching a plan being envisaged. The latter emphasizes a planned process, whether this be long-term or short-term.

Part of this emergence is *codification*: of the orthography and of the grammar. As we will see in particular in our discussion of French in Chapter 5, a solidly prescriptive approach can be assumed during this period in the standard's development, even when the process is circumstantial. More important, perhaps, is the enlargement of the functional sphere of the standard. Joseph sees this development as having a number of separate features. The standard, he claims (Joseph 1987: 72) will develop as the national symbol, particularly, perhaps, in those situations where two or more closely related varieties are associated with different nations. The emerging standard may also become the symbol of formality and solemnity, especially if associated with religious or philosophical tradition and scripture. It will, moreover, assume a *lingua franca* function, be used in writing and broadcasting to the near-total exclusion of all other dialects, and become the primary means of education, as well as the sole variety taught as representative of the vernacular.

The next stage in Joseph's model is a *maturing standard*. In the preceding stage the emerging standard's position within a number of functional domains is guaranteed. Nevertheless, the new standard may be faced with attitudes of inadequacy, particularly in terms of the language's 'elegance' (or lack thereof) and as a suitable tool for argumentation. The point is, however, that these attitudes are generally expressed in relation to the perceived merits of the former H language. Indeed, a number of the prescriptive norms of Standard English are products of just such feelings of inadequacy in relation to the perceived 'perfection' of Latin during the eighteenth century. The judgement of 'elegance' is not based on egalitarian notions.

Joseph makes a good case (1987: 88–90) for this process being due to a 'linguistic/cultural lag'. The linguistic avant-garde, having imbibed the cultural assumptions of the H culture, but wishing to express their new self-confidence in an elevated and standardized form of L, are faced with the problem that this new standard cannot – at least apparently, but often in actual fact – express all the nuances of connotative and denotative meaning which H can. In order to counter this, a maturing standard will regularly embark on a process of *elaboration*.

As Joseph describes it, elaboration can take a variety of forms, many of which will be referred to again in our discussion of *corpus planning*. Primarily, the elaborative process involves both actual borrowing of forms from the H variety (or varieties) and *calquing*, a form of loan translation. The level of which process takes place tends to be dependent on national or ethnic ideologies at a given time, as our discussion of *purism* in Chapter 6 will suggest. Nineteenth-century Romanian provides an example. At the time, the H variety, which had previously been Greek combined with Old Church Slavonic, switched, doubtless due to a combination of the ideology of Latinism (the idea that all speakers of Romance varieties are united in a common 'Latin' cause) and the association of France with radical causes and high culture, to French. The conflict between the nationalist, Romantic, fervour of which the language planning process formed a part and the particularly high prestige of French among the small number of literate people carrying out the planning, led to unusual levels of French influence on the standardizing form of Romanian, many features of which it has retained to the present day, despite their relative rarity in all but the most 'careful' forms of speech (Joseph 1987: 100).

Joseph makes a distinction (1987: 104–5) between *remedial* and *cosmetic* elaboration. Remedial elaborations, which can affect all areas of the language, not merely the lexical, fill an apparent (or real) gap in a language's usage. One example of this he gives is the importation of many Greek words and structures into Latin during the late Republican period, in order to enable Latin both to describe the flora and fauna of its new eastern Mediterranean territories, and achieve the level of nuanced distinction which Greek had accomplished through its dialectic tradition. Joseph contrasts this with cosmetic elaboration, which again may affect any part of a language. These are elaborations which are not at all necessary, but which may give the elite avant-garde in particular a sense of the 'worthiness' of the language. Some of the structural borrowings from French into Romanian could be seen as examples of this process. Another example Joseph cites (1987: 105) is the employment of Latin, Greek and (occasionally) Hebrew plural suffixes in English. The less than vital nature of these features can be seen both in the way in which the system of English finds it difficult to maintain their presence in the language (e.g., *stadiums* versus *stadia*; *cherubs* versus *cherubim*), and the fact that language arbiters (including non-elite representatives) for many other 'modern' languages frown upon such 'unnative' structures.

At its most banal level, cosmetic elaboration in English led, in the 1970s and 1980s, to the terminological preference for many people in the British Isles for *quiche* over *flan* for savoury tarts with an egg-based filling. It could be argued that this was actually remedial elaboration, since we can now distinguish between these savoury dishes and sweet flans. My own intuition is that this is an example of *post hoc* argumentation. The presence of both types of flan for centuries had not caused problems of definition until middle class British people began to make regular trips to the 'real' France beyond the holiday resorts in the 1960s. Attestations in the *Oxford English Dictionary* (s.v. *quiche*[1]) would support this view. The word appears first to have been used in written English in 1949 in a specifically culinary instruction context; until 1966, attestations are from cookery books entitled, for example, *French Country Cookery* and *French Provincial Cookery*. It is only from that date on that the word is used for the direct experience of eating various types of savoury flan. No cosmetic categorization of this type can last forever: I was offered a raspberry and citrus quiche in a restaurant recently. The problem, of course, is that *elaboration* can often lead to *over-elaboration*, particularly with cosmetic elaboration, as seen in seventeenth century France and England (Joseph 1987: 106; Barber 1993: 175–82 and Baugh and Cable 1994: 209–29).

Joseph's model does not end with the maturation process, however. He goes on to assume the gradual ossification of the mature standard. An originally living standard, capable of considerable variation, becomes an *absolute* standard (Joseph 1987: 160). As he points out, however, the presence of 'relative standards which are attainable by individual human beings' may maintain some of the vitality which the variety once possessed.

There are two potential conclusions to this process. The more positive one is that the guiding processes which created the standard do not 'come grinding to a halt. They may shift from an implementary to a maintenance level of intensity' (1987: 163). This is the situation we can observe with many contemporary European languages. The less favourable outcome (from the point of view of the standard's vitality) is that it may go through a process which leads to its becoming *classical* in status:

> By ceasing to be tied to a living community of speakers, by ceasing to change, classical languages give up much of what it means to be a language. They can nevertheless be maintained in limited but very prestigious functions for centuries. (Joseph 1987: 173)

An apposite example of this process at work can be found in the development of Classical Latin. The economic, ethnic and political tensions which led to the collapse of the western Roman Empire also led to the loss in many areas of a native Latin-speaking ruling class, and a diminution in the importance (and possibility) of urban life and trade, with a concomitant decline in literacy among all but highly circumscribed groups, such as the Church. Despite the fact that the local vernacular forms of Latin were already divergent, they might still have been kept under the 'roof' of Latin, as is the case today, to a considerable extent, with the highly differentiated varieties and monolithic standard (if not classical) form of Arabic, if it were not for these extra-linguistic factors. Indeed, Latin might still have continued as the 'ideal' form of at least some of the Romance vernaculars if it were not for the 'classicization' of Latin pronunciation and grammar carried out during the 'Carolingian Renaissance' of the eighth and ninth centuries, as we will see in our discussion of the standardization of French in Chapter 5.

4.3.1   Problems with Joseph's model

With so many theoretical and conceptual insights to work through, it is inevitable that queries over details arise. Joseph, for instance, questions the idea that some individuals within a given society may speak, and only speak, the standard variety of their language as a native dialect. In the English-speaking world, there are not many people who are monodialectal speakers of the standard variety; they do exist, however. In the British Isles, they tend to be associated with the present (and often former) ruling classes, with the upper echelons of the more traditional universities, and with the higher ranks of the Church of England. To be sure, membership of these groups does not necessarily mean that your language will be of this type; it is certainly more likely, however. How are we to bring this reality in line with Joseph's views?

Are we to assume that the privileged elite already mentioned continue to speak the synecdochic dialect, and that, along with all other speakers, the 'eloquence' of the standard is learned as part of the literacy process? The one proviso would be that speakers of the synecdochic dialect, being both source and analogue of the standard's central functional apparati, would be obliged to make a far less significant leap than would speakers of other dialects.

But can we speak in terms of an absolute split between synecdochic dialect and the standard? Those adults within this prestige community who acquired the standard variety in its written form would have employed it in their speech. Whilst conscious at first, those elements of the standard which were exclusive to it would rapidly have been transferred into the largely indistinguishable native code. More importantly, those in authority would quickly have begun to enforce these 'standard' usages in the speech of children both at school and, most significantly, at home. Whilst it is certainly true that the upper classes maintain certain features in their speech which could be described as non-standard (or *superstandard*, as Joseph suggests), that is not the case to such an extent with the upper middle class, the patrician class which forms the governing elite of most countries, or of their followers, the linguistically insecure lower middle classes.

Of course children – and adults – who speak only this standard would vary in their usage in speech depending on the subject they are discussing, and their usage would also alter over time, but this is surely a matter of register rather than actual dialectal distinctiveness. It may be that what Joseph has in mind here is the *relative standard* discussed above; if that is the case, he does not make this explicit, however.

Moreover, Joseph's views on the standardization process are elitist. This is not a criticism: the process as he describes it is founded upon the idea that elite groups of whatever type can dictate linguistic appropriateness within a speech community. A point which he does not discuss, however, is the manner in which the standard is diffused among a larger part of the populace of a given territory.

This is problematical, since it is difficult to see how we can call a prestige variety a standard without knowledge of its written form among a significant part of a population, or, as Suleiman (2003) points out for Arabic, the standard form is not associated both with 'pure' desert life and the word of God, expressed through a particularly vital ideology. If the knowledge of a standardized form of any language remains in the hands of the language planning elite, it is unlikely that it can be treated as anything other than a complex game, a point to which we will return in Chapter 8. In the past, however, in those periods where literacy has been low, we can probably speak of a micro-standardization process within the literate elite, where one element is sufficiently powerful or influential to establish its written form as equivalent to the written form of the language as a whole. A particularly apposite example of this process can be seen in the West Saxon *Schriftsprache* discussed in Chapter 5.

Interestingly, it is almost impossible to think of a standardization process, whether circumstantial or engineered, which has not taken place in a situation of expanding social horizons and growing potential for education and therefore literacy (at least among a potential or actual middle class), even if, as Crowley (1996) suggests, the process is often informed by fears over linguistic and social threats. The successful proto-standard form of English was established in a situation of growing urbanization, with an expanding middle class and the full-scale development of an early form of capitalism, including, in line with Anderson (1991), print capitalism as a means of 'imagining the nation'. The fact that the standardization process was carried out by an elite in the Royal Chancery and elsewhere in the centre should not blind us to the manner in which it spread among non-elite members of the community. This spread was only possible due to the spread of literacy among this middle class. The imposition of the standard throughout the English-speaking world was accomplished largely through mass education, producing literacy only in this variety. This might be termed the *no-alternative* strategy. It could, in fact, be argued that the standardized language actually requires this unquestioning adherence and application in order to be treated as standard.

In engineered standard language situations, where the standardization process is regularly much more rapid, many of the same precepts hold. In a colonial or post-colonial situation, it is likely to be the creole elite (the colonial middle class) who will be attracted to the new standard.

There must be a significant enough number of this expanding middle class sufficiently interested both in the language's status, and its transmission, to influence the level to which the new standard spreads. There also needs to be a receptive and willing mass audience (in terms of the territory and speech community) to receive the standard as the only acceptable form of the language.

4.4   Conclusion

The views of Kloss and Joseph are both complementary and also, apparently, opposed to each other. Joseph emphasizes the importance of the development of a literary culture as part of the elaboration and acculturation of a synecdochic dialect. Kloss, on the other hand, comes to the conclusion that the single most important element in the process of Ausbau is the use of the standardizing language in Sachprosa, non-literary, particularly official, prose. Both scholars, on the other hand, emphasize the importance of human agency, both individual and collective, in the development of standard varieties. In Chapter 5 we will test and illustrate some of their findings by a discussion of a number of standardization processes, viewed over a broad historical perspective.

5
Language Standardization: Testing the Models

In the previous chapter we discussed two models for the standardization process put forward by Kloss and Joseph. While some illustration for their views was given, no focus on the complete standardization process for any language over time was permitted. In this chapter, four standardizations will be considered – three successful and one failed – which will not only help to test Kloss' and Joseph's models, but also produce further understanding of the processes involved.

5.1 English

Of all the Germanic languages, English has the longest continuous written heritage; interestingly, it also represents their earliest example of an attempt at standardization, the late West Saxon Schriftsprache, 'written [or "writing"] language', which was used in the tenth and eleventh centuries, both within the West Saxon kingdom, centred intellectually on the chancery at Winchester, and in other centres outside the West Saxon dialect area (Gneuss 1972). Late West Saxon was employed in a number of genres at a time when these roles were normally assigned to Latin in other parts of western Europe, thereby suggesting an acculturation process which partly removed the previous superposition. Prior to this, local usages prevailed, emanating from monastery or cathedral scriptoria. It was not the case that, as Luick suggested, *man schrieb wie man sprach* 'you wrote as you spoke' (Stanley 1988); it must certainly be suspected that these local 'standards' did have a strong flavour of local language, however.

This Schriftsprache cannot be described as a fully fledged *standard*, however: primarily because a standard proper would only normally come into being in an era where literacy is spreading, particularly among a putative middle class. Whilst literacy was by no means uncommon in Anglo-Saxon England (Kelly 1990), there is no doubt that it was the province of a numerically insignificant (although socially influential) elite. Yet its influence over the rest of England's literate class bears many similarities to later standardization processes for English and other languages. We might put forward the term *micro-standardization*.

Along with manuscripts written in West Saxon from elsewhere in England, there are texts which hypercorrect – using features which the (non-West Saxon) scribe considers West Saxon, but which are actually based upon a conflict between the usage of that dialect and his own. This level of imitation beyond imitation represents, in the starkest way, what marks off standardization processes which proceeded by routes which Joseph would describe as *circumstantial* (that is, where it is impossible to distinguish individuals or groups acting as language planners) from *engineered* ones. These scribes must have considered their own usage to be inferior to the West Saxon one. It was, in some intangible sense, more 'correct', more 'English', than their own regional forms.

In the course of two or three generations after the Norman conquest of 1066, the Schriftsprache was gradually replaced, when English was written at all, by forms of writing which again were rooted in local scriptorial tradition. English was changing rapidly during the eleventh and twelfth centuries; indeed, when attempts at a form of writing representing the old model were made, these tend to demonstrate only a fitful understanding of certain of its orthographical, lexical and – above all – morphological features (Stanley 1969, 1988). As English re-surfaced, challenging the superposition of French, it did so in a variety of forms, depending on the provenance of author and scribe.

One of these local usages did demonstrate considerable spread during the late twelfth and early thirteenth centuries, however. Originally developing from the house styles of the scriptoria in the area around Hereford and Worcester, this usage, termed 'AB language' by Tolkien (as discussed by d'Ardenne (1961: 177–250)), is found in a wide range of texts, largely religious and didactic in nature, the most famous of which being *Ancrene Riwle*, 'a rule for anchorites'. What is interesting is that something approaching this 'house style' is to be found in texts written or copied a considerable distance outside its original heartland. There must have been a sense that this was a 'correct' way to write English, at least when it came to texts from this set of nested genres.

Why did this not become Standard English, therefore? In the first place, the south-west midlands were linguistically conservative, compared to areas both to the north and east; this meant that certain features found in the AB language, such as grammatical gender and case, would have had to be re-learned by speakers from many other areas, if the standard had spread (Millar 2002). The area was also 'peripheral' in a very real sense, exhibiting dialectal features which were unusual anywhere else in England.

Moreover, English was still not a prestigious enough language. Whilst it would be misleading to categorize it as the language of peasants, it was certainly not the language of choice for a significant element in the ruling classes. The *acculturation* process could not fully begin, therefore.

As Samuels (1989) suggests, a more likely candidate for the source of the standard developed in the late fourteenth century: the Wycliffite north-central midlands standard. Found in a wide range of texts, both from its base area and elsewhere in England, it is associated most strongly with the literary activities of the religious reformer John Wycliff and his followers. The fact that the usage had a supra-regional identity could only be of service to people who – on peril of their lives – would not have wished their dialectal provenance to be revealed. Interestingly, it was also used by their opponents in debates during the period, no matter their origin.

But whilst the use of this supra-regional form continued for a considerable period, there are very good reasons why it could not really compete with what was to become Standard English. Linguistically, the Wycliffite north-central midlands standard was too 'northern' for the majority of English people. Culturally, it cannot have helped that its primary users were viewed as heretics by the vast majority of the community. Yet its presence on the English scene might have encouraged the development of usages which were more linguistically and ideologically suitable.

By the mid-fourteenth century, London had developed into an entrepot. As the century proceeded, London texts gradually become more midlands in nature, as the flow of well-to-do immigrants from the central midlands increased. This can be seen in the way that the language used by Chaucer is more 'midlands' than that of London writers from a generation before, and the writing of his successors is more 'midlands' again. Indeed, the poet Lydgate (active in the second quarter of the fifteenth century) appears to be using a variety of language not dissimilar to a very early form of Standard English. Linguistically, therefore, a form of language which was associated both with southern and midlands speech would have been most approachable to any speaker of either, when writing. Yet this, while important, is not the primary reason why London English became Standard English.

Until around 1400, it was normal in London for all schooling to be in French and Latin. Around this time, the pointlessness of the use of French must have become evident, when it had ceased to be the native language of any English person. Many schools began to use English as the vehicle of primary instruction, therefore. After around 1425, the higher echelons of the royal administration were in the hands of people whose preferred means of written expression was English in its most recent London form. This group, as we might expect, had a house style of its own, generally termed the *Chancery Standard* after one of its central sources, the Royal Chancery. Fisher (1996) suggests that the development of this standard should be seen as part of an 'official language policy' of the Lancastrian usurpers of the English throne, to emphasize their 'Englishness' (Henry IV was the first 'English' king to be born in the country since 1066) in the face of renewed war with France. This is overstating the point; there is certainly a sense in which writers of the period and later perceived the era as pivotal to any construction of English identity, however.

During the course of the fifteenth century, people writing for assistance to the administration began to employ this usage, no matter their geographical origin. No doubt they assumed they would receive preferential treatment from the administration if they appeared to be members of its 'club' rather than outsiders. 'Provincial' writers then began to employ this usage even when writing to people from their own area. This can be seen in the *Paston Letters*, a collection of correspondence from members of a land-owning Norfolk family, largely to each other. As the fifteenth century progressed, fewer Norfolk forms were to be found in their writing, more and more Chancery forms (Davis 1952, 1954). This could be described as an almost archetypal choice of a synecdochic dialect by a speech community.

This is not to say, of course, that regional usages died out immediately. There was even an intermediate phase, for some writers, where a 'colourless regional' form of writing developed in which local features were gradually replaced by the more prestigious centralized norms, without there being a striking break with local tradition (Samuels 1989). From around 1450 on, however, most writers were at least aware of the Chancery usage, and must have considered it prestigious. This sense of dislocation from the local norm might have been encouraged by the civil wars which periodically engulfed England during the fifteenth century. If a local magnate was killed or imprisoned, scribes associated with his court would have had to seek employment elsewhere; often in areas where their regional norm would not have been acceptable. Technological means encouraged the process, however.

William Caxton, who introduced printing to England towards the end of the century, has been described as 'the Luther of English', suggesting that he standardized English in the same way that Luther standardized High German. On both occasions this is a gross over-simplification. Both men helped to stabilize and popularize an already emerging standard. In a manuscript culture, every written artefact is potentially different from every other, albeit normally in subtle ways; with the introduction of the printing press, however, scribes as a mediating vehicle ceased to have any importance. Acknowledging a low level of variation, generally caused by error, all versions of a given text were now essentially the same.

Caxton was at heart a businessman. For purely pragmatic reasons he would have preferred to use one variety of a language, in one (essential) orthography: if that usage was pleasing and prestigious in his customers' opinion, all to the better. Thus, while a Kentish man himself, he used the Chancery Standard, since this would be most readily comprehensible – and attractive – to the widest possible audience (Baugh and Cable 1993: 191–2).

We should pause here and review the extent to which the process described is fully blown standardization. Whilst, as we saw above, a degree of (minor) variation is possible within a standard written language, the 'Chancery Standard' here described and its descendants, well into the early modern period, demonstrate considerable variation at all linguistic levels. What we have here could be described as analogous to the development of a synecdochic dialect, in the sense that variation is confined to a rather limited set of alternatives drawn from an equally limited number of sources, rather than a standard proper. This is probably over-stating the point, however, since many of the elaborative and acculturative tendencies Joseph suggests as central to the production of a conscious standard are already present in the evolving, now printed, form of London English. Perhaps his concept of *emerging standard* would better serve the case.

In a discussion of the nature of Received Pronunciation (RP) within the broader framework of British English, Smith (1996: 63–4) provides an insight into the process:

> Received Pronunciation may be considered to be *standardised* or focused rather than *standard* or fixed: a centripetal norm towards which speakers tend, rather than a fixed collection of prescribed rules, from which any deviation at all is forbidden.

Extrapolating backwards in time, we might posit that the situation of Standard English in the early modern period is one of *focus* rather than *fixity*. The primary standardization goal of the period 1600–1800, as described in Stein and van Ostade (1994), was to achieve this fixity.

In the sixteenth and seventeenth centuries, the written standard continued to spread. It also continued to be elaborated. Moreover, there is evidence that many people both began to speak the standard in their own accents and to attempt to ape the speech of educated London and the two universities in terms of pronunciation, thus developing what could be described as the ancestor of RP (Dobson 1955). This apart, it would certainly be unusual to find anyone writing in anything other than the standard form by 1600 in England, and around 1700 in Scotland. Yet the Standard English used was still capable of rather more orthographic and morphological variation than it is today. Although English had gone through a process of standardization, it had not been fully *codified*. To use Joseph's term, the *control* process had not yet been fully triggered.

Whilst too much can be made of the encyclopaedic tendencies of scholars of the enlightenment, theirs was an era where absolutist ideals were brought to bear upon all western European languages, ideals which moreover were strongly influenced by earlier Latin and Greek models. Through the production of dictionaries, such as that of Johnson, as well as spelling and grammar books (for both children and adults), and books which gave lists of words and usages to avoid, English gradually became almost homogenous in its nature. Certainly there are differences between the usage of different countries within the English-speaking world, and even between rival prestigious publishing houses, but these are relatively minor. What is interesting about this is that this codification was achieved not by the institution of a language planning institute along the lines of the *Academie Française*, but, in terms of rhetoric, by prestige and good will as well as, in reality, by quite hard-line elitist authoritarianism, as Crowley (1989, 1996) argues most persuasively.

By the end of the nineteenth century, the expansion of the middle classes and large-scale literacy had led to the standard's pervasive identification as practically the sole permissible representation of English in writing and increasingly in speech. Part of this is associated with the importance of the schoolteacher in the eyes of the evolving middle classes, both as an instructor in the national language, and as its arbiter (Gellner 1983). With English, this new and often demotic interpretation of the originally elitist standard can be associated closely with 'democratic imperialism': the idea that all (white) subjects of the Queen-Empress shared their place in an increasingly egalitarian common enterprise, a point also emphasized by Clark (2001).

Many of these developments can be related to the ideas of both Kloss and Joseph. The (unconscious) selection of the synecdochic dialect and its elaboration, its conquest of various domains previously occupied by more prestigious languages, can be seen as a form of Ausbau (albeit one associated with significantly different media from those available in the modern era). We can also, in line with Joseph, see some of the initial stimulus for standardization coming from nationalism, later encouraged by imperialism, with, in the final spread of American English as a lingua franca in the late twentieth century, some degree of internationalism as well. Whilst there have been attempts to establish an *absolute standard*, especially in the eighteenth century, these have always been thwarted by ongoing change, both in the language and in the societies in which English is spoken. Because of differing histories and political models, different varieties of the standard have developed in different parts of the world. In general, the language community is very tolerant of this variation. All of these elements maintain and perhaps encourage the evolving nature of the standard. Thus Chancery Standard is often highly approachable to someone conversant with the contemporary standard (at least in comparison with the other dialects of English from that time). It is an ancestor in usage and practice of contemporary varieties of Standard English rather than its equivalent, however.

5.2 French

When discussing the history of the development of linguistic norms for French, we must recognize that this history is of considerably longer duration than is the case with English. For while there is no written form attested for the ancestral forms of English spoken before the Anglo-Saxons reached Britain, the ancestor of French, Latin, has been recorded widely, and often in confusing sociolinguistic detail, a point illustrated by Adams (2003).

The long-term history of what we now know as 'French' is one of competition between an original, and increasingly incomprehensible, High variety (Latin) and the various 'vulgar' Romance varieties of what had been Gaul. This rivalry was progressively complicated by the presence of further competition between these vernaculars (Lodge 1993: in particular, chapter 4). Both struggles were often ongoing simultaneously: French did not vanquish Latin as the High variety until well into the modern period, at which point the language of Paris had been generally accepted as the 'best' form of French, a situation achieved both by the informal means of association with prestigious functions and actual government *diktat.* Certainly, the influence of Latin spelling practice has been pervasive throughout the history of the French language (Pope 1952: 275–98).

Thus, from its very inception, standardization for French was strikingly different from its English equivalent. It is true that English was, in its early history, dominated by other languages, most notably Latin and French. But these languages were not close relatives of the vernacular. All Romance vernaculars in France were for a long period part of a continuum which included Latin at one end, and the vernacular at the other, with various forms of Latinized Romance in between. Although, as has been argued (by Pulgram (1950) among others), the reform of Latin pronunciation and writing associated with the court of Charlemagne led to an earlier breach of this continuum in northern France than anywhere else in the Romance world, this sense of inferiority was carried for a lengthy period by the French intellectuals who would nowadays be seen as language planners, and may explain some of the tendencies inherent in the planning of French up to the present day.

Further, the territory we now think of as 'France' did (and to some extent still does) not have anything like the linguistic homogeneity which England had even before standardization. No matter how apparently divergent one dialect of England is from another, there are very few people who would deny an 'English' identity to all of them (Scots is a special case, which will be dealt with in Section 5.4). It is debateable whether we should use the term 'French' to describe even those northern dialects of Romance which share much of their structural nature with the language of Paris. It would be dangerously deceptive to make any such claim for the southern dialects, which often have much more in common with Catalan or the northern dialects of Italy than they do with 'French'. Within a kingdom where feudal lords in the provinces often wielded more power than the king – in marked contrast to the more autocratic English state – these centrifugal forces would have been encouraged.

The triumph of the dialect of Paris over all the other Romance dialects of Gaul (and, eventually, over the non-Romance languages of France) is therefore part of the history of centralization in, and the increasing cultural dominance of, Paris, intrinsically connected to the sense of identity perceived in a country which often felt itself to be under external and internal threat.

Standard French, as Joseph (1987), among others, has pointed out, derived its particular characteristics from its origin in a period of great flux for France. Although, by the start of the sixteenth century, the variety used among the educated and powerful in the Paris region was increasingly regarded as the most 'French' form (*focussing*, to use Smith's term), the synecdochic variety, the actual process of codification, of elaboration and acculturation, was associated with a period where internal dissent within the country (over religion in particular) was matched by the threat from the territories of the Habsburg family, which had become phenomenally wealthy from their American possessions, in Spain and central Europe. Although it now seems inevitable that France should have entered the eighteenth century as the most powerful country in Europe, this may not have been obvious in the period immediately preceding. In a sense, the development of a highly centralized French matched (and was part of) the development of a highly centralized France. At its heart, the planning and standardization of Parisian French as the sole acceptable, and available, form of French was concerned with its being the 'best' French.

Lodge (1993) suggests that French went through two stages in its codification. On both occasions, there is considerable evidence of conscious individual and group intervention in the process. In Phase I, which he dates (Lodge 1993: 165) between 1500 and 1660, the chief concern was that '[t]he "best" French [was] the best because it [was] spoken by "the best people" '. This is the classic sociolinguistic approach to standardization. The association of Parisian French with the Royal court, which at the time was self-consciously increasing its prestige, the enforcement of the Royal variety as the sole vehicle of public discourse, even in the Occitan-speaking and writing south, and the concomitant shift in language use by the local power centres, inevitably led to the variety's use as the sole 'French' throughout the kingdom, at least in writing. Like English, a form of aristocratic standardization had taken place, which would, eventually, have led to 'leakage' into the day-to-day linguistic reality of all subjects of the King, even if, at the time of the Revolution, Abbé Gregoire's survey demonstrated the low level of knowledge of French among ordinary 'provincials' in France (Schiffman 1996: 97).

During this period, considerable numbers of prescriptive grammars and phonologies were published. Also notable is the foundation (or, in some senses, hijacking) by Cardinal Richelieu of what became the *Academie Française* in 1635. As Lodge (1993: 160–2) points out, too much can, perhaps, be made of the *Academie*'s importance as a language planner. Yet the fact of its presence, and its considerable fame in France and elsewhere, led language planning (or *engineering*, as Joseph prefers it) to have a particular prominence within the kingdom.

The second phase which Lodge identifies is that which he dates (Lodge 1993: 178) between 1660 and 1789, and defines as holding the view that '[t]he "best French" [was] the best because it [was] the language of reason and clarity'. This change in interpretation is very striking; it represents a view still held by Francophones and Francophiles. Certainly there are many today who would argue that 'reason' and 'clarity' are only to be found in the monodialectal use of the standard; its enforcement probably derives from the language planners of the French enlightenment, however. At the time, it is very likely that many writers saw their work as a 'honing' of French towards being a universalist language. Yet what was provided was a circular argument of some potency. Because Standard French was being used by the greatest minds in the kingdom (and elsewhere in Europe) to develop new and striking ideas which apparently 'liberated' humanity from medieval 'darkness', the arguments of reason must use the language of reason. Certainly, some of the more 'illogical' elements which every language contains were 'cleansed' from French; nonetheless, it was the fact that an association was made forcefully and then spread coherently that rendered the assumption irresistible.

It is also pertinent to the case that the intellectuals who formed and supported the French Revolution were almost all domiciled in Paris, and were themselves products of this view of French having a particular logical effectiveness. A unitary Republican people, throwing off the shackles of feudal superstition and embracing a cult of reason, was to be associated with a linguistic equivalent, as Balibar (1985) has suggested. Naturally, these opinions would only have carried weight among the literate. Yet as literacy grew in the nineteenth century, it was this view which prevailed among the overwhelming majority of the French people, even when they came from areas where the local dialect variety was very different from the Standard. It would be very easy to claim that this was achieved through the coercive power of the state; in fact, there is much evidence that a sense of French identity, whether established at school or at home, led people to embrace the Standard.

Inevitably, the process of Ausbau was rather more complex for French than it was for English. Being in competition with a close relative of considerable prestige meant that the struggle for domain dominance was much more taxing on the original Low variety. The elaboration and acculturation of French therefore aped Latin, whether that be visually (by making French look as much as possible like its mother language and by incorporating many Classical Latin lexical items within its Popular Latin framework), or in the ideological claim of French to be the primary post-classical form of Latin. Elements of the intolerance of variation, mentioned above, might be products of this dualism.

In this way, French and English, whose standardization processes began in such similar ways, eventually differed strikingly. Standard English remains at heart an aristocratic and rather inchoate usage; Standard French shed much of its aristocratic nature in favour of an elitist cult of reason in language which, ironically enough, was associated with the *equality* element of the Republican trinity. If everyone speaks and writes in a similar way, no one can be judged by their origin. Perhaps strangely, this egalitarian association has led to greater intolerance of spoken language variation in France and *Francophonie* in general in comparison with the attitude towards rural varieties in particular in the English-speaking world. This came about through the original nationalist (perhaps even nation-forming) purpose of this standardization, which was later reinterpreted for the purposes of imperialism, and eventually for something approaching internationalism, particularly as framed by the supporters of Francophonie in opposition to the hegemonic forces of English.

5.3   Greek

Greek has been recorded in an almost unbroken tradition for rather more than three millennia; it has amongst the oldest written heritages of any living language. This antiquity is both a glory and a burden. The language has gone through periods of standardization which are comparable with those through which either English or French passed, as well as, on at least one occasion, a fully planned set of standardizations which was inspired from the outset by ideology as much as language. Perhaps most strikingly, the history of Greek demonstrates the cyclical nature of standardization which Joseph puts forward, with the proviso that the prestige of earlier varieties of the Greek language will always have an effect upon later varieties and their development, even if this effect is a very self-conscious desire for 'modernization'.

The earliest forms of recorded Greek, written in the Linear B script associated with the Mycenaean civilization of the late second millennium BCE, appears not to show dialectal variation, no matter its original provenance (Palmer 1980: 53–6), despite the fact that we suspect considerable diversity at this point. Given the bureaucratic subject matter of the majority of Linear B materials, it has been suggested that this represents a chancery language. Whilst this seems highly likely, the relative paucity of information means that this can only be an informed guess, however.

The Mycenaean civilization crumbled beneath a series of disasters. The original literacy, probably confined to a very small clerkly caste who were expendable during such a collapse, was utterly forgotten. When Greek became a literary language again, around the eighth century BCE, the script used was adapted from a Semitic one, brought from the developing cities of the Syrian littoral. The breakdown had been so profound that no carry-over was possible between this prior standardization and the new dialect literacy. The new script was rapidly employed in a variety of often specialized and stylized registers derived from the different dialects which dominated Greek at this time (Buck 1955: 14–6; Palmer 1980: chapter 4). External political and economic developments were needed before the first 'modern' Greek standard could develop.

By the middle of the first millennium BCE, Greek civilization had developed in a variety of directions, depending on the cultural and political ideology embraced by a limited number of city states. Although to some extent these states cooperated with each other in the face of external threats such as Persia, these differences, exacerbated by interests which each of the major states had in the Mediterranean world, inevitably led to civil wars. The final, and most brutal, of these pitched the city of Athens and its allies against the city of Sparta and its allies.

The cultural differences which underlay this conflict included a linguistic dimension. Athens used the Attic dialect, which had considerable affinities with the Ionian dialects of the Aegean coasts. It was associated with commerce, but also with literature; in particular with the discussion of philosophy. In a sense, this variety can be perceived as a synecdochic dialect passing through acculturation, with the proviso that there was no prior dominant standard. Spartans spoke a Doric dialect associated with the Peloponnesian peninsula. Doric did have a number of literary functions in the stylized literary dialect use already mentioned; primarily its speakers were associated with a rather puritanical and archaic way of life. Both states were powerful enough for their form of language to be used by their allies (Browning 1983: 19–21). These varieties are known as *koinés*, 'common languages'. This final war was won by Sparta and its allies at terrible cost. A group of semi-barbarians, the Macedonians, were able to exploit the weakness engendered to stage a takeover of the Greek territories.

There is considerable debate over whether the Macedonians were originally Greek speakers, whether they spoke a closely related, but distinct, language, or whether they spoke a more distantly related (or entirely unrelated) language (Hock and Joseph 1996: 306). What is true, however, is that these conquerors were themselves conquered culturally by the

Hellenic way of life, especially as associated with Athens and the Aegean world. For the first time in almost a millennium, the Greek world was united.

The enhanced use of various koinés was inevitable. Even within the relatively small ambit of the Aegean world, not everyone was culturally Greek, never mind native speakers. Given the Hellenistic viewpoint of the new ruling class, however, the balance of power inevitably turned to Greek. The international nature of the Macedonian territories became even more obvious as the conquests of Philip of Macedon and his son Alexander incorporated the former Persian Empire, stretching into central Asia, to the river Indus and a considerable distance up the Nile. Thus, although the Macedonian Empire, and its successor states, remained Hellenistic in taste, and Greek in language (traits which were adopted by many of the conquered peoples of their dominions), it had to find a way to govern in that language without the need for the recognition of a variety of dialects used for different purposes in relatively small areas.

Over time, the Attic koiné of Athens – already highly prestigious intellectually – was developed (whether consciously or not) in such a way that it resembled the Ionic dialects of Asia Minor more. A number of the 'quirky' aspects of its grammar and phonology were jettisoned in favour of analogous simplification (Thomson 1960: 34; Palmer 1980: 189–93; Moleas 1989: 15–22). By the beginning of the Christian era, it had become the spoken and written lingua franca of a large part of the Mediterranean and Near Eastern world. Although originally a language of government and trade, it quickly came to be used in a variety of other registers and genres, the most famous of which being the Christian New Testament. So successful was its penetration that, with the exception of the Tsakonian dialect (Palmer 1980: 190), all of the Modern Greek dialects are descended from the koiné. Dialect convergence – perhaps even dialect blending – had taken place. This broadening in usage, coupled with fairly extensive literacy, encouraged a developing standard to become a mature one.

As Browning (1983) reports, although the Hellenic world gradually lost its autonomy, Greek in its koiné form did not lose its status. Indeed, its use in the western parts of the Roman territories is well documented. Naturally, the koiné did not remain static. From a very early period in its development we can see the evolution of different registers associated, perhaps, with different social and ethnic groups within the Hellenic world. The Christian New Testament, for instance, demonstrates considerable differences in the Greek used in its different parts (Palmer 1980: 194–6). Certainly, all of the books inhabit a linguistic space which is low register and probably highly demotic.

In its early centuries in particular (although it is a trait which has resurfaced on occasion throughout the religion's history), Christianity desired to speak to 'simple' people (or those who wished to be 'simple') in the language of their everyday lives. At the same time, becoming a major player in the urban society of the period in particular, the Church took on in its language use more of the trappings of the rhetorical, high register, variety of the koiné in an attempt to discuss and debate with philosophers. As both governmental and ecclesiastical power concentrated itself in Constantinople, and the rump of the Roman Empire became almost totally Greek in language, this new Christian Greek began to resemble increasingly the old Greek associated in its various registers with academic and governmental activity. Yet not quite: the prestige of the New Testament was so great that its original 'low' character was reinterpreted as being a norm for high style, in particular by the Church. This amalgam, associated with Byzantine government and church, remained largely unaltered throughout the medieval period.

That does not mean that the Greek spoken language remained static, naturally. But given that literacy outside the urban centres was relatively low, particularly as the Byzantine power-base contracted, those who wished for a radical reinterpretation of what 'Greek' should be were always in a very small minority. Thus, written forms which were originally close to the language of the people gradually become conservative in comparison. In Joseph's terms, they approached the status of absolute standard, perhaps straying into classical status. As Greek power in the Mediterranean collapsed in the later middle ages, a 'siege mentality' developed within this literate interpreter class. Under Ottoman rule, this was exacerbated both by a desire to continue writing as if the Empire were still in existence, and also because many members of this class became *de facto* rulers (under Turkish suzerainty) of other Christians in the Balkans. It would be only a minor overstatement to suggest that in the use of this language in their writing this class was presenting itself as 'Roman' in tradition, rather than 'Greek'. When an independent Greece brought itself into being in the early decades of the nineteenth century, this historical ruling class was, with notable exceptions, strikingly absent. Yet many of their linguistic ideas were very much present in the early days of the new 'Greece'.

This country was one of the poorest nations in Europe. Its inhabitants lived in some of the most marginal territory for agriculture possible on the north shore of the Mediterranean. Disease and famine were constant presences. Years of low-level banditry and war had left the economy in tatters. Literacy was low in what passed for urban centres, and practically non-existent in the countryside. Most Greek speakers did not live in 'Greece'. How, therefore, could the government of the new country develop its resources? What was holding it back?

The great divergence between the written and the spoken form struck many at the time. During the Ottoman period, this gap had grown even wider because most speakers, particularly those from urban centres and the east coast of the Aegean, had assimilated many Turkish words (and on occasion even phonological and syntactic features (Thomason and Kaufman 1988: 215–22)) into their Greek. What was to be done to ease the problem of literacy in the 'mother tongue'?

Three basic viewpoints were put forward during the nineteenth century. The first was the maintenance of the Byzantine-ecclesiastical 'high' variety as standard. Those who argued in favour of this standard claimed that this would connect the present Greeks with their 'glorious' past. Nevertheless, the manifest problems in teaching a highly archaic variety as first language to people who could not readily understand it meant that this view was never likely to gain acceptance; indeed, the only place where this type of Greek is still produced is within the Orthodox Church. That does not mean that the former standard did not have profound effects on the written forms of Greek which developed, however.

The other two views were based upon the precept that any standard form of Greek should be based upon the demotic speech of the people – although, as Browning (1983: 103–4) points out, the dialectal diversity present in Greece did not make this easy. How this standard was to be developed was (and remains) the main sticking point for planners and adherents of both standards. At one end of the spectrum were those who believed that modern Greek should be 'purified', both of its Turkicisms and of the 'corruptions' to which the language had been subjected since its days of glory: *Katharevousa* 'pure language' (Browning 1983: 102–3). In the early days of the newly independent state, this variety was the one normally considered 'Greek' by educational authorities and government. It had the advantage of being associated with an existing acculturation and elaboration process.

There were problems with Katharevousa, however. Many of the ostensibly 'ancient' reintroductions into the modern form were not morphologically or phonologically consistent with their surroundings; others were plain wrong in their interpretation and use. The variety was given to circumlocution under certain circumstances in certain hands. There were almost inevitable splits within the movement, with some writers claiming to be 'purer' than others in their usage. More striking, however, was the fact that the effort involved in learning Katharevousa as first language was considerable. The gap between spoken and written forms was still great. Some of the 'planners' of the variety may even have intended this. The greatest problem with Katharevousa was not strictly linguistic, however. In an era where democratization was becoming the norm, the variety became associated with – at worst – the reactionary end of politics or – at best – with the educational and governmental authorities at their most doctrinaire.

Demands for a more democratic standard grew, associated with Jean Psichari (1854–1929), who planned a standard named, provocatively, Dhimotiki 'speech of the people, demotic'. To linguistic (and social) conservatives, this form of written language was anathema (although it is significant that many of them probably spoke varieties very close to Dhimotiki). To many, dhimotiki was seen as a more pliable, more creative, variety than Katharevousa. Certainly its claim to be close to the people was true. It became associated with the more radical end of Greek politics.

A binary relationship existed between the two standards throughout the early twentieth century. As Trudgill (2000) points out, Katharevousa was used primarily in government and education, while dhimotiki was used more in the creative fields. When the political pendulum swung to the left, some Dhimotiki was permitted in written contexts in schools; when the political pendulum swung to the right, this process was reversed. On occasions when civilian government was completely suspended, such as during the military dictatorship of 1967–1975, Dhimotiki was forced underground. Yet this experience led to its final victory. Katharevousa is barely visible today in Greece, except in a few far-right publications. Its passing has not left Dhimotiki unchanged, nevertheless, since the latter standard has incorporated a number of the former's elements, perhaps to increase its register range. The process by which an emerging standard becomes a mature one is by no means straightforward.

When we consider each of the standardizations through which Greek has passed, it becomes apparent that many of Kloss' ideas on Ausbau are correct. It is the domains in which a language variety is used which affect that variety's status. Use by government and other authorities, such as the Church, enhances the standard's position in society. The koiné could have remained a trade language if it had not been associated with cultural, religious and political prestige. Indeed, with those standardization processes which we know much about, it is apparent that societal and cultural patterns and pressures are at the heart of whether a given language variety will succeed as a standard or not. This point will be even more apparent in our discussion of Scots.

5.4 A failed standardization: Scots

Throughout this book I have treated my mother-tongue, Scots, as if it were a language in its own right: as if it were a system analogous to languages such as French or Kiswahili, whose status as such no one would question. But many people would quarrel bitterly with such an association, preferring to see Scots as a dialect of English. We have already discussed some of the reasons for this discrepancy in Chapter 3, where the best term suggested by Kloss for situations such as this was *kin-tongue*. Both viewpoints are perfectly possible. What marks off Scots from other varieties is the fact that it is a failed example of language standardization. Scots came close to achieving systemic prescriptive regularity, only to have its distinctiveness gradually subsumed into the greater whole of written English. The purpose of this section is to demonstrate the extent to which economic, political and, to some extent, cultural power differences can affect the standardization process over an extended period of time.

As Macafee (2002) has pointed out, in the late fifteenth and early sixteenth centuries the native Germanic vernaculars of Scotland had achieved considerable status within the country as a whole. Over the preceding few centuries, the original Gaelic language hegemony had been replaced by one in which those in positions of political and economic power, in the Lowlands at least, would have been speakers of *Inglis*, the name then given to these Germanic vernaculars. At the same time, Inglis-speakers were producing a considerable body of literature in the language which is comparable to anything written in Europe at the time. Although Inglis was terminologically deemed equivalent to English, what is certain is that, by this stage in the development of the language, a combination of factors had made this variety different from dialects of English in England.

In the first place, Scots was the only 'dialect' of English to borrow independently and widely from contemporary languages of culture such as French, as well as from Latin and (to some extent) Greek. That this is the case is shown today in the existence of words such as *ashett* (French *assiette*), 'large plate', in many dialects of Scots, and of forms such as *propone* (rather than *propose*) in the language of Scots law (Macafee 1997, in particular pp. 206–7).

More important is the fact that speakers of Scots had developed a separate spelling system and prescriptive norms for the language (Meurman-Solin 1993, 1997; Kniezsa 1997), associated in the main with a metropolitan variety used in the court at Edinburgh. Other 'dialects' of

English also had distinctive spelling patterns; Scots managed to maintain and propagate its system well into the age of print, however. Indeed, the middle to late sixteenth century was when this separate system was most healthy. It was broadcast through the medium of print, and written both by considerable writers, and by some of the most prominent people in the country (Jack 1997).

At the same time, the terminological preference for Inglis to describe the national vernacular was gradually being replaced by one favouring *Scottis* (previously the preferred name for Gaelic, now, interestingly, termed *Erse*, 'Irish'). There was a growing self-confidence in the use of the written variety, suggesting the acculturation and elaboration of an emerging standard. It is quite possible to imagine a situation whereby Scots as a linguistic entity would have achieved as significant a degree of linguistic autonomy as Dutch did from Standard High German. But, as discussed, for instance, in Millar (2000, 2003, 2004b), the nationalist (and nationist) character of Scots was stripped away in the modern era, in favour of an association with locale and particular ways of life, thus producing an atomization into largely unwritten dialects, with Standard English as the diglossic High variety. It is not the purpose of this section to discuss the process of the decline of Scots as a standard language in any depth; nevertheless, elements of the process can aid us in our under-standing of standardization.

In effect, the roots of the decline were there even in its triumph. In the first place, extralinguistic developments led to a closer relationship between Scotland and England. The majority of the populations (and probably more importantly, the great part of the ruling classes) in both countries found themselves in the Protestant camp. Given that a central part of the Reformation process was a war of words using pamphlets and books, it was inevitable that a Protestant (or Catholic) controversialist would have used a language which would reach a larger audience. Since more people could read English, including all literate Scots speakers, than Scots, it made sense, from both a proselytizing and economic point of view, to use the majority language in print.

Secondly, no translation of the Bible into Scots was ever completed. Bible translations – even bad, temporary, translations – take time and economic stability to produce and disseminate: time and money which the Scottish Protestant reformers did not have. Moreover, many of the Scottish reformers had spent time in Geneva along with English Protestant refugees, and appear to have become both Anglophile and Anglophone in the process. The knock-on effects of the lack of this translation were profound for a society which viewed the Bible as a blueprint for all political and personal activity and behaviour. When the Gospel was in Latin in all churches, it did not really matter what language the people spoke (or wrote); when the language of one group was associated with the word of God, this had almost immediate, and rarely positive, effects upon any other variety's status. Similar slippage towards English was to be found in other forms of writing, although few writers were as systematic in their transliteration of Scottish into English norms as King James VI. His *Basilikon Doron* (Görlach 1991: 310–12) exists in both Scots manuscript and English print versions. Again, cultural prestige and economic dictates combined in favour of English.

This might only have been temporary if it had not been for political events leading, first, to a personal union of the crowns of the two kingdoms in 1603 and, after over a century of instability, to a political union of the parliaments in 1707. During this period, many Scots – particularly literate Scots of the governing classes – began to move linguistically (and politically) towards England. Whilst the overwhelming majority of non-Gaelic speaking Scottish people continued to speak Scots until towards the end of the eighteenth century, the trend towards Standard English in writing was almost complete by the beginning of that century. As Devitt (1989) and Meurman-Solin (in particular, 2000) have demonstrated, this was not, for many writers, a matter of overnight conversion from one system to the other; instead, throughout this 'long seventeenth century', Scottish writers gradually anglicized their writing, sometimes differing in the level of 'Englishness' from one written domain to another, with more personal domains remaining more Scottish until a remarkably late date (as can be seen, for instance, in the diaries of Sir Walter Scott).

On this occasion, the acculturative and elaborative process was abandoned by the linguistic avant-garde in favour of identification with a more prestigious standard. The nationalist function Joseph associated with a developing standard came into conflict with ideological and economic motivations. The fact that Scots and English are close relatives did not enhance the former's chances of autonomy or success.

5.5 Conclusion

It does seem, therefore, that both Kloss' and Joseph's analyses of the nature and process of standardization hold true. Joseph is correct in his assumption that the elaborative development of a synecdochic dialect inevitably leads to its being perceived as of a different type to all other dialects of a language. Standards which are associated with a strong and pervasive idea – political, cultural or religious – will be more likely to thrive. In a very real sense, standard languages encapsulate political and economic will and, in particular, power.

Joseph's concept of cyclical standardization, of standards following standards when the preceding standard becomes perceived as a classical language, is also convincing, although with one proviso. With languages such as Greek (and, to a lesser extent, the influence of Latin upon French), the classical language itself may exert such an influence upon the new standard as to stunt its development, or at least divert its development in otherwise unexpected directions, since they do not encourage a close connection between the spoken and written contemporary language.

Joseph is less convincing when he makes a case for the centrality of the literary development of a language, in distinction to Kloss' foregrounding of functional prose. Any successful standard language must be associated with literary endeavours of various types: this is without question. Any standard language which does not permanently, and unquestionably, occupy the domains associated with the governmental and educational apparatus will not be able to extend its use, however. In the past, this may have been different. Standard Italian, for instance, developed in a situation where its influence was felt through the status of great writers such as Dante, Petrarch and Boccaccio; it was not the language of a central organization, since no such organization existed. As we saw in Chapter 2, pre-modern states cannot be equated with the nations of the modern era; it is significant that Italian mass literacy developed only under unified governments, employing a single bureaucratic standard.

Nevertheless, it is striking that languages such as Greek have carried out the process generally when something approaching a centralized administration, with a desire for a largely uniform language, was in existence. The same can be said for each of the other three standardization processes discussed in this chapter. Initial prestige may well come from the association of the synecdochic dialect with a given set of literary or cultural virtues, as in the association of Attic with the philosophy of Athens; it is the bureaucracy who employ the standard and prescribe its use, however.

Yet this is not the whole story. As we saw in our discussion of Scots, a language with a lively literary heritage and a strong association with the state apparatus can eventually fail in its attempt to achieve full Ausbau, even when it is borderline Abstand. On this occasion, the end of autonomy for the polity in question, and the presence of a close relative, whose use was politically, ideologically and economically attractive for members of a powerful opinion-forming elite, was too much of a burden for the standard to survive; without the standard to act as 'roof', the still-existing dialects were in danger of being incorporated into the linguistic relationships of the new dominant exonormic standard.

One point which has only been tangentially touched upon is what the processes involved in planning for language standardization actually are. When painting such broad historical canvasses this is probably inevitable. In the following chapters, this question will be addressed, paying particular attention to the planning of languages in the modern period which did not have the luxury (and cushion) of a long written tradition, as well as for those, such as German, which do. Are there material differences between the two classes?

6
Language Planning: Process

6.1 Introduction

In recent years I have become increasingly aware of the use of the word *envision*, originally largely in American texts, but now increasingly in colleagues' speech. I take the word to mean 'gain a view of, predict'. It is entirely foreign to me: under these circumstances I would use the verb *envisage*, which originally meant 'to put a face to', but now generally has a similar meaning to what I infer for *envision*. If, at the end of the last century, I had been faced with a student's essay which used *envision*, I would have been quite likely to have questioned its use in some way or another. Given the levels of authority with which I associate the word, I would now be unlikely to do so. It is only a matter of time, perhaps, before I begin to use the word myself.[1]

Individual academics are very small cogs in a large educational and intellectual information wheel. Yet the constant correction supplied by a variety of authorities – educators, publishers (and, as Cameron points out (1995: Chapter 2), copy-editors), corporations and, in some countries, language academies or language boards – should not be underestimated. Sometimes language planning is unconscious, as in the case of my correcting a student's usage according to the norms which I have osmotically imbibed; sometimes the activity is highly conscious, as is often the case in countries where no standard, national, language is already in existence. In either event, language planning is a central feature in the development of literate societies.

6.2 The actors

It is natural that the purposes of language planning (and its final, intermediate and initial outcomes) will differ, depending on who the language planners are. Cooper (1989) suggests a distinction between a range of *actors*, all having some effect upon the development of a language.

Thus a group concerned with making language policy which is official or semi-official, such as *Noregs Mållag*, the protector and promoter of *Nynorsk* in Norway, will inevitably be different from one which is of considerable influence, but has no actual legal support, such as the *Academie Française*. Cooper would make a terminological distinction between *formal elites* and *influentials*. He comments (1989: 88): 'Formal elites are those who are officially empowered to make policy – presidents, governors, senators, congressional representatives, chief operating executives, school principals, teachers, and so on.'

Those individuals and institutions which have executive or legislative power differ from those which have didactic functions. The former grouping would have less formal ability in the administration of language planning initiatives than the latter; that need not necessarily stop attempts to influence linguistic behaviour, however. For instance, in the New Right discourse which dominated Britain in the 1980s, as discussed by Cameron (1995: chapter 3), government took a pivotal role in promoting 'traditional values', one of which was the 'preservation' of the English language from the depredations of change and decay. Demonstrating a lack of understanding of historical and contemporary variation, attempts were made to codify what was linguistically acceptable in schools. Its views were popular among the people as a whole and in particular among a large part of the class of educators; nevertheless, its recommendations amounted to little more than a long list of prejudices against the modern age (Crowley 1989: chapter 7). A further interesting, as well as enraging, example of this phenomenon can be found in works such as Honey (1989, 1997), where change in language is equated with the decay of 'British' values. In particular, any attempt to democratize the language of power in Britain is, in Honey's eyes, an attack on 'standards' which are not solely linguistic. His views and methods have been elegantly critiqued by Crowley (1999).

Similar to this (although inspired by the overt enemies of the New Right) was the 'first congress' of the Polish language, held in Szczecin in 1984. As Janicki and Jaworski (1993) suggest, a large part (if not all) of the background and content of this congress – from its choice of venue in the most westerly of the new/old cities of post-war Poland to its purist viewpoint – was intended to stress the military/communist regime's Polishness, and its commitment to Poland, rather than to the declining Soviet Bloc.[2] The power to legislate language use held latently by these elites should not be underestimated, no matter how ill informed the perpetrators can be.

Education authorities at various levels affect language planning. At the most global level, what languages are taught in a given territory is often the concern of the Ministry of Education, no matter how under pressure from other sources. An example of this is the changing views the education authorities in Scotland have taken towards Gaelic since the inception of mass education in the 1870s, as discussed by Durkacz (1983). More commonly, teachers and other educators affect language planning at the level of the 'chalk face'. The effects of idealistic teachers employing the local vernacular or a non-imperialist *lingua franca* in their classrooms in a post-colonial framework cannot be underestimated. Since literacy is generally introduced in school, the linguistic patterns and attitudes enforced during the first phase of education will inevitably have profound effects on children's written and spoken language. Naturally, this can have both positive and negative results. For instance, Catalan-speaking children living under the Franco dictatorship in Spain were told by teachers and other officials to 'speak Christian': in other words, Castilian Spanish (Fishman 1991: 297). No one should underestimate the power of linguistic prejudice on the part of schoolteachers (who have often had the same prejudices enforced upon them by *their* teachers); particularly in threatened, lesser-used, language situations. More positively, committed teachers are at the heart of any 'ethnic' revival.

Cooper's 'chief operating executives' could be seen as either governmental, or associated with business affairs. In many countries, business interests may have more 'clout' in everyday affairs than does the government; this is particularly the case in a post-colonial climate, or where a country has trade as its primary concern. Thus the Singapore Chamber of Commerce has considerable influence, and even, it might be argued, power, in the implementation of language planning in that country (Jernudd 1973: 18–19). Multinational corporations generally wish to work in as few languages as possible, something which, as Phillipson (2003: in particular, chapter 3) points out, is already affecting employment patterns in continental Europe in relation to the use of English.

Much of this could be taken as falling under Cooper's distinction of *influentials* (1989: 88). The power of the university presses of Oxford and Cambridge to dictate or guide usage within the (British and Commonwealth) English-speaking world is considerable, despite their having no statutory powers. The same is true for newspapers. *Aftenposten*, the main conservative newspaper in Norway, is (in effect) a language planner: its very conservative *Bokmål* acts as an alternative style pattern to those promulgated by the state language planning authorities.

The middle class in general – as teachers, religious ministers of the various denominations, members of the civil services and officials of corporate bodies – can be portrayed as influentials, often in affecting levels of change within a language, as part of its planning process. Well documented in English are the hyper-corrected, middle-class initiated, changes of pronunciation for words such as *forehead* and *housewife* which have been spread through the speech community because of that social group's influence over the education process, defined broadly (Joseph 1987: 66–7). In post-colonial sub-Saharan Africa, the middle class may affect language planning initiatives by their adherence to the language of imperialism as a marker of their prestige within the community; on the other hand they may become adherents of a given vernacular, and have the power to translate this adherence into action. The latter process could be interpreted as the actions of *counter-elites*.

In most societies a group of individuals exists who, while not strictly speaking part of the 'establishment', are able to derive their power and influence from the same resources. Even with movements which self-consciously derive their support from 'the masses', the main governing bodies tend to be dominated either by members of the middle classes or by working class people who, by dint of education and aspiration, have attained such status. In countries with a post-colonial legacy, such a state of affairs is almost inevitable, since a combination of elite-creation on the part of the colonial authorities and poverty led to literacy being confined to a relatively small cadre of 'creoles'. At one point in the 1970s, Jamaica's two main political parties, (literally) deadly rivals, were led by cousins. Counter-elites are therefore close to the centres of power, but are self-consciously apart from them.

Perhaps the most striking example of this conflict can be found in the early history of the Afrikaans language movement, as discussed by Holliday (1993). Afrikaans is a Netherlandic language which has diverged from mainstream Dutch by the development of a variety of features which many linguists (for instance, Trudgill 1983, 1989 and Holm 1988/1998: II, 338–52) would see as being analogous with creolization processes. There are a variety of different class and ethnic varieties of the language; the acrolect (that used in the most formal circumstances by the elite), at least, is mutually intelligible with Dutch. Although most people of Dutch origin in Southern Africa (as well as a significant number of 'coloured' people, whose views did not really enter this debate) have spoken Afrikaans varieties since the eighteenth century or earlier, the language of church and school remained Standard Dutch until the twentieth century. After the British conquest of the Cape during the Napoleonic Wars, the ties between the Dutch speakers of South Africa and those of the Netherlands were inevitably attenuated; at the same time, dislike of the new imperial masters led many of the most committed Afrikaners to *trek* inland to found new, independent, states. The sense of 'African' identity was therefore enhanced.

Yet not all Afrikaners loved their native language. The 'simplifications' which Dutch went through in Africa were inevitably seen as decay in a culture where both Latinate learning and Calvinism were predominant. Literacy and opinion-forming was also controlled by the Dutch Reformed Church, which had a vested interest in maintaining Dutch. Moreover, there was a taint of peasant life about Afrikaans – despite the same life also being celebrated. Most importantly, perhaps, 'coloured' Afrikaans speakers uncomfortably reminded many whites of what might now have seemed miscegenation to them. The elite therefore favoured the maintenance of Dutch as the standard.

Nevertheless, a powerful counter-elite existed who favoured Afrikaans. Interestingly, many of the strongest zealots for the disparaged language were descended not from Dutch settlers, but rather from French Protestant refugees. Their emotional attachment to European Dutch language and culture was therefore limited. Using a combination of procedures, ranging from an attempt at ubiquity by a presence in a considerable number of classrooms, through to a willingness to come to terms with the British authorities and (later) an association, ironically, with die-hard opposition to the compromises at the end of the South African War, the status of Afrikaans, in relation to Dutch, grew. The demographic shift of white speakers away from the Cape towards the less cosmopolitan heartland favoured it. Yet while strong emphasis was given by the language activists to this rural constituency and its virtues, it would be a mistake not to think of the prime movers as being members of an opinion-forming elite, albeit a counter-elite.

As Cooper points out, not all language planning is carried out by members of an elite. Individuals of all backgrounds can contribute to language planning, even if it is in terms of being part of the 'hidden hand' of linguistic change. Until the 1970s, it was generally unacceptable to say, in British English, '*Hopefully I will see him*', meaning, 'I hope I will see him', although it was perfectly acceptable in the American variety of the language. In these contexts, *hopefully* would have been interpreted by the *influentials* in British society as modifying *see*, and the sentence could therefore have been transformed as 'filled with hope, I will see him'. The new usage became almost universally accepted in a matter of years, despite considerable opposition from self-appointed arbiters of taste (Andersson and Trudgill 1992: 146–8). Indeed, so rapidly did the modification spread that people of my age are often quite surprised to hear that there was ever a controversy surrounding the usage. We cannot determine who began to spread this change through Britain (although conservative critics were very happy to point the finger at the mass media). For whatever range of reasons, a major modification to the ways in which the structure of British Standard English is analysed had been effected by consensus.

More conscious are those occasions where individuals and groups work towards the planning of a language in relative obscurity. An example of this is reported by Ascherson (1996: 203–9), where an obscure German scholar, Wolfgang Feurstein, and a group of like-minded people, are described as having essentially planned and revived the Lazuri language of north-east Turkey. People of this type probably do not have a hidden agenda of self-aggrandizement: they merely wish to right a historical wrong. Ironically, however, their very actions may make them members of an elite, albeit in a circumscribed field.

The importance of language to human society inevitably makes the planning of the 'best' variety a matter of struggle, compromise and even conflict between different elements of society. The process is itself also often part of greater political and economic forces at work regionally, nationally, perhaps even globally. The following sections will discuss what processes these actors initiate and encourage.

6.3 Types of language planning

The traditional view of language planning activities (based upon Kloss 1969, but with additions from Cooper 1989) is that these comprise three activities, as represented in schema as shown in Figure 6.1.

Corpus planners decide what is 'incorrect' or 'impure', and what is 'correct' or 'pure'; they decide what is the 'best' usage for a language, ideologically and linguistically. If new concepts develop, corpus planners attempt to produce a means to express this concept. Status planners attempt to achieve greater status for their language variety within a given polity in

Figure 6.1 The branches of language planning

relation to other language varieties. Acquisition planning is an activity designed to encourage the greater knowledge, and (eventually) native use, of a language variety. These activities can never be entirely separate, as Haugen (1983) points out. He rejects the more categorical aspects of the two-way split between status (and, by implication, acquisition) and corpus planning, seeing them instead as a mutually informative (and, it is to be hoped, enriching) relationship. Nevertheless, it is still fruitful to divide usage from promotion and implementation in our analysis.

6.4   Corpus planning

At the heart of any planning or standardization initiative lies the corpus of the language: its lexis, structure and (to some extent) phonology and, moreover, how these are to be represented. All speech (and, perhaps more significantly, writing) communities evince attitudes which are prescriptive on these matters. I have used the example already of my students' reaction to '*I have went to University*'. From a purely linguistic point of view, there is nothing wrong with this construction. Indeed, if linguistic attitudes had developed differently, it is quite possible that prescriptive grammarians would now celebrate the fact that *went* is used in both past tense and past participle, comparing it favourably with the 'needless complexity' of having both *went* and *gone*. If this seems far-fetched, it is worth comparing this situation with the occasionally expressed disdain by British commentators for the American (and dialectal) use of *got* and *gotten*, rather than the single *got*. The attitudes involved are largely learned responses due to training in appropriateness: in other words, corpus planning and enforcement. As we saw in Chapter 4, Joseph distinguished between two types of corpus planning: circumstantial and engineered. In the following, we will concentrate largely on the latter; that does not mean that the processes self-consciously employed by corpus planners may not actually mirror the attitudes towards different varieties of the language already held by the speech community, however.

Haugen suggests (1983: 275) that the first stage of conscious (or engineered) corpus planning is a selection process. This can be split into two parts: *identification of the problem* and *allocation of norms*. The first is based (Haugen 1983: 270) upon what Neustupny (1970) termed a 'language problem'. An actor or actors would have to perceive that a problem exists: a speech community, for instance, might not possess a means of expressing themselves in writing in their own language variety, instead employing another speech community's language. This might be seen as being disadvantageous to the first speech community. Yet even within the speech community, there may be important decisions to be made. For example, if two partly distinct groups, of near-equal status, speak different varieties of essentially the same language, planner(s) would have to decide the most effective means of communication: effective both in terms of mutual comprehension and the prestige values associated with a variety. The solution of the problem lies in the allocation of norms, which may appear to be a form of status planning, but involves elements of corpus planning. What would be acceptable lexis or structure? As we will see in Section 8.2, colonial and missionary authorities in east Africa made decisions about the standard variety of Kiswahili based upon their own attitudes towards authority, appropriateness and Islam.

At a more concrete level, an illustration can be found in my own speech community. My native word for 'child' is *wean*. Many Scots speakers would use the word *bairn* for the same concept. The two words are practically mutually exclusive geographically. Whilst a moderate approach would be to allow a degree of variation on this occasion, along the line of American English *faucet* and British English *tap*, a draconian language planning initiative would have to attempt to impose uniformity on one or other part of the speech community, at least in terms of their written use. Inevitably, there would be both winners and losers; many would be aggrieved at this state of affairs.

Beyond this is *codification*. A central element of this, according to Haugen, following Ferguson (1968: 29), is *graphization*: '[i]n areas where the concept of an alphabet, a syllabary, or a system of ideograms exists, a writing tradition can arise simply by the adaptation of a known system to the new language' (Haugen 1983: 271). He cites the adaptation of the Chinese *kanji* ideograms for Japanese in the early centuries of the Christian Era. Decisions of this type are not, of course, without ideological import. While kanji was doubtless convenient to the Japanese, the fact that it was associated with a dominant, and admired, culture from which Japan derived many central characteristics, can only have encouraged its position, despite the fact that Chinese script, designed for a largely isolating language, is not suitable for the often polysyllabic Japanese language. Indeed, it is striking when a culture does *not* readily borrow material and technological innovations of this type from its (culturally and politically) prestigious or dominant neighbours, or chooses to reject them, as was the case with Korean (Park 1989).

As Haugen points out: 'The typical product of all codification has been a prescriptive orthography, grammar, and dictionary.' Thus the notion of 'correctness' is enforced, and may, as he states (Haugen 1983: 271–2), in the case of French in particular,

> become an instrument of national policy, a linguistic code corre-
> sponding to the civil and religious code. ... It is significant that gram-
> matical deviations are still popularly known by terms of moral
> opprobrium: deviant forms are 'bad', 'wrong', 'incorrect', 'ugly', and
> 'vulgar'. Acceptable forms are 'good', 'right', 'correct', 'beautiful', and
> 'cultivated'. However meaningless such terms may seem to the scien-
> tific linguist, he is just as constrained in his usage of the language by
> the norms implied in these terms as is any other user.

This point is (probably unconsciously) echoed, with considerable bitterness, by Bourdieu (1991: 48–9).

Standardization (and language planning) are indeed designed to control
the language (and, implicitly, the behaviour) of a given populace, as both
Haugen and Bourdieu point out. Yet in a world dominated by a small
number of prestigious languages, it is difficult to imagine other languages
surviving *without* language planning.

Central to corpus planning is what Haugen (as well as, later, Joseph)
would term *elaboration*. In theory, of course, all language varieties
are equally suited to express ideas; the problem is, however, that not all
people are treated equally. Because, as Joseph (1987) pointed out, the
judgement of appropriateness and eloquence in the contemporary
social structure of the world is based on developments in the ancient
world, channelled through the western experience, language planners
who are guiding a 'new' language through the process of corpus development have to bear in mind what is needed for that particular language
in the modern world. They also have to pay some heed to the relationship
between that particular speech community and language and its neighbours, in terms of power differentials and culture.

Bearing this in mind, we will now turn to a discussion of how the elaboration process takes place, with particular reference to the levels at which
language planners perceive a threat to the 'purity' of a given language.

6.4.1   Corpus planning and purism

At the heart of most corpus planning initiatives is a debate among planners, and the speech community in general, over the perceived danger
from internal and external sources, and how to react to this: in other
words, a debate over linguistic purity. In Joseph's terms, this could
be seen as indicative of the avant-garde flexing its intellectual muscles.

In some speech communities the threat may be perceived as so great as to merit considerable purist efforts. In other speech communities, the reaction is less forceful. Yet the idea of building, and maintaining, boundaries around a language is central to the idea of Ausbau for that language, and of the building of a speech community into a nation.

6.4.1.1 Types of purism

Not all attempts to 'purify' a 'mother tongue' are the same. Reasons, processes and results differ greatly. Thomas (1991: 82) suggests the schematization shown in Figure 6.2 of puristic orientations. Basing his analysis on Ševčik (1974–1975), Thomas defines two perspectives for purism: *external*, looking outside the speech community of a language for reasons for its apparent 'corruption', and *internal*, motivations associated with apparent 'failings' in the language itself.

He links the external perspective to *xenophobic* forms of purism, arguably the form of purism which grabs headlines most readily. Naturally, in an era of mass communication, these fears are often justified by activists by the speed with which a high-status language can affect their own. This can be seen in the precautions taken within the French-speaking world to avoid (or even to excise) recently borrowed Anglicisms/Americanisms. It is a tradition of considerable antiquity, however. Thomas claims that purism of this type is unmarked, since a distrust (perhaps even dislike) of external material is often an accompanying feature of the nationalism which inspires many language (in particular, corpus) planning programmes.

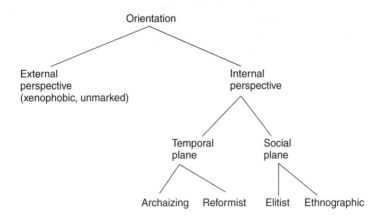

Figure 6.2 Purist orientations

With focus on the language itself, Thomas suggests that two viewpoints are possible: one of these, the *temporal plane*, is chiefly concerned with whether the language looks towards the past or the future, as seen in an ideological, rather than an actual, light. *Archaizing* purism 'can be manifested in an attempt to resuscitate the linguistic material of a past golden age, an exaggerated respect for past literary models, an excessive conservatism towards innovation or a recognition of the importance of literary tradition' (Thomas 1991: 76). This can be seen in the reverence which Icelandic language planners had for Old Norse and its literary tradition. Icelandic has maintained a historical, non-phonemic, spelling system which makes the 'language of the ancestors' seem much closer to the modern language than is actually the case (Groenke 1972); the same argument can be made for some written forms of modern Greek.

The 'recognition of literary tradition' is seen in the view expressed by Johnson, in the introduction to his *Dictionary* (1755), that the 'best' English is inevitably that of the past. He is not suggesting a return to the earliest possible sources, however. Rather, he sees the 'best' English as that used by canonical writers, as he perceives them, a view also held by the originators of the much more 'scientific' *Oxford English Dictionary*, although substantially abandoned in later editions (Murray 1977; Willinsky 1994; Mugglestone 2000). Arabic encapsulates all these features, probably due to the association the classical language has with divine inspiration (Thomas 1991: 77); this may explain why the classical language has been able to maintain itself as a living feature of literate Arabic speakers' lives (Suleiman 2003).

At the other end of this scale is *reformist* purism: 'an important constituent of the conscious efforts to reform, regenerate, renew or resuscitate a language' (Thomas 1991: 79), much associated with nineteenth-century language planning movements. Many 'planned' languages fall under this category: 'planning for modernization' has as a primary purpose the 'cleansing' of a language of its 'foreign' elements. Coming to terms with what has been produced in the language in earlier periods of its history is a subtle point. The phrase 'back to the future' could be used about these processes; this is particularly the case with Nynorsk, one of the two standard varieties of Norwegian, discussed in Chapter 7, where an apparent return to the medieval sources can actually be interpreted as a 'great leap forward' towards an envisaged peasant, egalitarian, democracy. Even today in Norway, speakers see a continuum between the most 'radical' forms of Nynorsk and the most 'conservative' forms of Bokmål (often termed *Riksmaal*). This is sociolinguistically correct; it still has some political truth underlying it (and had more such associations in the past); it is not true linguistically. This combination of archaizing and reformist aspirations is closely associated with ethnic nationalism, particularly in its romantic, largely nineteenth century, phase. It is also linked with the ethnographic purism discussed later in the section.

The *social plane* can be divided into two forms of purism: *elitist* and *ethnographic* purism. Thomas remarks (1991: 79) that the former

> is perhaps most often associated with the language of court, for which Versailles can be viewed as the paragon. Yet it should also be remembered that most modern standard languages display a liberal dose of elitism, particularly where prestige has to be defended against the democratising force of an army of newly literate speakers.

A striking example of this is to be found in the development of attitudes to the pronunciation of English in Britain in the eighteenth–nineteenth century.

With such a large part of its vocabulary not originally native, lexical purism in the English language is futile. It is with pronunciation that purism is strongest in English. Of course, tendencies of this type are by no means unknown for other languages. But the histories of both the English language and the English-speaking world make pronunciation particularly relevant to the topic.

Almost since the effective standardization of the written form of English in the fifteenth century, there has been a general view among educated people from the south of England that certain pronunciations used with the spoken form of the written standard were superior to others. Indeed, when a member of the ruling class did not speak with an accent (and probably also dialect) which was recognised as being a close approximation to the norm, as with Sir Walter Raleigh, this was often commented upon (Görlach 1999: 475). The great orthoepist outpourings of the seventeenth century, documented in Dobson (1968), must rest at least in part on concerns about the way that middle-class speakers – becoming, due to constitutional changes in England, a force of considerable importance – were perceived (or perceived themselves) in relation to the establishment.

Yet the discourse over this 'standard' pronunciation remained essentially elitist. Although literacy was rising in the eighteenth century in England, that does not mean that it was widespread. Intellectuals during the enlightenment cared passionately about 'propriety' in language; this propriety was confined to a limited number of their peers, however. The language of the great mass of the people was either of little concern to them or even to be encouraged in its 'provincialisms'.

A number of events and changes in modes of thought succeeded in altering this state of affairs. In the first place, revolutionary activity in France in particular associated, as we have seen, equality with uniformity in language. At the same time, the emerging lower middle classes became attracted to evangelical populism (as evinced in Methodism), a form of religion which fitted well with the individualist pieties of the age. All of these developments lent themselves to the spread of literacy: indeed they required it. Strangely, perhaps, given that these movements ushered in the age of the 'common man', they also encouraged the spread of previously elitist views and practices on pronunciation and usage, as Beal (1999), a study of the elocution strategies adopted by a political radical, demonstrates.

As has often been observed, it is members of this newly enfranchised (and empowered) lower middle classes who are the most lacking in linguistic confidence and given to hypercorrection. They are also not particularly well served by network ties to other members of their class and neighbourhood communities, given their general adherence to evolving dogmas of individualism, competition and the free market. In their turn they also became worried about their position in society, and their relationship both with their 'betters' and with the 'lower orders', a striking marker of such a relationship being linguistic.[3] The perceived threat from the 'democracy' also led to the cultural and political retrenchment of the former ruling (and intellectual) elite. Crowley (1989, 1996) analyses the ways in which an informal alliance of academics, litterateurs and politicians in England, from the late eighteenth century on, developed a discourse of the inherent superiority of what became known as Received Pronunciation (RP), and of spoken, monodialectal, Standard English, which eventually became associated with conservative values and the established order. It is interesting to note that these views were particularly focused during periods of socio-political change. Received Pronunciation as an ideal was established as a badge of association with a certain value system towards which many of the expanding middle classes aspired and which, whilst doubtless hated amongst the 'lower orders', became seen as both the 'norm' and the voice of assumed authority and command – the voice of 'truth', in other words.

Again, the apparent opposing pole is *ethnographic* purism. Thomas (1991: 77) cites Smith's observation (1971: 63) that while 'nationalistic movements are all urban-based ... their imagery is full of nostalgia and idealisation for the countryside and folk virtues'. Purism in the pronunciation of English in the United States appears to have taken this form. The official ideology of America, at least since the Jacksonian reforms of the 1830s, has been one which proscribes the creation of an elite and, at the same time, distrusts the idea of 'big government'. These views flourished in a nation which, until the technological developments of the twentieth century, had no one centre which was sufficiently dominant to control opinion-forming and intellectual currents, in the way that London does in England. The language of the 'common man' was inevitably identified as the norm, rather than that of an elite. That does not mean that American provincial elites in centres such as Boston, New York and Philadelphia did not fight a rearguard action in defence of their linguistic 'superiority'. But in a democracy (at least for white males), views of this type could not hold. Yet, as Bonfiglio (2002) points out, this idealization of the 'common man' was not quite as straightforward as it might seem. Who would the archetypal 'common man' be, in the first instance?

The lack of /r/ in medial and final position except before vowels – relatively widespread in the Eastern dialects of the United States in the early twentieth century, and also of some prestige, given its association with old elites in Boston, New York and the tidewater South – became unacceptable to opinion-forming elements within the American people because of, in the first place and historically, latent Anglophobia; its association with the speech of slaves and former slaves; and, finally, its association with the working classes of cities such as New York City, where 'native' Americans felt themselves being swamped by alien immigrants with distressing political and social ideas to go along with their 'appalling' accents. In these last two senses, the American and British developments of 'standard' pronunciation are not actually that different. The primary distinction is that, as has been pointed out by a variety of commentators, race is (or at least was) to the Americans what class is to the British.

Because of these associations, and because of the 'frontier mentality' so common in American intellectual and political life, the pronunciation of certain parts of the mid-western States came to be seen as 'General American': the language of a rural, hard-working, God-fearing people, generally perceived by people at the time (although perhaps mistakenly) to be, if not of Anglo-Saxon, at least of Teutonic 'bloodstock'. Carried west, as power and population flowed to the Pacific rim during the twentieth century, this view of America and its language has gained considerable potency, as we will see in Chapter 8.

From a linguistic point of view, the primary concern of ethnographic purism is a desire to move away from urban 'decadence' towards the 'pure' usage of the countryside. Other languages which have passed strongly through this stage of the standardization process include Icelandic, Finnish and Norwegian. As we will see, it is significant that ben Yehuda had been a *narod'nik*, a Russian populist: his Hebrew was an attempt to 'take the language to the people'. Indeed, the use in Israeli Hebrew of words and structures derived from other Semitic languages was an attempt, when no dialects of Hebrew survived, to achieve just such a purist result.

All of these aspects of the internal perspective can act in harmony. *Elitism* can be *archaic*; it can also be *reformist*. It can even be *ethnographic*. The Turkish language reform, as discussed in Chapter 7, had aspects of all four. It was driven from above by a small and powerful grouping who had faith in their own usage and coining skills; it harked back to a glorious 'Turanian' age; it was intended to modernize (explicitly, westernize and de-Islamize) Turkish; it claimed to be of the people and their dialects, rather than of the former, corrupt, Osmanlı ruling class and their language. Of course, it was difficult to give prominence to all these rhetorical, or ideological, positions at the same time; it was always borne in mind, however.

Equally importantly, the internal perspective does not rule out the presence of the external, xenophobic, perspective. In fact, it would be very unlikely for a purist effort to be initiated without there being a perceived external threat to the language. Sometimes this is seen in terms of the 'corruption' of the new urban society; it is very likely that this masks a fear of what has been imported into the city, and from where, a point which resonates with the nature of purism in American English.

6.4.1.2   The purism process

Purism can affect a language at any level of its structure (Thomas 1991: 67). A particular morphological or syntactic usage might be felt to be an importation from an undesired source. For example, adjectives in English normally pre-modify a noun, as in *a* happy *man*. As discussed by Markus (1997) and Moskowitch (2002), there are a number of occasions where a French (or at least Romance) pattern is followed, and adjectives should postmodify the noun. These tend generally to be stock phrases, such as *courts martial* (rather than *court martials*) or *sergeants major* (rather than *sergeant majors*). Generally, however, native speakers will avoid these 'aberrations', preferring, instead, the latter word orders which are unquestionably native (even if, pedantically, they might be seen as 'wrong' in terms of what is modifying what). The avoidance of appearing pretentious could be glossed as a form of purism. It is striking, however, that an opposing, elitist, tradition is also present with this usage.

Thomas would argue (1991: 73), however, that the unmarked part of the structure of a language upon which purism, and, by extension, corpus planning, is expected to play is the lexis. He would assign the hierarchy shown in Figure 6.3 to the phenomenon. Purist coinages can be divided by whether the new term is perceived as foreign or not. If the coinage is not foreign, it can represent a *neologism*, completely novel to the written variety. These neologisms can derive from standard word formation practice, as can be seen, for instance, in German *Wasserstoff* 'hydrogen', or in the nineteenth-century innovation *foreword*, in place of (or in tandem with) *preface* (Thomas 1991: 93–4). If the neologism derives from a non-standard source, this can be either an *archaism* or a *dialectalism*, although the boundary between the two is not always clear. An infamous example of the former is the resurrection of the term *Gau*, 'region' or 'territory', along with its derivative, *Gauleiter*, 'regional party boss', by the Nazi party in Germany between the wars, thus stressing the organic (and pseudo-mystical) relationship between leader and followers (and their territory), along the same lines (as they perceived it) as the relationship between ancient Germanic tribal leader and his retinue.[4]

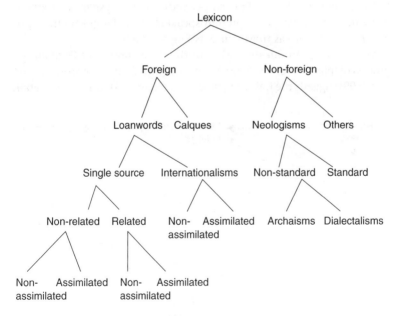

Figure 6.3 The hierarchy of lexical purism
Source: Adapted from Thomas 1991: 73.

Dialectalisms are also frequently sources for purist word-formation, a particularly powerful source in the planning of Norwegian, where some dialects were considered 'purer' than were others.

If the coinage *is* foreign to the system, there is a basic split between *loanwords* and *calques*. The latter are often concept by concept translations of a foreign source word or phrase. Thus English *skyscraper* is represented by German *Wolkenkranzer*, literally, 'scraper of the cloud'. In Québécois French at least, *hot dog* is calqued as *chien chaud*.

On the other hand, language planning actors may choose to borrow from the sources directly. Some actors appear content to use loanwords derived from a highly prestigious *international* source. In Western European terms, these languages of high prestige are Latin and Greek (and, to some extent, Hebrew). Elsewhere in the world, languages of prestige include Arabic, Chinese, Persian or Sanskrit. Many languages (or their planners) are happier with these borrowings if they are assimilated phonologically or morphologically to the native system. Sometimes this assimilation can even be represented orthographically. Thus Scottish Gaelic *telefon* and Manx *challvane* are pronounced in a similar manner, but the latter's planners have chosen to assimilate the internationalism to the language's (largely English-derived) spelling system, probably to dissuade learners (the only present speakers of the language) from pronouncing the word as they would its English equivalent.

As we will see in our discussion of the development of German, the process of 'purification' is by no means straightforward, however. Thomas (1991: 99) suggests the following flow chart (Figure 6.4) as a representation.

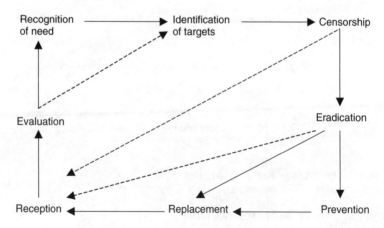

Figure 6.4   The purism process

In order for a purist effort to work, some speakers must believe that it is necessary, a point most effectively demonstrated by there being little in the way of impetus for lexical purism in English, despite a number of attempts to achieve this in the nineteenth and twentieth centuries (Thomas 1991: 93–4). It is unlikely to proceed if what is to be purified, or even excised, is not identified. Which of the levels of language is considered to be problematical from the point of view of its 'purity'? To take the French language for the moment, it can be argued that the primary problem associated by some speakers with the language from the Second World War on was the perceived threat from the importation of English lexis, this being connected with the power of Anglo-American (popular) culture.

Conscious attempts must be made by speakers both as individuals and groups not to use certain features of the language as it exists at present, however. Thomas suggests that the majority process is in the first place one of *censorship*, followed by *eradication*. Although it is true that a great deal of this initial censorship must inevitably be self-censorship, this is often played out in the correction of features in the usage of others.

Eradication implies that this censorship can be imposed (or, more positively, disseminated) – both personally and collectively – as a norm. One French speaker, or a number of them, may decide not to use the borrowing *weekend*. That does not *eradicate* the usage unless wider acceptance is forthcoming. In order for this to be carried through, there have to be mechanisms for *prevention* and *replacement*. These two processes work closely together, as they do with eradication. A usage cannot be eradicated unless further usages of that type can be prevented; by the same token, native speakers must be presented with a replacement. In the case of the unsuccessful eradication of *weekend* in French, an attempt was made both to prevent further English borrowings of this type, and to replace them with equivalent French coinages, many of them calques, such as *fin de semaine* 'end of week'. Activities of this type might be carried out either by influential individuals, or by a language planning authority. Yet its success very much depends on its *reception* among the wider community. This process, along with others discussed in this section, have as much to do with status and acquisition planning as with corpus planning.

The reception stage is at the centre of any purism-motivated corpus planning process. As well as the main route from replacement to reception, there are also opportunities for feedback from all stages after the censorship process has begun. No corpus planning is productive if it is not accepted by its intended audience. This is particularly the case with purism, since a speech community is being asked to give up elements of its language in favour of new usages (even when these are couched in terms of ethnic antiquarianism). Given that people are naturally conservative about language, there will need to be considerable consensus, among at least opinion-forming elements of the community, that the activity being undertaken is worthwhile. Thus, Czech purism was most acceptable when the Czech speakers of Bohemia and Moravia both felt themselves to be under attack by German language hegemony in central Europe, *and* nationalism in its most romantic form was at its zenith in the area. As we will see in our discussion of Turkish, and was seen in our treatment of the development of French during the reigns of Louis XIV and XV, an innovation's reception is aided by its association with a charismatic leadership and ideology which have the potential to establish these innovations by force.

Language planners must *evaluate* the success of the process. Any language planning effort is an ongoing process; this is particularly the case with purism. If an effort has been successful, there may be a temptation to carry out further efforts which had previously been considered unlikely to succeed for societal reasons. At the same time, an identification of targets must also be carried out, because any new activity must be considered thoroughly to have any likelihood of success. This is, perhaps, even more the case when a previous effort at 'purification' has not been successful. Inevitably, questions will be raised about whether the perceived need was genuine (in the eyes of the great mass of speakers) or not.

6.5   Discussion

Corpus planning is, by its nature, very attractive to both professional and amateur linguists. But as our discussion of the purism process has demonstrated, it is doomed to remain a hobby, unless the corpus planning is associated with outreach ventures connected to both the native speakers of the language variety in question and, quite possibly, the members of an ethnic group who do not speak the ethnic group language, but would like to. These developments, associated with status and acquisition planning, are in many ways more nebulous than is corpus planning; they are vital to it, nonetheless.

6.6   Status and acquisition planning

As Haugen suggested, the dividing line between corpus planning and status planning is convenient rather than natural. Under most circumstances the two processes go hand in hand. Acquisition planning can also be seen as the most developed form of status planning. Although it is tempting to portray corpus planning as being at the heart of language planning, the inequalities of status which affect the chances of survival of many languages today actively demand status and acquisition planning rather more. Indeed, the feedback loops suggested by Thomas in his model enforce this.

Language varieties seem locked in a Darwinian struggle for survival. In this competition, there will inevitably be winners, but there will equally inevitably be losers. As was already noted in Chapter 2, the ecology supporting a particular language variety can be extremely fragile. In her study of the gradual shift away from their ancestral language by ethnic Hungarians in the Austrian town of Oberwart, Gal (1979) discovered that the effects of two world wars, industrialization (connected with immigration of monolingual German speakers) and the association (particularly among younger women) of Magyar with a low prestige lifestyle, had left that language as largely the preserve of the older generation. Dorian's 1981 study of 'language death' in relation to the Gaelic of East Sutherland in Scotland associated this development with similar phenomena. Analogous changes can be analysed throughout the world.

Where closely related varieties are in competition with each other, as studies such as Macafee (1994) demonstrate, the phenomenon is particularly acute. For speakers of the disparaged, or displaced, variety, there is little choice but to accommodate towards the more prestigious variety, in particular in writing. This latter phenomenon, of language displacement, submersion and merger, is especially common when one dialect becomes synecdochic within a dialect continuum.

Naturally, supporters of the displaced variety often resist this process. Much effort is expended in the planning of language revitalization; since it grabs attention, this activity is aimed more towards corpus planning, in an attempt to establish the disparaged variety as equivalent in domain use and prestige to the dominant variety. Yet corpus planning cannot be successful of itself. Status and acquisition planning can be of equal, if not greater, importance.

Efforts to support and enhance the status of a disparaged language can often be heroic; sadly, they are not always successful. As Fishman (1991, 2001) points out, the recovery from a variety which may be practically moribund to one which itself is dominant can pass through a variety of stages, the crucial points of which are the achievement of intergenerational transfer of the oral variety, and the presence of a developed written form in a number of domains associated with Ausbau in the wider society.

That this achievement is by no means a straightforward process can be seen in the following chapter, however, where, with one exception, none of the high-profile status and acquisition planning efforts discussed can be said to be an unqualified success.

6.7   Conclusion

In the following chapter, attention will be given to a range of language planning situations, stretching from situations where the process has been ongoing and only semi-conscious over a large part of its history, to other languages which have been planned in a highly conscious manner, in the matter of a few years. Although the first set of examples is largely concerned with corpus planning, the other with status and acquisition planning, it will become increasingly evident that one form of planning is unlikely to succeed unless it is associated with the other two.

7
Language Planning: Testing the Models

In the preceding chapter, a number of different planning processes were discussed, using relatively small-scale examples to illustrate them. This chapter will test the models suggested, as well as redressing the balance towards status and acquisition planning. It should be noted from the outset, however, that, although corpus planning and status and acquisition planning have been discussed in separate sections, the application of one cannot proceed without the others. This is particularly the case with corpus planning which, as we will see, can never work without there being status and acquisition planning in support of it.

7.1 Corpus planning

7.1.1 German

The strength of Germany and its people within Europe is recent. For most of the early modern era, for instance, Germany, divided by religious and political allegiances and with a 'patchwork' of states, many of which were physically small and politically weak, was at the mercy of more powerful neighbours, most notably France. The German language, now a major regional language within the European Union and elsewhere, associated with high quality literature and culture as well as with a proud academic tradition, was, until around two hundred and fifty years ago, disparaged by both internal and external observers. A 'siege mentality', lending itself to purism, has sometimes been visible in relation to the language even when Germany has been at its most powerful in political, military or cultural terms, therefore.[1] Although, as Langer (2001) points out, German purism has sometimes focused on the 'impurity' of elements of its structure, in general its primary focus has been on the connection between pronunciation and lexis, and the nativization of lexis.

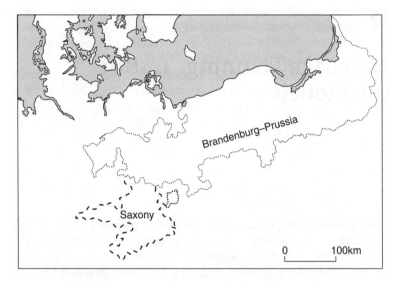

Map 3   Northern Germany in the early eighteenth century

What we now think of as the German-speaking world is, as we might expect, deeply heterogeneous linguistically. Without Standard High German, it would be largely impossible for someone who spoke the dialect of the Graubünden region of Switzerland to understand someone from Vorpommern in northern Germany. Unlike the situation in England during the middle ages, moreover, no central authority was strong enough to demand linguistic centralization.

This did not mean that 'one wrote as one spoke', naturally; local styles of writing, largely reflecting local norms, did develop. Under these circumstances, strong external influences would have been exerted upon the language as written by individuals. When French culture was dominant across the western and central parts of Europe, elements of this language had a considerable influence upon varieties of German, albeit to a lesser degree than with English. Predictably, Latin influence at a variety of levels was highly prevalent.

These local 'house styles' were not necessarily equal in status, however. Within the loose structures of the Holy Roman Empire particular territories were highly significant in the development of a more general written language. Most strikingly, the place where the imperial chancery was situated had some effect upon the language used elsewhere. In the sixteenth century, the local writing styles of Saxony were foregrounded by their association with the ideas of Luther. Similar, although lesser, positive associations were present for the Upper German employed by Swiss reformers such as Zwingli. Given that (conservative) Protestantism was associated with an emerging, literate, middle class, the connection of these varieties with the mass-production of print capitalism cannot be over-emphasized, particularly as an element in the creation of the equation of language with nation, and nation with language. These 'standards' were generally consistent internally; given the differences of pronunciation to be found in the German-speaking world, it was difficult to decide which particular 'peculiarities' were to be permitted, however.

During the course of the seventeenth and eighteenth centuries, general opinion reinforced the idea of representing a Saxon pronunciation of the written form, established through the orthography (Blackall 1959), despite rearguard actions by both Silesian and Swabian/Swiss partisans. Considerable numbers of literate Germans must have believed that this particular variety in some way encapsulated the 'best', least 'aberrant', of the varieties of German available. By the start of the nineteenth century, the previously commonplace orthographic variation had been displaced by much more unitary usage.

Lexical planning for the new standard has a longer, and more fraught, history, however. Whilst moderate purism was present from an early period, from the seventeenth-century German writers became increasingly worried about the status of extraneous elements in the language; it is very striking that this should have begun in the brutal aftermath of the Thirty Years War, which promoted France to the status of the most powerful country in Europe.

At its inception, German lexical purism was localized, associated with small-scale clubs in urban centres. But in the course of the eighteenth century a number of these associations began to expand and become more influential. Again, this activity was associated quite strongly with the Saxon area, although the growing might of Brandenburg–Prussia to its north should not be underestimated.[2] Strenuous efforts began to be made in lexicography and literature for the nativization of the language.

The period when this was taking place was particularly crucial, because the predominant status of French as a world language was making itself felt in fashionable circles throughout Germany. There may even have been revulsion towards German in some very elevated circles: as we saw in Chapter 2, Frederick the Great of Prussia, admittedly an exceptional case in so many ways, was only marginally a German speaker, had little sympathy for the idea of a 'German' culture or nation, and preferred French as a means of communication both inside and outside his country.

Inevitably, reaction against this cultural obsequiousness would eventually make itself felt.

The Revolutionary and Napoleonic wars exacerbated this. It would be a mistake to see the German nation as being united in its opposition to this external threat; far from it, in fact, since many of the German states, both great and small, were largely willing allies of the French expansion until its collapse. Nonetheless, a reaction based on the prevailing trends of romanticism and nationalism, as discussed in Chapter 2, set in, in particular in the newly reconstituted Prussia. The previous desire to appear 'refined', and part of the European mainstream, was now perceived by progressive circles in government and education as being an affectation which distanced you from the German people in their purist, rural form.

Nevertheless, the purist replacement of 'foreign' elements with 'good' native equivalents, along with the preference for native rather than internationalist terms for new coinages, was patchy until the unification of 'little Germany' in 1870–1871. It is difficult in the context of much that happened afterwards to imagine the explosion of popular sentiment which the unification caused; this became particularly the case during the long reign of Kaiser Wilhelm II, where the monarch's own personal obsessions with being equal (if not actually superior) to all other monarchs, ruling a 'progressive' nation, clashed with his strange sense of inferiority in ruling over a country with such a short pedigree of unity. Indeed, how better to express this unity than by nativizing the national language? This purism process was encouraged by a variety of language associations and pressure groups, most notably the *Allgemeiner Deutscher Sprachverein*; it would have got nowhere without the active participation of members of the federal and state governments and bureaucracies in the process, however (Wells 1985: 397–8). In fact, in the period between unification and 1918, German experienced a radical shift towards native sources which was carried through by all elements of the now highly literate German population, both from elite and non-elite positions.

In the aftermath of the war and the perceived inadequacies of the peace settlement, this purist train was not derailed, even if, in some of the larger cities of the Weimar Republic, there may have been moves towards greater internationalization. This was seen as decadent by more nationalist members of the purist movement. With the advent of the National Socialist dictatorship in 1933, many of these more extreme purists confidently developed their radical agenda, often casting their nativism in the light of anti-Semitism or anti-bolshevism. Surprisingly, the upper echelons of the Nazi movement had little time for these views; the purist movement was itself targeted as being ideologically suspect (Ehrlich 1989; Hutton 1999). Nevertheless, the concepts with which 'purity' had come to be associated during the period did not do linguistic purism any favours in Germany in the immediate post-war period.

The general tenor of the times led to a growth in the borrowing of foreign lexical items, particularly from English. Inevitably this influx – especially of words such as *Handy*, 'mobile telephone', which do not even exist in English – produced heightened levels of purism, particularly in official circles. Popular usage is less likely to follow this official process than it was in the period 1870–1919, however. In general, most purist organizations have avoided political associations, although there is some evidence for far right sympathies among some fringe movements (Pfalzgraf 2003).

In recent years, the emphasis in German language planning circles has returned to the question of spelling. In many ways, the reforms suggested by the *Zwischenstaatliche Kommision für deutsche Rechtschreibung*, 'Cross-border commission on German spelling', are relatively minor, as in the suggested replacement of <ß>, originally pronounced /sts/, but now /s/, with <ss>, in words such as *Straße/Strasse*, 'street', although other reforms may not be as straightforward in their implementation as the planning actors envisaged. Nevertheless, even the most casual trawl of the internet indicates that a large part of the opinion-forming classes – journalists, politicians and teachers – are incensed by at least some of the proposals. This dissatisfaction seems to be reflected in a large part of the populations of all the German-speaking countries. In some ways this reaction can be seen as *archaistic*, whilst the reform process is perceived, rightly or wrongly, as *elitist*. Perhaps *populist* purism could be suggested as a separate category in post-romantic, highly literate, contexts. It may be no coincidence that the self-confidence associated with (West) Germany in the post-war period has been undermined by the unexpected costs of sudden reunification, the 'federalization' of the European Union and even, perhaps, the replacement of the 'strong' Mark by the Euro. French speakers are often considered to have adopted a siege mentality in relation to their language; perhaps the same is also true for some speakers of German.

We can therefore argue that German, which started out by having elitist language planning, both of circumstantial and engineered types, gradually shifted over to a more ethnographic or archaistic approach; as Thomas has taught us to expect, however, much of this apparently non-elite and rurally oriented planning was actually carried out by academic, urban, elite groupings.

7.1.2 Norwegian

Today, Norwegian has two standard varieties, termed Nynorsk 'modern Norwegian' and Bokmål 'book, written language'. These varieties are mutually intelligible. Why, therefore, should a nation of little more than four million people have arrived at such a situation? What marks off one variety from the other linguistically? Why should this division be perpetuated?

The historical linguistic ecology of the country is one of the central issues. The dialects of North Germanic spoken in what is now Norway have always been highly divergent: particularly in the west and centre of the country. Furthermore, a bundle of isoglosses runs through the eastern parts of central Norway. Simplifying somewhat, the eastern dialects share much with Swedish and Danish, while the western dialects bear similarities to Icelandic and Faeroese. Moreover, the western dialects tend to be more morphologically (and therefore grammatically) conservative than are the eastern. All of the dialects are undoubtedly Norwegian, from both a linguistic and sociolinguistic point of view; nevertheless, the differences cannot be ignored.

This is particularly the case because of the position of the two main population centres, both in the past and present, of the country. In the middle ages, it was Bergen, with its western dialect, which dominated. At the time, the country looked west towards its north Atlantic possessions. The royal administration was largely concentrated there; inevitably, the local scribal style came to have synecdochic status. In the course of the fourteenth and fifteenth centuries, power shifted east towards the Oslo fjord area. The personal union of the kingdoms of Norway and Denmark led eventually to a political union of the two countries which, in the aftermath of the Protestant Reformation, brought about considerable centralization, at first in Oslo, later in Copenhagen. This was accompanied by a Danicization of the court language, although remnants of the old synecdochic Norwegian lingered (Haugen 1976: 329–32). At the same time, all of the Scandinavian languages were coming under considerable influence from the Low German of the Hanseatic League, as demonstrated in many of the papers collected in Ureland (1987) and Jahr (1995).

To most Norwegians, of course, changing the official language made little difference. It was the governmental and trading classes who were primarily affected in both the ways that they wrote and, to an increasing degree, spoke. Inevitably, Norwegian speakers who wished to 'get on' in the union began to assimilate their spoken and written idiolects towards the dominant language; this accommodation was only occasionally total, however, given the differences between the languages. Danish and Norwegian are to some extent mutually intelligible. Nevertheless, certain developments in the former language, such as the voicing and spirantization of voiceless stops, are only found peripherally in Norway.

By the time at which Norway became independent of Denmark, but in personal union with Sweden (1814), Haugen (1966: 31–2) distinguishes

> roughly the following types of oral expression: (1) *Pure Danish*, used by a small number of immigrated Danish officials and merchants, and on the stage, which was dominated by Danish actors; (2) *Literary Standard*, a Norwegian reading pronunciation of Danish used on solemn occasions by Norwegian-born pastors and officials, in its most exaggerated form by country schoolmasters when instructing the young; (3) *Colloquial Standard*, the daily speech of the educated classes, a compromise between the preceding and the following types, varying in style according to the occasion and the speaker's origin; (4) *Urban Substandard*, spoken by artisans and working-class people, varying from city to city, but showing many characteristics in common with the surrounding rural dialects; (5) *Rural dialect*, spoken by the farming and fishing population, varying from parish to parish, with an intricate network of isoglosses crisscrossing the country, but falling into broad dialectal areas determined by the lines of communication. Between the extremes of stage Danish and the remoter rural dialects there was a gulf which effectively prevented communication. But from one type to the next of those listed above there was extensive communication and mutual adaptation.

The spoken sociolinguistic situation was complex; the written situation was straightforward, however. With the exception of a few 'folk' representations, the written language of the newly autonomous country was Danish. This situation had the benefit of prestige and historical pedigree; it did not suit the prerequisites of nationalism, particularly of a romantic cast, so common in northern Europe in the nineteenth century, however. Almost all Norwegians were agreed that a 'Norwegian' language must be reborn. The solution obviously lay in corpus planning; the problem in the linguistic and sociolinguistic patterns of the country. What was Norwegian? Whose speech should be represented in writing?

Since this awakening, Norwegian language planning has taken two courses. One school, the purist, or maximalist, party, has tended to favour the development of a language form which is aggressively different from the pre-existing standard, associating itself with the 'best' dialects and literary achievements of 'the ancestors'. The other view is embraced by the minimalist, or pragmatic, party. According to this view, 'Norwegian' would develop incrementally through the gradual nativization of the existing standard. It would be tempting to see the former view as being representative of the party within the Norwegian language community which promotes what is now called Nynorsk, the latter with the promoters of Bokmål (and *Riksmaal*, a distinction to which we will return in the following). This is a truism, however, since the history of the Norwegian 'language war' of the twentieth century includes examples of both tendencies among members of both camps. It is not the purpose of this section to describe in detail what was often a rather unedifying process (interested readers are directed to Haugen (1966)); nevertheless, some understanding of the processes involved in the corpus planning of both national varieties is necessary.

To the original maximalist party of the mid-nineteenth century, a 'back to the future' mindset was necessary for the development of a new form of Norwegian. In the romantic climate of the time, folk traditions and rural language were valued above the corrupt values and language of urban areas. Where, therefore, would you seek out such uncorrupted forms of language? The most obvious place was the west of the country, where the most conservative dialects were spoken. This would have been particularly attractive to many corpus planners because of the archaic tendencies inherent in language planning during the Romantic period. Indeed, the chief agent of this movement, Ivar Aasen, gradually became more purist and archaistic in his approach as he grew older (Linn 1997). Moreover, as Bucken-Knapp (2003: chapter 2) points out, the ideology of purity and nationhood became a powerful symbolic element in the achievement of *elite* status by the Liberal party in the course of the 1880s and the following decades, often in concert with the print media, even when elements of the new ruling party who came from social or geographical background not consonant with Aasen's sources may not have been as keen on the one-nation, two-languages policy then espoused.

Corpus planning for *Landsmaal*, which can be translated as either 'language of the countryside' or 'language of the country', an ambiguity which was probably entirely intentional, had three goals: (1) a complete break with the use of (Low) German vocabulary in the new standard language and, when possible, the replacement of Danish-style formations with 'native' ones; (2) the replacement of what was seen as an artificial and elitist standard form with one which was close to the 'people'; (3) a return to the language of the 'golden age' of Norse literature and Norwegian power in the North Atlantic area. Naturally, these goals were not entirely mutually compatible. Excluding non-native vocabulary (particularly since the habits of prefixation and suffixation in traditional Norwegian are strikingly different from Low German) was relatively straightforward. But it is difficult both to coin new vocabulary (or extend the meaning of previously existing vocabulary) and to encourage speakers to use the new vocabulary item for a concept for which they already know a word. It is unlikely that native speakers, rather than corpus planners, regularly care (or even know) whether a current word is 'native' or not.

'Taking the language to the people' is laudable; it is also problematical, however. This is particularly the case where the dialects of even relatively small areas are divergent. Whose forms and structures are to be chosen? A planner could concentrate on the language of only one area, considering it to be in some way most representative of the national language, or an ostensibly more democratic approach might be taken, using forms and structures derived from a number of different areas which are considered to be the 'best' form of the language. The latter was the course chosen by Aasen and his successors. A natural dialectologist, Aasen established connections between a variety of different dialects, interpreted in an ethnographic and archaistic light.

The disadvantage of this discovery of the 'best', however, was that the new standard did not actually represent any one dialect's usage completely; therefore, any putative learner of Landsmaal would have had to learn usages which were naturally foreign to him or her. The design of the standard, with its intended bias towards the dialects of the west and centre of Norway, would still have made it closer to the language of any speaker of this region than the Danish-based existing standard, however. But this linguistic proximity had to be weighed against the sociolinguistic claims of the two standard varieties.

The archaizing tendency was arguably the most problematical factor in the development of Landsmaal. Old Norse had a complex system of noun and adjective declension; the verb system was also rather synthetic. By the nineteenth century, a large part of this was no longer current for most dialects. It would therefore take an unlikely effort on the part of the speaker to reintroduce either case or number marking to the language. Wisely, Aasen concentrated on those features which were current in a number of dialects, such as the use of *me* instead of *vi* for 'we', rather than on features which were now highly marginal. Nevertheless, outside the dialect areas which Aasen believed to be the most 'genuine' representatives of Norwegian, elements of the new standard were still considered too archaic by the great majority. Speakers could therefore object to the new standard on linguistic grounds; many speakers would have had a strong (although rarely enunciated) aversion to employing the 'language of peasants' in writing, however, so that sociolinguistic arguments would have been very likely to come into play as well.

Landsmaal as a social project was remarkably successful, particularly in its first half century. It had earned equal status with the other standard. This achievement was largely due to an astute combination of status and acquisition planning in line with the increasingly democratic nature of the country, as well as the agency of dedicated schoolteachers and officials who helped to promulgate Landsmaal, to a newly literate population, as the only acceptable form of Norwegian. Yet there were also problems with the associations the variety had, not least the fact that its active espousal (rather than passive acceptance) was practically confined to the centre and west. This partial acceptance led to understandable fear that a future government might rescind the guaranteed equality between the two varieties.

Nevertheless, the cultural environment which produced Landsmaal, as well as its initial success, did have repercussions for Danish in Norway, generally referred to as Riksmaal, the 'language of the kingdom'. The users and promoters of Riksmaal, and its successors, can be split into two parties, although the membership of either party fluctuated according to time. The *ultras* generally stood for the status quo as it existed at the time their particular programme was put forward (generally this meant the situation before the reforms suggested at that time). There were members of this grouping who accepted no change from Danish, but they have usually been marginalized. The other party were (and are) the *moderates*, who generally accept change, but only as a gradual process.[3]

Most adherents of Riksmaal also supported the idea of producing a more Norwegian standard form. To some, this might have been merely the tolerance of Norwegian features regularly used in speech even by the ruling class. Many would also have supported the gradual introduction of a spelling system which represented everyday pronunciation more readily. Thus Danish *bog* 'book' would be replaced by Norwegian *bok*; *nu* 'now' by *nå*. Many of these changes were generally accepted, although some, such as the change from *sprog* 'language' to *språk*, were resisted,

Language Planning: Testing the Models 125

probably because of the symbolic importance of its meaning. Other proposed changes were much more problematical, however.

By the time of Norway's full independence in 1906, therefore, Riksmaal had become more Norwegian. Its acceptance as a fully fledged variety of Norwegian was rather less convincing than with Landsmaal, however. On the other hand, its supporters did not have to try as hard to proselytize. Riksmaal already had considerable status; furthermore, it was the spoken variety of a small but significant part of the population, while Landsmaal had no native speakers. Moreover, the dialects of south-eastern Norway bore some resemblance to the Norwegian/radical end of this Riksmaal continuum. As urbanization increased, this set of varieties gained considerable importance, particularly with the rise of politicized organized labour. Any twentieth-century planner had to decide how to represent this changing linguistic situation. Increasingly, central government called for the end to the split between the two official varieties, to be replaced by *Samnnorsk*, 'together Norwegian' or 'common Norwegian', which represented the 'best' features of both pre-existing standards without alienating supporters of either. As Bucken-Knapp (2003: in particular, chapter 3) points out, the Norwegian Labour Party, as it strove for power in the 1930s, found it expedient to embrace this policy (rather than maintain its previous neutrality on the language issue) as a pragmatic means to encourage support from the countryside, while not dividing their traditional urban working-class support.

From the point of view of the Landsmaal side of this convergence, it was generally felt that more eastern forms of the language could be introduced into the language, now known as Nynorsk. Thus the form for 'we', which was represented solely by *me* earlier, was replaced as primary form by *vi*, the eastern form. It was hoped that these changes would make the standard more acceptable to speakers from elsewhere than Landsmaal's heartland.

At the same time, successive government-inspired committees attempted to make Riksmaal (or, as it came to be termed, at least by the government and its supporters, Bokmål, 'book/written language') more like Nynorsk in terms of morphology, and, in particular, the phonology underlying the orthography. Typically Norwegian (or, rather, West Norse) diphthongs were introduced into the standard, so that, for example, the indefinite article used with members of the historical neuter gender class, which traditionally in Riksmaal had been represented by *et*, was now to be written *eit*.

It is very unlikely that the successive government committees which suggested these reforms would have been so naïve as to assume that they would be accepted by either side without argument. In fact, the resultant furore threatened to reduce the language use of the country to chaos from the 1930s to the 1960s and beyond.

The reform commissions were serious in their intentions, however. Norway is a democracy, so that an enforced change, along the lines of the Turkish spelling reform discussed in Section 7.1.3, was never likely to succeed. Nevertheless, the power of central government was employed. Haugen (1966: 143) presents the following schematization (Figure 7.1) of the preference given in civil service and school usage, based upon *A* being the best possible form, and *F* being utterly unacceptable.

These distinctions were policed. Any publication which employed forms other than the *A, B* or *C* forms would potentially be fined. *B* and *C* forms did co-exist, but *B* was preferred. On those occasions where only *A* forms were officially permitted, no alternates were allowed. Thus there was some room for variation, but this was generally based on the idea of a short-term compromise; it was certainly biased in terms of preference towards the use of the new standard forms, with the partial exception of the writing of schoolchildren, where non-standard features were acceptable as a temporary compromise to lead children into the standard forms.

Even after a succession of these reforms, the two standards were still separate, although some parts of the educational and political establishment planned to achieve Samnnorsk in the next set of reforms (probably intended for the late 1960s). This did not happen, however, precisely because of the linguistic destabilization which happened during this period. Opposition was particularly vociferous from the Riksmaal platform, which saw Bokmål as an attempt to strip away the 'cultured'

A	Sole Form (*eneform*)	Obligatory (*obligatorisk*)	In all writing
B	Main form (*hovedform*)	Obligatory (*obligatorisk*)	In textbooks only
C	Alternate or doublet (*jamstilt, dobbeltform*)	Optional (*valgfri*)	In all writing
D	Side form (*sideform*)	Optional (*valgfri*)	In pupils' work only
F	Excluded		In all writing

Figure 7.1   Degrees of acceptability for Norwegian usage

history of their language. Instead of the expected conjunction of the two national varieties, interim linguistic states began to develop, whilst a long-standing language committee continued to attempt compromise (an attempt which ended in the committee being wound-up, without reaching a solution, in Spring 2003). In general, language use is defined in terms of a radical or conservative adherence to a norm, along the lines of the following continuum:

> [Høgnorsk] Nynorsk radical Bokmål moderate/conservative Bokmål [Riksmål]

Samnnorsk would have been established between radical Bokmål and Nynorsk. A representation of these distinctions can be found in the following examples, extended from those of Braunmüller (1998: 105):

Danish	Jeg gik	frem og skrev	på tavlen.
Riksmål	Jeg gikk	frem og skrev	på tavlen.
Moderate Bokmål	Jeg gikk	fram og skrev	på tavlen/ tavla.
Radical Bokmål	Jeg gikk/gjekk	fram og skreiv	på tavla.
Conservative Nynorsk	Eg gikk	fram og skreiv	på tavla.
Radical Nynorsk	Eg gjekk	fram og skreiv	på tavla (på tavli).
Høgnorsk	Eg gjekk	fram og skreiv	på tavli.

'I went forward and wrote on the blackboard'

This short sentence in all (or practically all) written varieties of 'Norwegian' which can be found in Norway demonstrates a number of the features already mentioned: the movement towards diphthongs, as found with *skreiv* as against *skrev*; the preference of feminine (*tavla*, or *tavli*, the original Landsmaal form) over common gender forms (*tavlen*), and so on. It is also possible to see more radical and conservative forms of Nynorsk represented by *gjekk* (Western) and *gikk* (Eastern), but both containing the iconic *eg*, 'I'. Considerable tolerance of variation is necessary (although not always forthcoming) on all sides.

As Jahr (2003) points out, the general acceptance of the end of Samnnorsk as an objective (whether long-term or short-term) by the end of the 1960s, along with considerable financial help from supporters of a more conservative outlook (whether linguistic or political) led to a rejection of the move towards a more radical Bokmål, with new norms harking back somewhat to a more Riksmaal pre-war form. At around the same time, planners for Nynorsk also halted the coalescence. Lying behind both compromises and the rigorous opposition to merger are power struggles between various elites and counter-elites in Norwegian society (not all based upon views on language).

Stasis appears now to have been achieved between the Norwegian varieties. Moderate/conservative and radical forms of both national standard varieties exist. Nynorsk has constitutionally guaranteed rights and privileges in official and educational contexts. Since Norway operates a highly localized form of democracy, decisions on what national language variety is used are taken at the level of *kommune*, 'parish'. Yet there is evidence that Nynorsk is in decline. Fewer and fewer local communities choose this variety as their preferred norm; fewer and fewer young people declare for that variety when entering higher education or the armed forces; fewer and fewer tax returns are made out in that language variety. Nynorsk's imminent demise is not anticipated. It *has* been marginalized, however: the attempted break-out from western Norway never happened. Even in Landsmaal's original heartlands, Bokmål is often to be found in its place in the official function.

That does not mean that the corpus planning involved has been a wasted effort. The presence of an aggressively ethnographic and archaistic Norwegian variety in the country during the formative nation-building period helped to accelerate the nationalizing corpus planning processes for the other local standard. Although Samnnorsk as a goal has now been officially abandoned, it does seem likely that radical Bokmål will assume that role eventually. If Nynorsk disappeared tomorrow as an independent variety, its influence would continue to be felt.

7.1.3 Turkish

The sources of the Turkish language reform lie in the histories and cultures of the areas involved. It also can only be understood in terms of the character and actions of the first president of the Turkish Republic, Mustafa Kemal, surnamed *Atatürk*, 'father of the Turks', towards the end of his life, and the (at least overt) reverence felt towards him in Turkey.

When Turks gained power in Asia Minor in the eleventh–thirteenth centuries, they were a relatively unsophisticated nomadic people from central Asia. At the heart of their social structure was the idea of inter-connection with the leader through membership of a clan. Although the ruling classes adopted many of the cultural practices of the peoples they conquered – Persians, Arabs, Armenians and Greeks, among others – this sense of inter-relationship was never abandoned. This clan unity was always somewhat at odds with the idea of the unity of all Moslems, however. Language and ethnic background should not affect anyone's right to consider himself or herself as a brother or sister of all other Moslems. Along with these connections come mutual obligations to support the Moslem cause, both individually, and as part of a group. This egalitarianism and internationalism is problematical for any group which wishes to emphasize its ethnic and cultural identity by the foregrounding of a national language. Part of this problem can be seen in the figure of the Ottoman Emperor himself. The Emperor derived his initial power as leader of the Turks from his position as chieftain of the Osmanlı clan; his rule was accepted among the non-Turkish Moslem majority of his empire because he was *caliph*, the lieutenant of the Prophet.

The leaders of the Turks therefore altered their very ethnic and cultural orientations. Something of this can be seen in the ways in which the later ruling class analysed the word *türk* (Glenny 1999: 99). To these noblemen, Turks were peasants, beneath the dignity of the Ottoman warrior. This change in orientation for the ruling class can be seen in their language, also termed Ottoman, replete with Arabic and Persian idiom. It is thus even more shocking when the nationalists of Anatolia and Rumelia, often, although not always, from this very Osmanlı background,[4] began to call themselves Turks.

A specifically Turkish form of nationalism was slow to develop, therefore; indeed the idea of being an Ottoman continued to spread well into the nineteenth century (Wheatcroft 1995b). As with all feudal systems, all power was in theory concentrated in one person at the centre; considerable devolution of power was necessary, however. In order to maintain power effectively, the concept of being a member of the extended Ottoman family was promoted among civil and military members of the sultan's household. These notional slaves were generally loyal through perception of being part of a single enterprise. Indeed, the first moves towards a 'modern' Turkish nationalism were taken in the name of *osmanlık*, being Ottoman: a privilege which reformers overtly wished to spread to all subjects of the Sultan, no matter their ethnic, religious or linguistic background.

Throughout the nineteenth century, the Ottoman Empire attempted to reform; yet these attempts were often half-hearted. As the regime's foreign debt grew, its ability to express an independent osmanlık became limited. Even more importantly, the level of stability necessary to achieve a unificatory ideology was lacking. In effect, both ethnic and linguistic divisions rendered the Ottoman ideal not merely unrealistic, but actively against the tenor of the times.

Until the middle of the eighteenth century, the Ottoman Empire managed to maintain, and perpetuate, itself fairly successfully by means of the *millet* system. The religious leaders of the various confessional allegiances within the Empire governed their respective communities, in accordance with the will of the Sultan. Although absolutely open to abuse, this system did manage on the whole to maintain the peace. It also ensured a very limited level of contact between communities. In the nineteenth-century 'liberalization' of the Empire, this separation, of necessity, became unacceptable. If all were to be Ottomans, all were to be citizens rather than subjects, then these boundaries based upon religion had to be dissolved. But the underlying ethnic and linguistic distinctions were much more difficult (if not impossible) to resolve.

Expectations rose to unrealistic heights for all Ottoman subjects. To those emotionally connected to the Ottoman state and its apparatus of rule, the hope was that the new sense of unity would be continued, as all of the former millets became one Ottoman nation; to members of the ethnic groups, this new liberalism was equated with greater autonomy for 'national' groups. The distance between centripetal and centrifugal concepts of justice and equality inevitably grew. This was particularly acute in the Balkans, where Christians of various ethnic and linguistic backgrounds, as well as a number of Moslems who did not have Turkish as their native language, were in the majority.

The 'Young Turk' movement, which gained power in 1908, learned from the previous mistakes; it made the equation between loyalty and being a Turk (defined in terms of language). In the ensuing wars and bloody interludes, a large part of the Christian population of the Empire formed new nation-states. With the exception of the majority Moslem Albanians, who remained within the Empire for as long as there was a connection on Turkish soil between Thrace and Epirus, the Moslems of Europe under Turkish control had become overwhelmingly Turkish in language.

In the majority Moslem areas of the Empire, the same process was slower, but no less inevitable. Throughout the nineteenth and early twentieth centuries, the Arab African territories were gradually incorporated into the overseas empires of various European powers. In Asia, the process had already been initiated by the temporary 'liberation' of the holy sites of Islam by the ibn Saud family (Winder 1965).

By the end of the Great War, Ottoman power was effectively confined to areas where Turkish speakers were in a majority. In the years that followed, the two main Christian populations of the area – Armenians and Greeks – were ejected from large parts of the territory, often (particularly in the case of the Armenians) with evidence of their long-term residence being erased. In the case of the Greeks, their eventual departure had the advantage (for Turkish nationalism) of being open to analysis as a war of liberation. With the exception of the other large Moslem ethnic group of Anatolia, the Kurds, the territory of the new Turkish Republic of 1922–1924 had become overwhelmingly monolingual and monocultural. The problem, as many nationalists would have seen it, was that the written language of the former Empire, Osmanlı, with its elitist indebtedness to Arabic and Persian forms of utterance, was not suited to a new state whose founding father's central principles began with *halkçılık*, 'populism' (Shaw and Shaw 1977: II, 378–84). How could a 'new Turkish' be formed?

Turkish nationalists had been affected by the trends of European nationalism in the nineteenth century. Along with a Social Darwinian focus on purity of 'blood' and the 'survival of the fittest' (in social and ethnic terms), they had accepted the idea of the 'fittest' language being the purest, that is, the one which had least foreign influence exerted upon it. As we have seen, Turks suffered from a 'cultural cringe' in comparison with their Arab, Persian and Greek subjects. Often the reaction under such circumstances is to retreat into clichéd images of the pure-blooded tiller of the soil (or the warrior) in distinction to the cosmopolitan (and effete) populations surrounding. This dialectic is, in fact, at least as old as the work of the historian and cultural commentator Herodotus (Hartog 1988).

At the time at which Turkish nationalism embraced language reform, the position was particularly acute. Turkey was suffering under the punitive provisions of the peace treaties which followed the Great War. With some justification, the Turks believed that their non-European status had led them to be treated more harshly than the other, Christian, Central Powers. With the exception of some French military leaders, none of the victor powers seriously envisaged the partition of the ethnic heartlands of the Germans, Austrians and Hungarians; precisely such plans were afoot with the 'Oriental' Ottoman Empire, including those areas where Turks were the dominant ethnic group. The Sultan and his government were supine in Constantinople.

In order to address this problem, and maintain the essential territory of the Turkish nation, both victory in the field, which was established crushingly against the Greeks, and a complete break with the Ottoman past, had to be achieved. Because the 'Oriental' background of the 'bloody Turk' had been particularly harmful to the Turkish cause, this break, inevitably, was aimed towards the European model which so many of the 'Young Turks' had admired; the perceived collaboration of the Sultan–Caliph led both to a rejection of his family Osmanlı state and of his language.

Inter-related to this desire to 'develop' was an awareness among progressive nationalists that general standards of literacy in what was left of the Empire were too low for full-scale acceptance as a European power. These relatively low levels of literacy were probably caused by the inefficiencies of an empire which was contracting in geographical and economic extent and where a great deal of what revenue there was was either squandered at the centre or used to feed payment on the foreign debts which the Empire had accumulated; to many nationalists, however, including Kemal, the illiteracy problem was caused by the use of a developed Persian version of the Arabic alphabet for the Turkish language. This script could not fully represent some of the nuances of Turkish phonology; in particular the rich vowel system, often used in word-initial position. To these critics, this problem was significantly exacerbated by the Arabic and Persian words and structures which had been incorporated into the Ottoman standard language, distinguishing this variety from the everyday speech of the people. For all of these reasons, the new Turkish Republic, and, in particular, Kemal and his advisers, was heavily committed to language reform. Ideological factors propelled the reform process in a populist/ethnographic direction.

The first stage of the language reform (and arguably the most successful) was the implementation of the new alphabet. With a few minor exceptions, the Turkish version of the Roman alphabet is as close to a symbol to sound correspondence phonemic system as possible. What makes this particularly impressive is that the process was achieved and implemented so rapidly and, apparently, so successfully.

Although there had been some prior discussion over the implementation of a Turkish Roman alphabet, and there appears to have been cross-fertilization between this Romanization and that ongoing in Soviet Central Asia, the actual planning process lasted some three months, beginning in June 1928 (Lewis 1999: 32–6). The process was encouraged by Kemal's keen participation, teaching the new alphabet himself to groups of villagers from the area around Ankara. Remarkably, the nation shifted from one graphic representation of their language to another in a matter of months. It does not in any way lessen the achievement to recognize that, for many adult Turks, this alphabet was the first to which they were introduced. Less successful, however, was the corpus planning of which the change of alphabet was a relatively small part.

Under the aegis of Kemal's overall reform programme, a general move towards 'pure Turkish' began. Arabic and Persian usages were to be excised; instead, 'pure Turkish' usages would be encouraged, with proper respect given to Turkish dialects and the means by which they coined new words. If a term could not be found in Turkish proper, then recourse was to be made to other Turkic languages, and even to other members of the debateable Altaic group. Turkish language planners were more open ideologically to Western influence and borrowings than they were to 'Islamic' influences. The importance of individuals in the process was considerable. The peculiar respect given by Turkish society to journalists and creative writers led to many of their innovations being at least considered, and often incorporated, into the language. In relation to Thomas' findings, we can see connections to a form of archaistic and ethnographic purism, which claimed to be populist, but actually contained significant elements of elitism. Interestingly (European) internationalisms were generally preferred over the prior borrowings from previously prestigious unrelated sources such as Arabic and Persian, as a sign of the ideology of the new state.

The Turkish language reform proceeded eccentrically. If a language's planners choose the purist route of development, they will inevitably have to coin neologisms. Normally those who introduce these neologisms will give much thought to the form these neologisms will take, how they will be introduced to the general public, and the level to which they can be brought into the language. All of these concerns were certainly addressed by some Turkish language planners. Given the speed of change through which Turkey passed in the first half of the twentieth century, and some of the more eccentric ideas which the Turkish leadership promoted,[5] neologisms were piled upon neologisms. Many Turks suffered from sensory overload when it came to language; not helped by the shifts in political allegiance to which the Turkish Republic has been subject in its history. When more conservative forces have been in power, the process of language reform often went into reverse, with more Ottoman usages becoming acceptable (although it is noteworthy that none but the most conservative critic of the reform would suggest a return to the Arabic script). The process is most certainly not over yet. But has it been a success?

If the aim was to 'return the language to the people', then it is difficult to answer 'yes'. Certainly, some elements of the Turkicization process did lead to greater comprehension of the standard form by the people in general. Yet the use of neologisms in large numbers, as well as shifts in what particular forms were favoured at a given time, has led to confusion and frustration among the people the reform was supposed to help.

On the other hand, if the aim was to distance the present from the past, then the reform has been immensely successful. All Turks need to learn another alphabet to read Arabic, which they do not need to do in order to read, for instance, French. This would have been entirely to Atatürk's taste. Moreover, the level of change has led even transliterated Turkish literature from the relatively recent past to be virtually opaque to younger Turks, to the extent that many classics of the early twentieth century are more readily available in 'translated' editions than in their original form. It would be almost impossible to imagine this in any other country in the world. Cultured Turks regret this, but the distance produced has certainly served the ideological purpose of the Republic's founders.

Many more conservative Turks also claim that the rigidity of the imposition of the language reform led to a loss of semantic nuance, in comparison with its Ottoman predecessor. The often highly artificial official variety of the language probably bears this out. Yet the very variability of the language has led to creativity in the improvisation of individual speakers and writers. Although this variability has hindered the task of educators, been costly in the production of textbooks and a logistical nightmare for administrators, its final product may well be a new language variety created to a considerable extent by the people themselves. Elite language planning actors can therefore act as catalysts for non-elite planning.

7.1.4   Israeli Hebrew corpus planning

It is illuminating to turn from one language which has been micro-managed, and from another where corpus planning has been employed for ideological purposes, to one whose corpus planning seems at times to have been improvised. Of course we have to remember that Hebrew had had no native speakers as such for millennia: when everyone is a novice, there will be opportunities for non-specialists to contribute. Nevertheless, it is sometimes difficult to judge *who* did the planning. For instance, the Hebrew word for non-commissioned officer comes from an acronym of a shaky translation of the English expression, coined in the traumatic circumstances of the foundation of the state of Israel (Kutscher 1982: 268). Terms for 'passport' or 'visa', previously unnecessary in a Jewish context, could apparently be 'ordered' from an unnamed wordsmith by the Foreign Minister (Kutscher 1982: 242).

Once the momentum for planning of this type gets moving, improvisation may well proceed in a similar direction. In the case of Hebrew, this can be seen in the ways in which the language has used the resources which Eliezer ben Yehuda envisaged for it according to a cline of appropriateness: moving from the 'purity' of Biblical Hebrew through later forms of written Hebrew, from the period after it had ceased to be a mother tongue, and then to other Semitic languages, most notably Aramaic, which had an honourable history of use in commentary on the Scriptures, as well as being the first of the major diaspora languages, and Arabic, which had the advantage of being a relatively closely related modern language from which words could be borrowed and reworked, which was both a Jewish vehicular language and the everyday lingua franca in Palestine. Only after these Semitic sources were exhausted was recourse made to European languages, whether this be the common use of Latin, or especially Greek, roots (internationalisms, in other words), or from contemporary languages. Many of these developments were suggested by the various language planning agencies; many were not, however. At times, a mass improvisation seems to be taking place, although, even so, much of it is close to the typology of purism put forward by Thomas.[6]

Israeli Hebrew is a particularly fascinating case, of course, because in living memory (indeed for many speakers, within their own experience) the language was practically no one's first language. Although, as we will see in Section 7.2.2, the language was not 'dead' in any meaningful sense, the effort involved in planning it was greater than with most language planning efforts, particularly because of the language's secular and religious ideological associations. The process involved both mass-learning and mass-planning.

For instance, many of the Semitic phonological features which were central to Sephardic and Arabic Hebrew spoken usage, such as the preservation of the distinction between velar and pharyngeal consonants, are strikingly absent in most native pronunciations of Israeli Hebrew (Kutscher 1982: 247–51). This 'simplification' has been compared to a creolization process, although *koinéization* is probably a more apt term: elements of a number of separate pronunciations have been combined, in the process finding a 'common denominator'.

One of the problems caused by this koinéization process is the *graphization* of Hebrew. For ideological reasons, the alphabet used by Israeli Hebrew today cannot be significantly different from that used for holy scripture; indeed, one advantage which this language planning process had over many other acquisition type strategies is the fact that a large part of the male Jewish population, no matter their native tongues, was literate in Hebrew. Moreover, many Jewish vehicular languages used the Hebrew script in writing. Yet the present Hebrew language is faced with a situation not dissimilar to that found for Turkish before its spelling reform: an alphabet which does not suit its phonemic structure well. Thus an archaizing form of purism can be seen to be at least partly counter-productive.

Perhaps the most trying aspect of this is in the treatment of the phonemes /b/ and /v/. In many varieties of Hebrew before its revival, the letter ב 'bet' was capable of both a plosive /b/ and a fricative /v/ pronunciation. The problem was that ו 'waw', which many Sephardic and Oriental Jews pronounced /w/, was pronounced /v/ by many Ashkenazi Jews. In the koinéization process, the /v/ variant for 'waw' was preferred. This caused problems for children learning the phoneme–symbol correspondence, however.

Problems of this type are not uncommon in languages. In English, for instance, many speakers do not make a distinction between the initial consonants in *watt* and *what*, making the words homonyms, rather than the minimal pairs they are for other native speakers. Children (and non-native speakers) find the written distinction extremely difficult to learn. The difference between that situation and the early days of revived Hebrew is that, in the latter situation, everybody was a non-native learner; most of the learners were children. To get round this, a group of teachers in the Galilee area in the early twentieth century, the most charismatic of whom was Simhah Hayyim Wilkomitz (significantly referred to as *Ha-moréh* 'the teacher' by his pupils), decided to teach children only the plosive /b/ pronunciation for ב in all environments (bar-Adon 1975). Because of their isolation, this pronunciation was adopted by children for a generation or so. Many retained it into later life. The more mainstream pronunciation, although actually a less elegant solution to the problem, eventually triumphed, however. Nonetheless, the Galilean pronunciation demonstrates the ways in which language planners may encourage the development of new and divergent varieties through a belief in their own intuition as the only solution.

7.1.5   Discussion

Corpus planning is a complex, and confused, process. Agency for the planning is generally shared among a great many people. Corpus planners may set the process in motion; they may also attempt to control the planning process, employing the feedback mechanisms suggested by Thomas. Success or failure is controlled by the socially embedded attitudes of native speakers. Non-elite language planning appears often to be as effective as the consciously engineered equivalent.

There is, of course, a continuum between planning states which are controlled and planned by government (or equivalent) inspired actors and those which appear improvised by consensus by the speech community itself. Many languages, perhaps inevitably, exhibit the full range of these features in their (planned) histories. A primary point remains true throughout, however. The direction which a language's corpus planning process is taking in relation to purism is intrinsically connected to the ideological appreciation by the speech community involved of itself in relation to its neighbours. It is to this point which we will now turn in our discussion of language planning initiatives which are most closely associated with status and acquisition.

7.2 Examples of status and acquisition planning

7.2.1 French in Québec[7]

From the 1960s on, the provincial government of Québec attempted to implement legislation designed to enhance the status of the French language both in the province as a whole (where the language's majority was guaranteed) and the city of Montreal, where English speakers were in almost equal proportion to French, and were culturally and economically dominant.

Prior to this, many of the French speakers in Québec and their opinion-forming elite had accepted this situation, since it maintained the 'purity' of Québécois culture in the rural heartland. French speakers who wished to succeed accommodated towards the dominant culture and language; most did so quite willingly. This pattern changed after the Second World War. Greater educational opportunities, and a move towards more mainstream North American values, led the generation which came to maturity in the intellectual foment of the late 1960s to question the structure of their society and its bias towards an urban, English-speaking, ruling class.

In the age of the steamship, Montreal was often the first stop for European immigrants to North America. Many stayed there. Given the majority language of the continent, and the sociolinguistic pattern of Montreal, most of these immigrants gravitated towards English rather than French. The French-speaking population felt themselves being 'squeezed out' by two forces: the English-speaking economic elite, and the immigrants.

This was particularly the case with the school system. In Montreal this was denominational rather than linguistic: Catholic or Protestant schools were the norm. The overwhelming majority of Protestants in the city were English speakers; most Irish Canadians were English-speaking Catholics, however. Provision was therefore made within the Catholic school system for 'English schools'. The problem was that many immigrants of southern European origin lived in those working class districts of eastern Montreal whose inhabitants were traditionally French-speaking. They also wanted their children's Catholic education to be in English. This change in the demographic situation in the city was bound, it was felt by activists, to undermine the influence of French in the chief city of a primarily French-speaking province.

During the 1970s, the ruling parties of the province increasingly encouraged Francisization. Simplifying somewhat: in the school system, only those children whose parents came from Canadian English-speaking backgrounds could be enrolled in schools which taught in English as the primary medium of instruction; everyone else was obliged to send their children to French-medium schools. At the same time, the visual appearance of Montreal changed, with French becoming the sole, or the most dominant, language in the discourse of shop and street signs, and advertising. Province-wide, French became the primary vehicle of provincial and local government; whilst English was allowed in communications, it assumed the role of translation rather than authoritative text. Naturally, these changes did not pass entirely unopposed. Nor is it possible to tell whether they actually halted and reversed the anticipated 'decline' of French, although this would not be unexpected. Yet no-one could question their effectiveness in establishing the Québécois identity of both the city and the province.

7.2.2   Israeli Hebrew acquisition planning

It is much easier to judge the success of Israeli Hebrew, since the planning involved fell much closer to the acquisition end of the status continuum. Nevertheless, the development of this language had to deal with many of the same issues faced by French in Québec. Language planners for Hebrew had an overwhelming advantage, however: a sense of nationhood born out of millennia of suffering.

Some scholars, such as Fellman (1973: 12), date the 'death' of Hebrew as a spoken tongue to around 200 CE, connected to the final 'ethnic cleansing' of Judea. It is likely that even before this the everyday language of the overwhelming majority of Jewish people would have been Aramaic (another Semitic language, the lingua franca of the pre-Hellenistic Middle East), however (Weinreich 1973: 54–7, in particular).

In this final diaspora, the connection between Jewish people and their sacred national language was attenuated, not severed (in marked contrast to many similar emigrant experiences). The exile communities were inevitably obliged to take up the languages of the territories in which they lived. Yet as Fellman (1973: 12–13) and Fishman (1991: 289–90) point out, Hebrew continued to be spoken by Jews. It was the language of prayer of a highly literate population, regularly of sacred scholarship, and was even used between Jews of different geographical backgrounds who had no other common tongue. Although these conversations were often extremely uncomfortable for the speakers, it is this last function which had the most profound effect upon Hebrew as it developed as a fully fledged spoken language again in the late nineteenth century.

It was once customary to date the revival of Modern Hebrew as a living language to the decision taken by Eliezer ben Yehuda (1858–1922) to speak Hebrew, and only Hebrew, within his family circle in Jerusalem. The decision for this switch to Hebrew, as expressed by ben Yehuda himself (ben Yehuda 1948, as quoted in Saulson 1978: 16–17), is resounding:

> concerning the contention that Jews were not now a nation and that they could not become one because they did not speak a single language, I responded with political argumentation based on the existence of other nations which do not speak a single language, such as the Swiss or the Belgians. But to the same degree that my political sentiment increased and strengthened with me, I increasingly sensed what language means to a people; and I soon concluded that, with respect to the argument in the matter of language, I myself was not satisfied with my political argumentation and it racked my brain. I answered myself with a more natural and simple rejoinder, which was really the simplest of answers; just as the Jews cannot really become a living nation other than through their return to the land of their fathers, so too, they are not able to become a living nation other than through their return to the language of the Fathers and by using it not just in books, not only in things holy or scientific as Peretz ben-Moshe the editor of Hashahar claimed, but rather through the spoken word, spoken by young and old, women and children, boy and girl, in all affairs of life, day and night, like every other nation.
>
> This was the important, the decisive moment in my life. I soon discovered what I immediately had to do. I realized that without two things Jews could not become a nation, and these were: the land and the language.

ben Yehuda was tapping into the European tradition of Romantic and post-Romantic nationalism, with a radical edge (prior to his conversion to Zionism, he had been a *narod'nik*, one of a mass of Russian students who believed that they could effect radical change, if not actual revolution, through a 'return to the land' with the peasants (Fellman 1973: 20)). Yet the reality of the situation was somewhat more complex than what he is suggesting here.

It is impossible to dismiss ben Yehuda's role in the revival and planning of Israeli Hebrew. The revival would have been most unlikely without him. Yet his symbolic status should not blind us either to the Hebrew milieu in which he lived, or his failings as a linguist and a language planner.

It might be more pleasing to imagine the history of Hebrew as being one of utter collapse followed by around two thousand years of silence, and then a miraculous rebirth. But this is not the case. ben Yehuda inhabited a linguistic world where Hebrew continued to have a position of central importance in the emotional and spiritual lives of most Jewish people. In the hundred years before ben Yehuda's birth, the language had also developed an intellectual life beyond the confines of traditional scholarship. Ausbau had already begun.

The revival of Hebrew as a spoken living language must be placed in the context of the intellectual and political history of European Jewry. During the eighteenth century, two intellectual streams flowed through the intellectual life of (primarily) Ashkenazi Jews. In rural districts of central and eastern Europe, a considerable, often heated, rebirth in orthodox Jewish life took place. The disputes which reflected this renaissance were regularly conducted in Hebrew. Many within the movements encouraged the pious return to the 'land of Israel', and especially Jerusalem, so that a growing Ashkenazi community was present in the ancestral homeland. Since there was already a considerable Sephardic and Oriental Jewish population present, speaking a variety of Jewish vernaculars, the oral use of Hebrew became prevalent under certain conditions.

At the same time, many Jews in central and western Europe began to question the tradition of Jewish exclusiveness. The majority Christian population had also begun to question its own tradition of exclusivity and assumed superiority in relation to Jews. Many Jews wished to be included in a common, European, secular culture which had abandoned what they would have considered medieval notions. This enlightenment is termed the *haskalah* in Hebrew, its adherents the *maskilim*. A central prop of the haskalah, at least in its initial phase, was the use of Hebrew as a language of new scholarship.

Since most maskilim understood Yiddish, the 'national language' of the Ashkenazim, using Hebrew was a cultural act. Just as many 'enlightened' Christians were embarrassed by events in their recent past, such as the persecution of 'witches', for many 'enlightened' Jews, Yiddish was associated with the religious reform movements mentioned earlier, which they would have considered especially obscurantist (Kutscher 1982: 183–4). Using a language of high prestige beyond their own community along with the 'national' language of their country was in many senses a move towards integration. Perhaps most significantly, Hebrew was used to discuss subjects which did not have an immediate relationship to traditional Jewish scholarship, including fictional material which, whilst normally dealing with Jewish life, was not necessarily open to a traditional moral interpretation. This inevitably led to considerable corpus planning.

Yet there were contradictions in both the haskalah platform and its reception in non-Jewish circles. Many of the movement's adherents became so involved in the mainstream of European intellectual life that they, or their children, converted to Christianity, as part of a full-scale assimilation process (Vital 1975: chapter 2; Lacqueur 1976: chapter 1). The use of Hebrew as a vehicle of enlightenment was often a victim of this process. Assimilated and enlightened Jews used the national vernacular of the country in which they lived (and of which, as the nineteenth century progressed, they increasingly considered themselves citizens); this became marked in the pervasive nationalist environment.

A further problem came from outside the Jewish community. No matter how hard 'enlightened' Jews attempted to assimilate, no matter how many liberal regimes included their Jewish inhabitants within their general citizenry, anti-Semitism remained. This led many Jews to assimilate even more, abandoning residual ties with their ancestral faith or its language; many other Jews who had also learned the lessons of the enlightenment, and of nineteenth-century liberal nationalism, derived a different moral from the experience. The Jewish people were a people in themselves, separate from all other peoples.

Given the intellectual pieties of the time (and also its violent realities), such a separate identity necessitated a separate homeland. Its separate identity, it was felt by many, also demanded a separate Jewish language. To these Zionists, as they came to be known, who had also generally accepted the haskalah prejudice against the Jewish vernaculars, the normal (although not the only) choice for this national symbol was Hebrew.

When ben Yehuda and his wife arrived in Ottoman Palestine in 1881, there was therefore a sizeable population who could speak Hebrew, even if this was not their mother tongue. His major contribution to the revival of the language was both the encouragement of others to use Hebrew in their everyday lives and, most importantly, to apply this to his own life and family. To those who subscribe to the view that ben Yehuda single-handedly revived spoken Hebrew, it is from this source that all modern Hebrew springs. In fact, as a number of scholars have pointed out (in particular Fellman), ben Yehuda represented an example of how the process could be carried out, and also a useful symbol. The fact that he was also an inspiring journalist did not do his cause – and his stature – any harm. There was a period when he *was* Hebrew in Palestine. His practical contribution to the revival of Hebrew, and to its planning, is debateable, however.

Fellman suggests (1973: 36 ff.) that ben Yehuda's programme was made up of seven steps:

1. The first Hebrew-speaking household,
2. the call to the diaspora and to the local population,
3. the Hebrew-speaking societies,
4. Hebrew through Hebrew in the schools,
5. the newspaper,
6. the *Dictionary of the Hebrew Language, Ancient and Modern*, and
7. the Language Council.

Each of these points was achieved, although a number of them did not have ben Yehuda as the primary cause for their success. For instance, the symbolic importance of ben Yehuda's creation of a Hebrew-speaking household in Jerusalem should not obscure the fact that this city was not suited to the programme and its promotion. Since the majority of Jews in Jerusalem were, for various ideological reasons, opposed to the secular use of what to them was a divine language, beyond a limited set of temporary domains, the chances of the new variety spreading into the surrounding community were limited. If he had been situated on the coast, it might have been more effective: most of the settlers in this area were secularists. They were also much more committed to Zionism.

Further, this geographical distance was eventually associated with ideological distance from the newer waves of settlement. To many of these radical immigrants, ben Yehuda's paternalistic form of liberalism was foreign. This distance was most obvious in the newspapers of the Zionist community, which derived a great deal of their impetus from ben Yehuda's work, but eventually outstripped and replaced it.

ben Yehuda's other great contribution is his dictionary. Given, on his own admission, that he had no scholarly background in lexicography, the extent to which he constructed an effective dictionary is impressive. Nevertheless, by the time at which the dictionary was published (1923), the Hebrew revival was already advanced.

The 'call to the Diaspora' had considerably greater success in propaganda terms; nevertheless, the spread of Hebrew among young Zionists who intended to 'return' to Palestine was often autonomous, even if it was encouraged by ben Yehuda's example. The same is true of the Hebrew-speaking societies and the Language Council. Both efforts were undertaken; both eventually succeeded. But the organizations which ben Yehuda set up were not successful; rather, they tended to stumble along for a few years before collapsing through lack of interest or funds (or both). The eventually successful organizations certainly learned from ben Yehuda's attempts; this was often a case of how not to carry out change of this type, however.

ben Yehuda certainly possessed considerable moral stature when it came to the question of how to teach Hebrew in schools. In the diaspora, the generally accepted method was by means of translation, as with all other classical tongues. ben Yehuda, among others, realized that teaching of this type would be unlikely to encourage anything other than passive knowledge. In essence, Hebrew language planners were the inventors of immersion teaching. Yet ben Yehuda did very little of the actual teaching. When it came to the major struggles for the language in schools before the First World War, such as whether French or German should be used for all but 'Jewish' subjects in the curriculum, it was others (including the student body) who were most directly involved, and who effected the most radical changes. Again we can see that a dedicated cadre of activists, some members of the ben Yehuda circle, some not, were the actual leaders of the revival.

Indeed, the acquisition process itself seems to be as much to do with the desire both of the new immigrants themselves and their children to create an identity for their new project and community (bar-Adon 1975: 43–4). The willpower involved in this process cannot be exaggerated. It is part of a package which included a particularly powerful and unusual form of idealistic nationalism (combining both religious and secular elements, even with the most unreligious of Jews) joined, for many immigrants, with revulsion for the past, and for the languages used in exile. By the end of the First World War, when the likelihood of a Jewish Nation state became greater, Hebrew had become a language, vitally associated with Zionism, with a critical mass of native speakers.

7.2.3 Irish

Irish language planners were – and are – faced with a different, but comparable problem. The results of their planning were different in almost every way, however. The reasons for this can be traced to the histories and cultures of the inhabitants of Ireland over the last thousand years.

Irish was the first truly standardized post-classical language in Europe; indeed, some have gone so far as to attribute the origin of what we now understand as western civilization to the activities of speakers of Irish, employing both their native tongue and a particularly 'pure' form of Latin (Cahill 1995). Whilst this may be overstating the case somewhat, it is certainly true that early medieval Ireland had developed cultural and educational institutions which were uniquely progressive for their time. Nevertheless, as western Europe began to centralize and urbanize in the eleventh and twelfth centuries, the decentralized, inherently rural, traditions of the great part of Irish society could not fail but be perceived by outsiders as aberrant, if not heretical.

From the very beginning of the Anglo-Norman invasions and settlement of Ireland in the twelfth century, this immigration (often achieved through conquest) produced, for both natives and incomers, a sense of the presence of 'the other' in greater parts of the island than had been affected by the earlier Norse settlements. Certainly, the English-speaking inhabitants of Ireland (sometimes referred to as the 'civil Irish' or 'Old English'), as well as the English 'at home', appear regularly to have worried that they might merge with, 'stoop to the level of', the natives (the 'savage Irish'). Indeed, there is considerable evidence that this took place, as documents such as the Statutes of Kilkenny (1366; as cited and discussed in Crowley 2000: 12–16) suggest, in their condemnation of the practice.

From the beginning of the seventeenth century, in fact, Gaelic culture and (to a lesser extent) language was in retreat in the face of encroaching English models and speech. Primarily, this can be attributed to the series of setbacks which the Irish (and largely Catholic) cause suffered at the hands of the English-speaking (and Protestant) *Ascendancy*: the flight (or conversion) of a large part of the native nobility and gentry, in the face of military defeat; the plantation of Ulster (previously the most Catholic province) with Protestant settlers from Scotland and England, speaking various English or Scots Dialects; and the attempted expulsion of Catholic Irish speakers to areas west of the River Shannon, into the most marginal areas.

Although there were both political and cultural attempts at resistance throughout the seventeenth and eighteenth centuries, the level of demoralization endured by native Irish speakers by the end of the latter century cannot be exaggerated. Indeed, the period ended with an attempted insurrection under a Protestant leader who appears to have interpreted the idea of Irishness according to birth, rather than culture, and the subsequent union of the Irish Parliament (a body entirely dominated by Protestants) with the Parliament of Great Britain, thus incorporating a largely Catholic and Gaelic country into a state dominated numerically, as well as culturally, by English-speaking Protestants.

Irish nationalism of various sorts never disappeared, naturally. Yet the nationalism espoused was one which played either upon the Catholic nature of Ireland (rather than its language and attendant culture), or the common grievances felt by all (or many) of the inhabitants of the island, no matter their language or religious affiliation. The former trend can be associated with Daniel O'Connell, whose experience as a native speaker of Irish actually led him to abandon its use in political meetings, because of the potentially alienating effects it had on Irish speakers of English (Crowley 1996: 110–11). The latter tendency can be associated with Charles Stewart Parnell, a sympathetic, rather Anglicized, Protestant, and in the Irish Parliamentary Party in general, no matter their linguistic backgrounds.[8]

At the same time, the large part of the monolingual Irish-speaking population had been caught up in a series of disasters which can only be described as catastrophic, both for them personally, and for their language. These events – overpopulation, division of farmland to all children equally, reliance on a single crop (potatoes) as a staple (often the only element) of their diet, and the famine and disease caused by the failure of that crop for three years in the 1840s – affected all inhabitants of Ireland, no matter their language or religious profession. Their effects were most disastrously felt by Catholic Irish-speaking monoglots, however, since they were generally the most reliant on the potato crop, lived in the most marginal areas in any event, and were culturally out of favour with the free-trade pieties of the state in which they lived. Those who were lucky were able to emigrate, to North America, or Britain, or the cities of Dublin and Belfast. It is impossible to calculate exactly how many people died, or left, during this period, but it numbers in the millions. A commentator on these events, and their linguistic aftermath, refers to them as *The Great Silence* (de Fréine 1965); certainly a large part of Gaelic Ireland perished with the famine. Although reforms were made to agricultural practice, and the lot of the Catholics who survived and remained improved, particularly if you were able to join the middle classes, Ireland was irreparably altered.

It is to these middle class Catholics that we now turn. As Pašeta (1999) demonstrates, the general political bent of this new class (some of whom became very wealthy or influential indeed) was nationalist (although the bogeyman of the cultural separatists, the collaborationist *Seánin*, was much feared by the Church and the community in general).

Nevertheless, the great majority of the generation who were educated in the 1880s and 1890s, and many of those who were educated in the first decade of the twentieth century, could envisage themselves as being part of a self-governing province of a great empire, from which they hoped to derive some advancement in the civil services or professions of its various other provinces, even when, often simultaneously, they were repulsed by the idea (a not uncommon experience for members of a developing colonial elite). The schools and university colleges which were initiated by this new class were designed to make their children the equals, if not, in an inimical world, the intellectual betters, of their Protestant peers. As Pašeta (1999: 120) reports, 'Moran [a cultural as well as political nationalist journalist] came closest to addressing this confusion of priorities by lamenting that Catholics wanted both Home Rule and an English accent'.

Inevitably, there was a reaction to this assimilative process. Suspicions of Irish Catholics becoming 'West Britons' (a derogatory term, still occasionally heard, for those inhabitants of Dublin whose cultural and linguistic affiliations, no matter their confessional loyalties, were more with England than Ireland) led to the foundation of the Gaelic Athletics Association (*Cumann Lúthchlas Gael*), dedicated to the revival of traditional Irish sports, running counter to the interest in rugby and cricket developing among the middle classes, and in association football among the workers, and particularly the Gaelic League (*Conradh na Gaeilge*), which stood for the maintenance, revival and promotion of Irish, as a cultural instrument of Irishness. Although both organizations continued to stress their non-political agenda well into the revolutionary period, there can be little doubt that the overwhelming majority of their members would have embraced a more radical form of nationalism than did other Irish people. These organizations were particularly popular among younger members of the middle classes at the beginning of the twentieth century, who may have been disillusioned both by the ongoing stalemate over Irish Home Rule, and the growing awareness of a 'glass ceiling' for aspirant Irish Catholics within the British Empire. These organizations would probably not have had the effects they had without the destabilization of Ireland in the period before the Great War, and the events which followed the beginning of that war, however.

In the early years of the twentieth century, it became increasingly apparent that Irish was in a perilous situation. There were still a considerable number of speakers, but the *Gaeltacht* areas were no longer contiguous with each other, and were generally associated with a way of life which was no longer economically tenable; out-migration continued at a frightening pace. Many of the speakers were now bilingual (although monolingualism survived well into the twentieth century in some isolated communities); as often happens in situations where there are inequalities of power between speakers of different languages within the same communities, bilingual parents were choosing not to pass on the disparaged language to their children, in order to give them 'a better start in life'. To the cultural and political radicals of the nationalist movement, this ongoing language shift was particularly painful, because the connection between the Irish people and their language and culture was a central plank of their separatist programme.

Ironically, the status of the Irish language – because of its antiquity as a literary language and its association with nationhood – had never been higher. As Crowley (1996) points out, this adulation had a ridiculous side, as when the poet and dramatist W.B. Yeats – who spoke no Irish – wrote plays on Gaelic subjects which were written in an archaic, heightened English prose, intended to represent the 'ancient beauty' of the national language. It also had an unpleasant side, since the promotion of Irish was often connected to rather exclusivist attitudes to other races and languages. At times there is a feverish, mystical, quality to discussions of the language, a vision of a spiritual marriage between language and people which is reminiscent (probably consciously) of the Catholic image of the Church being married to Christ. At the heart of this mysticism was Padraig Pearse, sometime schoolteacher, republican visionary and, eventually, martyr.

Other related groups were less interested in this mystical connection, but still viewed the Irish language – in particular its revival – as a central feature of the disengagement of Ireland from what we might now term globalization, a homogenization of language and culture within a global free trade system, favouring the major economic powers over the primary producers in less developed nations. The most significant of these groups (at least with the benefit of hindsight) was Sinn Féin. The name of the party is significant in two ways. The use of Irish in its title is symbolic of its wish for separation, even if you do not speak Irish; in a sense, therefore, the actual meaning of the phrase – 'ourselves alone' – is also carried by its appearance.[9] The party, in its initial phase, stood for self-help and cultural self-confidence, in an essentially protectionist economic state. Unsuccessful, it had practically disappeared by the end of the first decade of the twentieth century (Laffan 1999).

Indeed, despite these undercurrents of cultural and linguistic radicalism in the nationalist camp, it is quite likely that these views would never have reached the political mainstream in Ireland if it had not been for events in the second decade of the twentieth century. A relatively radical Liberal administration had come to power in the United Kingdom, maintained in office by the Irish (Nationalist) Party. The likelihood of the achievement of Irish Home Rule – low in the preceding decades, because of the presence of Conservative and Liberal Unionist governments – became considerable. Although these measures passed through the two Houses of Parliament, it became apparent that the majority of Protestants in the north-east of Ireland would not accept Home Rule, and appeared to be willing to fight for this, setting up the paramilitary Ulster Volunteer Force in 1911. Elements within both the British establishment, especially the army, appeared willing to turn a blind eye to these rebellious activities (which included receiving weapons and tactical assistance from Britain's deadliest rival and, eventually, enemy, Germany), and perhaps even to support their separatist ambitions. This level of tolerance was never available to the Irish Volunteers, formed in response to these unionist activities, or to the Irish Citizen Army, the paramilitary wing of the Irish Labour Party. If it had not been for the outbreak of the Great War in 1914, there is every chance that civil war would have broken out.

Irish nationalists were faced with a quandary. The parliamentary moderates had achieved most of what they had set out to do: Home Rule was on the statute books, even if it included the possibility of exclusion for the six counties in the north-east, and its implementation had been suspended until the end of hostilities. Nevertheless, how nationalists should react to the conflict became a thorny problem. The parliamentarians encouraged the Irish Volunteers to volunteer for active service in the British forces, to demonstrate their willingness to act in concert with their erstwhile opponents, as well as to help guarantee Home Rule, preferably on their terms, at the end. The majority of the Volunteers did so, willingly or under duress. The radical nationalists could not countenance such a compromise, and continued to organize and train. With the moderates mainly ruled out of the national equation, the radicals were able to set the agenda – which included the linguistic agenda. This they did to particular effect in 1916.

They attempted insurrection in Dublin in Easter week of that year; savage reprisals were taken against them. Initial defeat and unpopularity among the overwhelming majority of Irish people was transformed into adulation through martyrdom. This new movement, which took the name (as well as many of the personnel) from the original Sinn Féin, became, in the succeeding years, the political mainstream of a radicalized Ireland. Part of this radicalization was linguistic.

A striking example of the prioritization given to Irish within the Republican platform is the fact that, throughout the chaotic circumstances of the first and second Dáil, the Anglo-Irish war and the civil war between the pro-treaty and anti-treaty factions of the IRA (1918–1923), the Irish government, even when in hiding, continued to legislate for the re-establishment of Irish in Ireland as the primary language, a commitment emphasized in the constituions of both the Free State and, later, the Irish Republic. Irish is given higher status than English; it is treated as original, with English as translation. Throughout the first 40 years of the state's existence, this commitment to the return to Irish in Ireland was repeated and emphasized, in particular by governments dominated by Fianna Fáil. In a country which suffered lengthy economic birth pangs, a considerable percentage of gross national product went towards language maintenance and revitalization. Yet, by the end of the 1960s, Irish, as a language with native speakers, was in a perilous state. There has been little sign of revitalization since then, even if the methodology for preservation and spread has changed. Why had this come about?

The first question which has to be asked is whether this apparent collapse in native speaker numbers was actually as disastrous as it is often taken to be? The short answer is both 'yes' and 'no'. As the figures presented in Fishman (1991: 127) and Ó Riagáin (2001: 199–201) demonstrate, the knowledge of Irish among non-native speakers is considerable, and has meant that some Irish was understood in many places where it had not been spoken, at least since the early nineteenth century, and often (as in the case of Dublin) for centuries. When we delve deeper, however, we find that the level of knowledge of Irish among non-native speakers, whilst impressive individually, is often highly superficial for the mass of this group. Moreover, surveys of various sorts have shown that knowledge of Irish among non-native speakers seems to decline the older a person gets. This suggests that many people leave school with a considerable knowledge of Irish, but that this is not supported and maintained by later use.

Part of the problem, as discussed by Kelly (2002), actually stems from the methodologies employed in schools in the teaching of Irish. Until the late 1950s at least, despite repeated statements by governments, educational authorities and language planning actors that the revival of Irish would have to come through oral use, the emphasis in the school curriculum was on written use, with the 'stick' being the fact that entrance to university, college and the civil service (as well as promotion in the last) was predicated upon demonstrated ability in these skills. What was frustrating for even the most nationally minded person was the fact that, once these hurdles were passed, there was little, or no, opportunity for the language to be used in any of the professions. The problem was even more acute among the urban working class. At the time, many critics of the system noted that the time taken in many schools for the teaching of Irish – not an easy language for a speaker of English to learn – was to the detriment of other subjects which might, it was argued, have served the children better in later life. Many parents were very aware of this problem; by the mid-1960s, the compulsory study of Irish, as a central gating feature of the school system, had been shown to be counter-productive.

There was also the problem that the language, over which so much money and labour was spent in the education system, was not reinforced in the wider world. It may be that the language planning actors (of whatever type) thought it likely that the language would have been taught by the children to their parents, as had happened with Hebrew in Palestine. There was a vital difference, however. Whilst Hebrew was a unifying factor for Jewish people who did not necessarily share a common vernacular, and had a strong of sense of having come out of 'bondage', part of which included, for many, the rejection of these vernaculars as *zhargon*, all Irish people, by the middle of the twentieth century, had access to English, the major hegemonic language of the time, which was also the native language of the countries which acted as pull factors for potential emigrants.

Central to the language planning initiatives of the time was that the Gaeltacht areas be encouraged to expand into the populations of those areas which were losing, or had lost, the language. At the same time, however, it was becoming increasingly obvious that many of the Gaeltacht areas were economically untenable. Successive governments attempted to encourage the movement of new industries into the Gaeltacht; although well intended, this often meant that native Irish speakers became outnumbered by speakers of English, who had been attracted by the prospect of employment (a problem also encountered in similar initiatives in the Scottish *Gaidhealtachd* in the 1970s). Attempts to form what were, in essence, small-scale Gaeltachts in the eastern cities foundered on the fact that, in a liberal democracy, it is nearly impossible to force someone to live in a specified place.

Since the 1970s, successive Irish governments have maintained their commitment to Irish, while at the same time removing many of the levels of compulsion which were present in the past in the education and civil service systems. Instead, the cultural qualities of Gaelic Ireland have been evoked through a commitment to oral Irish use in fun activities, both in the Gaeltacht and the *Galltacht* (the English speaking parts of Ireland), including the opportunity of mixing with young people from all parts of the island. Whilst this is undoubtedly a positive feature, it does seem unlikely that genuine revitalization will spring from it. Although few would admit it, it seems that the authorities have accepted this.

Does that mean that Irish will die in Ireland? There can be little doubt that the Gaeltacht areas are contracting; native speakers are not, in general, being produced by the revitalization activities. On the other hand, it seems unlikely that the Irish language, as a symbol of Irish identity, will ever disappear. What is often seen as tokenism in its use in a few political and public contexts will probably guarantee its future presence within the Irish state. As we will see in greater depth in the case-studies in Chapter 8, the potential of language promotion to become a central feature of nation building can never be underestimated.

7.2.4 Esperanto

With most languages, centuries of development have normally passed before scholars became interested in their planning and standardization processes. One exception to this can be found with *auxiliary* languages. With most, if not all, of these, we can actually observe a language in a fully standardized state springing fully formed from its inventor's head onto the page, purely through human ingenuity.

The most famous example of an artificial language is Esperanto, 'invented' in the second half of the nineteenth century by Ludwig Lazar Zamenhof, a medical doctor and polymath born and educated in Russian-occupied Poland into an enlightened Jewish family. He based his language's lexis largely on Romance roots, with a phonology and grammar which derived much of its logic from both German and the Slavonic languages. As Forster (1982) relates, the language's striking (albeit largely temporary) success was supported by its founder's belief in the project as a practical possibility, which could be coupled with his abilities as a publicist for the language and the idealism he associated with it, as well as Esperanto's accessibility to its target audience, many, if not most, of whom would have had some exposure to Latin, or one of the Romance languages, at school. Most important, perhaps, is the fact that in its final form the language was remarkably well planned.

Yet many of these strengths masked weaknesses. A completely planned language, which everyone has to learn from first principles, must be entirely free from variation. But evidence of 'national' varieties of the language was already present at the first Esperanto congress held in Boulogne in 1905. The only means of controlling these centrifugal forces would have been to have an authoritarian centre to the language. But although Zamenhof proved himself to be a shrewd negotiator, determined to maintain 'his' language in 'his image', the liberal and democratic views he espoused would have made such authoritarianism difficult.

Zamenhof may not have been a natural dictator; there were, however, a number of personalities within the French Esperanto movement in particular who took highly doctrinaire positions about the new language. In the end, the language's chances of being widely accepted were negated by a major schism within the movement, which led to the creation of a new standard form, Ido. This attracted radical and intellectual parties within the movement (the 'elite', to use Cooper's phrase), although most enthusiasts remained loyal to the vision of the founder. The acquisition and proselytizing process was irreparably damaged by the schism; it led to more energy being devoted to the internal debate than to the spread of the language. This very public dispute did not help the language and its enthusiasts to shake their reputation for eccentricity, bordering on crankishness.

This reputation derived again from the character of the founder, and his disciples, within the movement. Whilst recognizing at the height of enthusiasm for the language that Esperanto could be capable of being used for trade, politics or even 'base purposes', Zamenhof himself had quasi-religious views about his creation, coupled with a deeply felt desire for understanding between peoples. But whilst these views may have attracted many to the 'cause', they repelled many more. The messianic quality of some of his claims for the language may have encouraged 'rationalists' within the movement to turn to Ido, with its ostensibly scientific committee and origin.

Another factor was beyond the control of any founder or committee: the international political and cultural climate. In its early stages, Esperanto was generally associated with potential disloyalty by the authorities in the Russian Empire. Its proponents suffered from occasional – if petty – harassment. Many of the early adherents to the language's cause in the Empire were Jews of liberal–radical persuasion: never a favourable viewpoint in Russia. This shifted the language's 'centre of gravity' to France, leading to the circumstances discussed earlier. Moreover, whilst the Esperanto movement's commitment to internationalism and negotiation based on mutual comprehension was prescient in a Europe of growing tensions, in the nationalist fervour of the First World War, and in the dictatorial regimes which sprouted in its aftermath in Europe and elsewhere, such views may have been even more suspect than they had been in Tsarist Russia. Finally, the outcome of the war irrevocably shifted the centre of power towards the United States. The world no longer needed an auxiliary language, since the English language's hegemony was guaranteed.

Many languages have dealt with similar problems. Several have faced competing standards; some have both benefited and suffered from the support of an eccentric proselytizer; many have been considered suspect by a given regime. The point is, however, that it is easier to face these tribulations with native speakers. Although language shift is not uncommon, many languages have survived much more threatening circumstances than those faced by Esperanto. But Esperanto had no native speakers. Its acquisition was based on idealism and good will; its spread relied on relative and essentially progressive stability. Sadly, these qualities were often in short supply in the twentieth century. Attempts at too elevated a status conspired with dissent – and history – to damage acquisition planning almost fatally.

7.3 Conclusion

Corpus planning is a difficult and painstaking process. It involves considerable skills both in language and ability to compromise. Status and acquisition planning are regularly downplayed by corpus planners, whose interest in purity is not well suited to mass movements. Yet without popular endorsement, language planning fails. Any corpus planning programme which neglects status and acquisition as part of its general remit is deluded.

The examples of planning discussed in this chapter share a central feature. No matter how detailed planning of whatever sort has been, it is the conjunction between the actors and their time, place and position in society, along with the receptiveness of the speech community itself (affected by the same factors), which decides the success, or failure, of the initiative. This point will be returned to in the next chapter, when we consider the relationship between language planning (and policy) and nation-building.

8
Language and Nation-building

8.1 Introduction

In most of the case-studies in Chapters 5 and 7, emphasis was given to linguistic and national groupings which either possessed from an early period a strongly developed sense of their linguistic cohesion, or where ideological foregrounding of a significant majority and their language in the modern era has led, to a large extent, to such a conclusion. As we saw in Chapter 2, however, the situation on the ground is often rather messier than this would suggest.

What happens, for instance, in those circumstances where a nation, or set of nations, has to be created quickly? How is it possible to construct a connection between language and nation in contexts where there is linguistic diversity, and little cultural homogeneity? What is to be done if a multilingual polity either wishes, or is forced, to maintain unification, but the ideology of past regimes has been abnegated? Finally, what can be done for a people beginning to seek a new political identity whose original linguistic symbol is in disarray?

8.2 Language and nation-building in a post-colonial context: east Africa

Even the briefest glance at a map of Africa illustrates the complexity of the relationship between ethnicity and nationality on that continent. It is practically unknown for a nation to have an overwhelmingly numerically dominant language. Of course, many polities have had to wrestle with the problem of a multilingual population. But African nations, often with severe economic problems, have had to create a viable polity, culturally, socially and linguistically, in a short period of time. Moreover, both

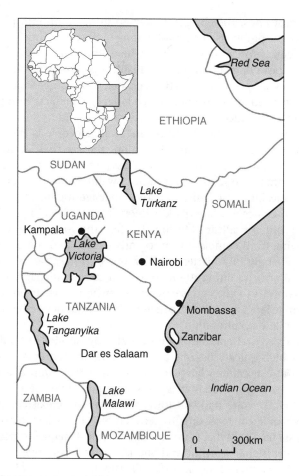

Map 4 Contemporary East Africa

the former imperialists and the world in general have expected that
everything be carried out in a democratic fashion, largely copied from
the modern planning strategies of nations whose rulers, in the past, had
dealt with problems of the same type in an authoritarian manner.

The situation is further complicated by the presence of languages of
former imperialism: English, French, Portuguese, Spanish and, to some
extent, German. As we saw in Chapter 2, post-colonial nations were
faced with the decision of whether to use a native language for nationalist
ends, potentially imperilling relationships within the nation between
different ethnic groups, or to use the language of the former imperialists

for nationist ends, thereby practically ensuring short-term peace, but increasing the problems of nation-building in the long term. This section will concentrate on an area of Africa where ethnic diversity is great, but a non-European lingua franca was available: Kiswahili. The differing fortunes of this language in the nations created by the imperial powers tell us a great deal about the ways in which language interacts with personal and group power, ideology and the history of a nation.

The original native heartland of the Swahili people is the Zanzibar archipelago and a narrow strip of land along the east coast of the African mainland, including the cities of Mombassa (in present-day Kenya) and Dar-es-Salaam (in present-day Tanzania). Swahili identity is fluid, associated with speaking Kiswahili as a native language and, to a lesser extent, with an adherence to Islam (Parkin 1994). Thus all Swahili people speak Kiswahili, but not all are Muslim. Further, the Arab conquerors and settlers who, until comparatively recently, dominated the coastal strip shifted, generally in a matter of generations, to the near-exclusive use of Kiswahili, maintaining Arabic only as a sacred language. This is in marked contrast to analogous contexts elsewhere, such as north Africa, where native languages were gradually subsumed under Arabic as part of conversion and acculturation.

The Arab coastal colonies found an already developed Swahili oral culture, which quickly became a literary one, written in Arabic script. Kiswahili also became a language of Islamic scholarship and popular devotion (in Islam, the latter is more common than the former with vernaculars). No one standard form of the language existed, although a number of local focussing, synecdochic, dialects had considerable prestige, such as Ki-Mvita, from Mombassa, or Ki-Unguja, from Zanzibar, representing Islamic learning and political power respectively.

Immediately preceding, and during, the achievement of European hegemony across the continent, Kiswahili spread rapidly through east and central Africa as a lingua franca, particularly useful in a region dominated by small-scale ethnic and linguistic units. Whilst large-scale mutual intelligibility between the Bantu languages is not possible, there is sufficient structural similarity for a relatively straightforward transfer from one language to another. Moreover, the multilingual nature of Africa, and the economic necessity which induces people to learn the languages of their neighbours, must be borne in mind, as must another factor: the prestige and power of speakers of Kiswahili during the period.

To westerners, speakers of Kiswahili were representatives of the 'Arab slave trade', which caused a furore in the nineteenth century. This mercantile empire and its trade routes led far into the African heartland, to the

Great Rift Valley and beyond. Yet leaving aside the gross hypocrisy of a culture which had only recently itself abandoned a far more brutal form of slavery, and which instituted one of the most exploitative regimes Africa has ever witnessed, the Congo Free State, ostensibly to protect the 'poor benighted blacks' from the machinations of the 'Arabs' (Hochschild 1998), the slave trade can only have been part of the reason for the prestige which Kiswahili carried. There is some evidence, in fact, that it was associated with resistance. Certainly, many of the leaders of armed insurrection against Europeans in central Africa were Kiswahili speakers (Lewis 1988). This association was carried into the colonial period in east Africa. Mazrui, A. A. and Mazrui, A. M. (1995: 39) report Kiswahili's prominence as a propaganda-spreading device, and as a means of organization in insurrectionary units in a number of anti-colonial risings.

Interestingly, the colonial powers and other resident Europeans in east Africa also employed Kiswahili, although there were considerable differences in the extent to which this was done. The administration in German East Africa (the mainland portion of Tanzania) employed Kiswahili rather more at different levels of the educational and administrative systems than did the British in Zanzibar, Kenya and Uganda. Partly this was a product of the world-view of the various imperialists. Whilst Germans generally preferred those they ruled not to learn their language, which they saw as a marker of their superior exclusivity, the British colonial authorities, as evinced in Macaulay's (in)famous minute of 1834 in relation to India, desired to produce a 'class of persons, Indians in blood and colour, but English in taste, in opinion, in morals and in intellect' (quoted in Khubchandani 1977: 35). Thus English was given rather more prominence in education and administration.

The dynamics of ethnic politics within these disparate territories must also be borne in mind. Whilst German East Africa had many small-scale ethnic/linguistic groups, none of which would have been capable of dominating the territory, this was not the case with Kenya, where the Kikuyu and the Luo are both populous and self-confident, in African terms. Uganda is a particularly complex case, because the dominant ethnic group used Luganda, itself a regional lingua franca. Since the Bantu people of the area were also largely converts to Christianity, there may have been a suspicion of Kiswahili because of its perceived Muslim origin. Moreover, Uganda had (and has) a considerable population speaking non-Bantu languages. The peculiar linguistic nature of the administration of German East Africa was continued to quite a large extent when the territory was reincorporated as the League of Nations (later, United Nations) mandated British Protectorate of Tanganyika, in the wake of the First World War.

A further factor can be discerned, however: Muslim and Christian missionary activities. Both religions and their proselytizers were present in considerable numbers in east Africa; they were very much in competition with each other; both were equally religions of revelation through the written word. In the case of Islam, the Qur'an was available in Arabic – the revealed language – only. As we have seen, however, there was both a considerable tradition of Islamic scholarship in Kiswahili, and a sense of 'special status' for the Swahili cultural group in the context of east African Islam. When coupled with the already considerable status, and both passive and active competence, which the language enjoyed among people across a large part of the territory in question, it is unsurprising that the language should have spread along with the religion.

In linguistic terms, Christian missionary activity took similar forms. Interpretation and preaching should have all been in the vernacular. But there are (and were) a number of problems associated with too great a degree of vernacularization. The ethnic and linguistic diversity of the region would have produced a proliferation of printed material, often costly to translate and produce. It would also have been both expensive and difficult to find not only linguistically able European pastors but also, in the long term, an acceptable number of native preachers who were both theologically adept and ideologically acceptable to the church authorities in the region and 'at home'. Whilst often heroic efforts were made to carry out the vernacularization programme, pragmatism generally dictated that a lingua franca of whatever type should be sought. Over a large area of east Africa, Kiswahili was already present, and had considerable status already endowed upon it as a language of religion (as well as many religious terms acceptable to monotheistic religion) by its association with Islam.

Yet this very association would have caused problems for any Christian language planner. The negative associations which Islam and the east African slave trade had for westerners would have made the use of any language normally written in Arabic script problematical. The Mombassa Ki-Mvita synecdochic proto-standard was particularly suspect, given its associations with Islamic scholarship. Instead, a standard based upon the politically prestigious Ki-Unguja dialect of Zanzibar, associated with a traditional and authoritarian form of government which may have been amenable to bureaucrats and missionaries alike, but written in Roman script, was preferred, and generally promulgated.

By the period between the World Wars, a combination of events and processes had led to Kiswahili's prominence throughout east Africa, albeit with differing levels of status in the different territories. This tendency would only be encouraged by events which would take place following the Second World War.

Even before the advent of either Middle Eastern or European imperialism, there is considerable evidence for long-range trading in east Africa, with concomitant implications for language knowledge, both individually and in larger communities. The gradual inclusion of east Africa within the global capitalist system inevitably sped up this process. Everywhere in the world people move in search of work or better prospects. In east Africa this resulted in a mixing of peoples in the developing urban and industrial areas. Naturally, people living side by side had to find a means of communicating; the most useful lingua franca was Kiswahili. At the same time, the lower, 'native', levels of the colonial bureaucracy, and the colonial forces of British East Africa, were ethnically mixed. A bureaucrat in a new station, or a soldier a great distance from home, would have turned to Kiswahili in one of its forms: often the new 'European' standard.

This ethnic mixing, and the creation of an urban proletariat, was used by the growing trade union and independence movements in Tanzania in particular as a means of expanding Pan-African consciousness among the dislocated and disenfranchised. Central to this was Kiswahili. Unlike many other independence movements, activists possessed a ready-made 'national' language with very little colonial stigma attached to it. Yet the planned and actual position of Kiswahili in the post-colonial period in the three countries under discussion was strikingly different.

Large parts of Uganda already had Luganda as its lingua franca, a language associated with both the native monarchy and the growing middle classes. Kiswahili should have achieved nothing more than a peripheral position in this country after independence. Yet, largely due to the political instability which has plagued Uganda, it was accorded considerable status. In the period immediately prior to independence, the army had assumed a position of importance in east Africa as a means by which poor men from rural backgrounds could achieve some advancement and education. In Uganda, a considerable number of members of the minority Nilotic communities from the north were involved. Although their native languages were not Bantu, they nevertheless adhered to their army Kiswahili as a counterweight to the majority Luganda. Kiswahili might also have been attractive to the many Muslims in these communities.

Many of the disenfranchised members of the Luganda-speaking community had also come into contact, through travel and work, with the proletarian Kiswahili lingua franca of British East Africa. In any struggle against the 'feudal oppression' of the old, royal, order, it was inevitable that these two groups would band together, using Kiswahili. This can be seen in the populist regimes of Obote and Amin. Although their rule was disastrous for Uganda, the linguistic policies initiated by Amin in particular had profound effects on the visibility of Kiswahili in the media and education. Many of these innovations have not been reversed in subsequent years.

Kenya presents a different set of circumstances. The great part of the population is linguistically Bantu, thus making Kiswahili rather more attractive than in Uganda. Nonetheless, a small number of ethnic/ linguistic groups predominate. According to Mazrui, A. A. and Mazrui, A. M. (1995: 15–18), the Mau Mau insurgency of the 1950s led to the dominance of Kikuyu leaders, aware of the need to pacify the large Luo population. A number of Kenyan politicians expressed their dislike for Kiswahili because of its Moslem and 'Arabic' origin. These views were not wholly shared by the majority of the Kenyan ruling class (Jomo Kenyatta, the country's leader until his death in 1978, was considerably less anti-Kiswahili than were many of his supporters). But their combination of a distrust for a divisive, ostensibly 'foreign' and 'Muslim', language in a professedly unitary and, for a long period, one-party state is probably indicative of the suspicions of many close to the centre of power. Given the deadlock between the two main ethnic groups, and the unattractiveness of Kiswahili, it was inevitable that the ruling elites should decide largely to promote English as the 'national' language.

Another reason for this preference was political. On independence, Kenya became a loyal member of the Western camp, enthusiastically embracing global capitalism. Bearing this in mind, it is again inevitable that the ruling elite should promote English in favour of Kiswahili, particularly since the latter had become associated with Tanzania and its – to them – flirtation with 'communism' (in Tanzanian eyes, their ideological position would have been one of non-aligned radicalism, with the adoption of Kiswahili as a symbol of the country's African identity).

Yet at a lower level in the Kenyan hierarchy, Kiswahili was welcomed as part of a planned response to the problem of vernacular education (at least at primary level) and of low-level administration (thus continuing the British response to the 'problem'), since the cost of more than basic provision in all the native languages of the country would have been prohibitive. The previously fairly anti-Muslim and anti-Kiswahili ideology of the ruling elite gradually lessened under the leadership of Daniel arap Moi, who, although Christian, is himself a member of a minority community (Parkin 1994).

Given its different history, ethnic make-up and development, Tanzania's language policy after independence diverged from its two sister nations. From an early stage in the process, Kiswahili was promoted aggressively as an African language for Africans. Unlike Kenya, its status as lingua franca was never in doubt.

Under the leadership of Julius Nyerere, a policy of *ujamaa*, 'African socialism, African familyhood', was attempted. All Tanzanians were not only to have theoretical and judicial equality within the state, but also to have actual equal opportunities in education and economic life. One of the central props of this policy was the planned extension of Kiswahili to all non-tertiary forms of education. This was enthusiastically encouraged by Nyerere who, although not culturally Swahili, was one of the language's greatest propagandists, himself translating a number of Shakespeare's plays into Kiswahili. In a similar way to revolutionary France, the new order's egalitarianism would be equated to unity through language. This never achieved fully blown authoritarianism, however, Nyerere himself casting doubts on the wisdom of Kiswahili being the main language of instruction in Tanzania's universities, when the academic world elsewhere was increasingly dominated by English. Although the ujamaa experiment eventually proved unsuccessful, as discussed by Wright (2004: 4.3), its linguistic consequences are still felt in Tanzania. English does have considerable status in the country; Kiswahili remains its linguistic and political bedrock, and a central part of its vision for itself, especially in terms of primary and secondary education.

In recent years, the three countries discussed have moved closer together in economic and political terms. One of the main props of this détente is the continuing spread of Kiswahili in both elite and non-elite spheres.

Eastern Africa can therefore be analysed as a region where language planning (in particular status and acquisition planning) has played an integral part in the conflict between ideologies, both indigenous and imported. Each of the three nations discussed was committed to a process of nation-building; no doubt all three would have preferred a nationalist language policy. Ethnic complexity made this unlikely to be successful, however. Unlike many parts of Africa, a viable indigenous alternative to the language of the former imperial power was available as a nationist solution, however. Kiswahili provides an elegant means of combining elements of nationism and nationalism, because of its African origin and association with struggle against imperialism.

Another force was present in the language planning process, however. The elite agents of change (which included language development) in each of these countries had different political goals. The egalitarian goals of the elite in Tanzania were in stark contrast to the globalization goals of their equivalent in Kenya; in Uganda, there was considerable conflict between an elite which supported Luganda, and a developing counter-elite who promoted the neutralization of this elite. Part of this neutralization process was associated with the growth in use of Kiswahili.

At the same time, non-elite status planning was also under way in all three countries. The need for mass education, coupled with the proselytizing initiative begun by Europeans or people from the Middle East and carried on indigenously, implied literacy in languages other than the mother tongue. Economic and pragmatic forces could not be ignored in this development. To many teachers, Kiswahili was a profoundly useful tool in the spread of literacy, no matter the ideology of the state.

8.3   Language, equality and ideology: the United States

Nation-building is not, of course, a peculiarity of post-colonial environments. Most states have carried out programmes of this type. Particularly interesting, however, are the nation-building activities of, countries, such as the United States, which are the product of mass immigration. In these contexts, the desire for unity also comes from a need to achieve a viable society as quickly as possible. Unlike a post-colonial situation, however, these immigrant nations generally have a fully developed standard language to hand: usually that of the initial conquerors and colonizers. New countries of this type are inclined to celebrate their fresh start as an ideology. In the case of the United States, the desire for unity, as emphasized in one of its mottoes, *e pluribus unum* 'from many one', is to some extent in direct conflict with the country's primary founding ideology of 'liberty'. What are the linguistic consequences of this conflict to a nation of immigrants? To what extent must we take into consideration the 'founder effect' (Mufwene 1991; Trudgill 2004: 163–4) on later language policy and use? In order to understand what happened later in the republic's history, we must consider in the first place what forces shaped the American variety of English.

8.3.1   American English: unity and diversity

Naturally, the English brought by colonists to north America, from the seventeenth century on, would have been representative of the speech of their home territories in the British Isles (although it is worth noting that, among the Protestant sectarians who made up a large part of the immigrants to New England, Delaware and Pennsylvania, the 'culture of the Book', along with group literacy, may have made their awareness of Standard English greater than would have been the case for most of their contemporaries in the 'mother country'). Because of the separate immigrations (of differing times and types) which established the original colonies, several scholars, most notably Krapp (1925), Fischer (1989) and, to some extent, Fisher (2001) have derived much of the present variation to be found in American English from these original settlers' point of departure. Other scholars, most notably Montgomery (in particular, 1989, 1997, 1998, 2001) have questioned the idea of straightforward transfer between the 'old country' and north America, although not denying that transfer of various sorts was both possible and real.

This must be distinguished from a number of more nationalist-minded writers from the United States from the Revolutionary period on, who have wished to distance their language from that of the 'colonial oppressor', a matter commented upon in considerable detail in Dillard (1985), Simpson (1986), Dillard (1992) and Bonfiglio (2002). Part of this ideological shift seems to have been a desire for linguistic unity, through the loss of dialectal diversity.

In fact, as a number of scholars report, many (particularly eighteenth century) British visitors to what became the United States did comment on the linguistic uniformity of their inhabitants. It is, as can be readily imagined, difficult to ascertain what these commentators meant (or to whom they were listening); this is particularly the case when it is recognized that many other commentators from the same, and slightly later, period commented on the difference they found between British English and its American offshoot, and on diversity – cultural in the first instance, but also linguistic – between different parts of the emerging nation.

The evidence could be sifted in a variety of different ways. In the first place, the persons with whom educated people on official missions spoke might have been very different from the 'ordinary' people with whom travellers and settlers dealt in everyday situations. The former category would, in particular, not have been representative of the linguistic behaviour of English-speakers as a whole, particularly since, up to and including the revolutionary generation, close ties of education and kinship existed for the property-owning classes across the Atlantic (in marked contrast to the rather feeble connections felt between, for instance, New England and Virginia). Moreover, when hearing a foreign accent (particularly that which was recognized as the authoritative/authoritarian voice of the present or recent imperial power), many speakers might also have been on their linguistic 'best behaviour', in an eighteenth-century representation of the 'observer's paradox', a point I have suggested for Scotland during the same period (Millar 2000). On the other hand, there is considerable evidence from contemporary studies that 'new' societies, whether that be urban enclaves or larger-scale units, take a considerable period to settle down linguistically, developing a relatively uniform variety which has incomplete concordances with any existing variety (Kerswill 1994; Williams and Kerswill 1999; Trudgill 2004). These problems should not in any way invalidate the desire on the part of many Americans for linguistic unity, however.

In terms of the 'native dialects' of United States English, the relationship between linguistic centre and periphery is in many ways no different from what it is in any other country in which mass literacy is present. As has been shown in the work of Preston and his collaborators (for instance, Preston 1996; Niedzielski and Preston 2003), strong opinions can be provoked over where 'bad' English exists in the United States; interestingly (although perhaps not surprisingly), the centre for this usage is the heart of the former Confederacy (a view not shared by southerners) and the language use of the great eastern cities, particularly New York (a view which *is* shared by many New Yorkers). Not only are both these varieties highly distinctive in terms of the United States as a whole; they also represent histories and ideologies (at least in the minds of outsiders) which run counter to the 'American way', a point already touched upon in Section 6.4.1.1, in our discussion of purism in relation to American pronunciation.

Yet there is more to this than merely fear of the internal 'other' (powerful though such a fear might be). Although, or perhaps because, the United States has a long tradition of democracy, a rather authoritarian language policy has prevailed, particularly in the ways in which English is taught in childhood (a point perhaps supported by the use of the term *Grammar School* for institutions of primary education, in contrast to the meaning of the term in England). From the very beginnings of English settlement in north America, the primer tradition, as well as the paramount authority of the dictionary, has been particularly strong, a point supported by the amount of space given in any discussion of American English to the views and practices of Noah Webster, for instance. This dependence upon prescriptive authority may be seen in the preference of many middle-class Americans for usages such as *this is she* (rather than *this is her*) or *To whom am I speaking?* (rather than *Who am I speaking to?*), even in informal contexts, usages which often appear over-fastidious to

British English speakers. Indeed, eighteenth century views on 'good' English have often had more profound influence upon the American consciousness than upon the British.

Of course, much of this could also be said about many other polities, particularly in Europe. But standardizing influences may have had more effect in a situation where an immigrant population was gradually expanding across a continent (thereby coming into more contact with speakers of different varieties of the same language than might otherwise have been possible); where social cohesion was largely supplied by lower middle class authorities, such as schoolteachers and religious ministers, during this formative pioneer period, and the national ideology was one of unity and special election for the nation. This may explain the rather apologetic nature of discussions of employing dialect and teaching dialect awareness, in American schools, as found, for instance, in Wolfram *et al.* (1999). For most 'Anglo-Saxon' (or 'Nordic') Americans, this unificatory koinéization process was probably neither foreign nor burdensome. Two groups have always fared less well within this linguistic melting pot, however: African Americans, and the most recent (and poorest) immigrant communities at any given time.

8.3.2   African American Vernacular English

African Americans are marked off from all other non-native citizens of the United States by the fact that the overwhelming majority of their African ancestors were brought to America in chattel bondage from which, at least in the southern states in the eighteenth and early nineteenth centuries, there was no real escape. Although many of the ancestors of European and Asian Americans may have been less than 'free' when they reached their new home, it was always understood that any lack of liberty would be temporary. As the ideological grip of slavery tightened around the south, the idea of even eventual liberty for Africans and their descendants became unthinkable to the vast majority of whites (Berlin 1998). Even after 'liberation' in the 1860s, African Americans had to suffer great injustice, leaving many in a position not dissimilar to peonage well into the twentieth century. In a country founded upon precepts of liberty and equality, the perpetuation of this manifest inequality was (and is) a damning indictment, only being permitted by the willingness on the part of the majority of power-brokers in the north and the developing west to acquiesce in the actions of hegemonic white forces in the south (Wormser 2003). The fact that the structures which held Jim Crowism in place were eventually overthrown (often with the help, it should be acknowledged, of liberal white southerners) is symbolic both of the perseverance of African Americans in the pursuit of their egalitarian goal and the recognition of severe injustice on the part of the vast majority of all Americans.

One issue which was not solved by this set of events was the status of the varieties of English used by African Americans. These had regularly been mocked by white supremacists, and frowned upon by the educational establishment – both black and white – as 'broken' and 'wrong', perhaps even of demonstrating lower levels of intelligence on the part of the speaker (a regularly expressed opinion on the part of even otherwise progressive linguists and sociologists well into the twentieth century).

The origin of African American Vernacular English (the most distinctive set of varieties spoken by African Americans) is an extremely vexed question which can provoke considerable disagreement between scholars; it is not the purpose of this book to enter the debate (a good, if ideologically charged, introduction to the controversy can be found in Mufwene 2001a). It is sufficient that we recognize that African American Vernacular English is the most distinctive, and also often considered the most divergent from mainstream norms, of any variety of American English, perhaps as much because of the 'race' of its speakers than any actual linguistic distance. Indeed, there is considerable evidence for mutual influence (in the early days of colonization in particular) between the language of poor whites and blacks in the south, as discussed by, among others, Mufwene (2001b) and Bailey (2001); part of the feeling of distaste provoked by African American Vernacular English may actually be its reminder of this close relationship (which naturally included an element of intermarriage), viewed from a period where a form of apartheid reigned in the south. Indeed, there are similarities between the views of the respectable Afrikaner community towards Afrikaans, with its many 'coloured' speakers, in the nineteenth century, as discussed in Section 6.2, and language attitudes throughout the United States towards African American Vernacular English, well into the middle of the twentieth century, if not beyond.

In fact, the suggestion that it was African Americans' use of language – rather than their inherent lack of intelligence, as racist science had previously held – which 'held them back' in mainstream society originated at a time when such overt racist attitudes became academically and socially unacceptable. Used by certain writers – not necessarily the language deficit model's original promoter, Bernstein (1972) – this model may have become a means of maintaining covert racist attitudes towards African Americans. It was towards these views that Labov (1969) addressed himself, pointing out that there was a logic to the structure of all non-standard varieties (specifically African American Vernacular English), which makes them the communicative equal of the standard; in no way a restricted code. This view has been carried forward, and developed, by the scholarly community; its success in passing over to the mainstream has been limited, however. Partly we can associate the lack of success with doubt, on the part of the educational community, over the manner in which to translate Labov and his successors' insights into successful pedagogical practice; partly, because many of the speakers of African American Vernacular English lived (and live) in socially deprived areas where there may already be considerable pressures upon educational budgets; partly, it could be claimed, lack of interest in (rather than any genuine animus towards) the topic.

This deadlock probably explains why the School Board of Oakland, California, chose, in late 1996, to make a declaration which appeared to recognize *Ebonics* (in their interpretation, equivalent to African American Vernacular English) as a language separate from English (indeed, of African origin in terms of structure and phonology in particular), and therefore liable to federal bilingual education funding (most education funding in the United States is derived from state budgets). It also explains the levels of vituperation provoked by the announcement from both the general public (including many African Americans) and significant portions of state and federal government. As Baugh (2000) points out, the original statement was not particularly well thought out; nevertheless, the criticism which followed it seemed not to have understood the position which underlay it. In permitting, indeed encouraging, speakers of African American Vernacular English to use their language in school, educationalists believed that there would be a less traumatic transfer to the use of Standard English in writing and, when the context made its use socially or economically beneficial to the individual, in speech, a point which is rarely pedagogically controversial. But as well as throwing up some rather unpleasant examples of both covert and overt racism among a vocal minority of Americans, the reaction to the Ebonics controversy re-emphasized the commitment on the part of most Americans to an egalitarian ideology which frowns upon the formation of special groups within the society as a whole. The appropriateness of such an ideology to a situation where citizens' ancestors were involuntary immigrants does not seem often to have entered the debate.

The reactions throughout the United States to the Oaklands declaration bear striking similarities to attitudes about the language use of immigrants and the status of English in the United States. Again, the different viewpoints on these matters reach towards the heart of the question: what is equality?

8.3.3   Constitutional English and the language of immigrants

In the last 20 years, a process has been initiated which may result in the constitutional highlighting of English as the official language of the United States. Is this merely a symbolic *de jure* recognition of a *de facto* reality, or are those who promote this goal attempting to mask more sinister anti-foreigner sentiments by appearing to promote unity?

Successive waves of immigrants have been admitted into what is now the United States; each grouping has contributed to the exceptional growth and success of America. Yet almost from the beginning of this movement, there has been concern among those who were native (or less recent in their arrival) about the effects which the most recent wave of immigration would have on the country's ethnic make-up, to its institutions and, perhaps as a symbol of them all, to the language used by the first mass immigrants: English. Bennett (1988) discusses the more radical elements of those who feared 'alien' immigration, demonstrating continuities among the 'Know-Nothings' of the 1840s, the Ku-Klux-Klan of the 1920s, the communist scare of the 1950s and the New Right from the 1970s on. He suggests that nativism at this level could be termed 'The Party of Fear'. Of course most Americans do not subscribe to the extreme views held by these movements; nevertheless, nativism does have a long pedigree in American life, a fact touched upon by Lippi-Green (1997) in her discussion of prejudice against immigrant varieties of English.

The targets for this fear of the alien and their culture have changed over time, particularly as western society has moved away from religious towards ethnic and cultural targets as subjects of mistrust. At times it has been Germans, Irish people, Italians, Poles or Jews who have been believed to threaten the American status quo by their cultures, religious practices and use of language. In more recent years, the highest levels of mistrust have been directed towards immigrants of Asian and Hispanic origin.

As a number of commentators, such as Barron (1990), have pointed out, one of the greatest fears expressed about 'alien' immigration has been, throughout the history of the United States, that people who do not speak the English language will not be able to understand the institutions and political processes of their new country. This has led a number of states in the past to make a knowledge of English compulsory for the full exercise of citizen's rights. Supremacist ideas often underlay this type of legislation. The idea that America has a special and elect nature can sometimes degenerate into the idea that only certain types of American are fully capable of exercising these rights. But many liberal Americans may also feel deep discomfort over the idea of uninformed ethnic bloc votes cast at the behest of a corrupt local 'boss', seeing this as a mockery of the ingrained American ideal of the educated, individualist, citizen exercising his or her democratic rights in an open and fair way (Woolard 1990). The present situation is exacerbated somewhat by the fact that, unlike most earlier non-Anglophone populations in the United States, a significant part of the Hispanic population did not so much enter America, as were entered by that country. Unlike earlier 'problem' populations, many of these Spanish speakers are American citizens by right from birth. This does not stop some commentators from fearing 'submersion' in an 'alien' sea, however.

Throughout its history, the United States has wrestled with what should be done with residents – indeed, citizens – who do not speak the majority language. At times, the prevailing view has moved towards a liberal interpretation; at others, it has veered towards exclusionism. Nevertheless, even in its most isolationist phases, general opinion has consistently (albeit eventually) veered towards the protection of individuals who speak another language in the exercise of their individual rights, as detailed in Del Valle (2003) in particular. What has not always been fully accomplished is the recognition of collective rights of language.

In the 1960s the United States embarked on a period of enthusiasm in the application of social engineering: poverty was to be conquered by the Great Society programme; institutional racism was overthrown. At the same time, there was considerable awareness that children from non-mainstream backgrounds were much more likely to fail in school than other children. For this reason, bilingual education programmes were instituted in a range of locales where there was felt to be a problem. Despite their critics' assertions that these programmes were intended to encourage maintenance of 'ethnic' languages, instead of the learning of the 'national language', the overwhelming majority of these initiatives were designed to establish sufficient English knowledge for children to join the mainstream as early as possible.

Nevertheless, critics saw these initiatives as being an attempt to replace American equality with particularism. As the New Right began to flourish in the late 1970s, it became increasingly fashionable to criticize these initiatives as being a primary source of many of the social problems which the United States had begun to face. Some claimed that, unlike previous generations of immigrants, the Hispanic population, in particular, were being treated as a special case, and were therefore being permitted to remain outside the mainstream. Some might even have thought – although few said – that this exceptionalism was caused by 'laziness' on the part of the immigrants.

It is in this context that the ongoing debate over whether English be made the official language of the United States should be read. The overt viewpoint of those who favour an initiative of this type is that such a statement would be an elegant representation of the unity of all Americans under one language, as they live under the protection of one flag and one constitution. This has considerable symbolic worth; what is striking about most of the proposals of this type which have been made is that they appear to have 'teeth', however. Whilst some of the scare-mongering on the part of those opposed to this change is without basis, such as the contention that this would stop someone from using their native language in any official, governmental or employment contexts, it is possible to imagine that a less pragmatic view of language use would be mandated by its acceptance.

What is ironic is that there is little or no evidence that more recent immigrants to the United States have maintained their native languages any better than have earlier (Fishman *et al.* 1985). At the very least, recent immigrants have embraced a creative bilingualism (Veltman 1983). At a certain point in the parabola of immigration from a particular source, some Americans have always expressed fears that these newcomers would never learn what is perceived as the national language. But most immigrants have made considerable efforts to learn English, for both idealistic and mercenary reasons. By the third generation, ancestral languages are generally in retreat. Strangely enough, the activity which many English language activists in America most believe will encourage people to learn the language quickly – the end to bilingual education in any meaningful sense (actually accomplished in the early years of the twenty-first century) – may make it more difficult for people to achieve this goal. This, however, is fundamentally different in its desired end result from the ratification of English as official language; the problem is, however, that the two programmes are often condensed into one: as if official English implied English only.[1] Sadly, in the climate of fear after 11 September 2001, it is unlikely that the distrust of 'the other' felt by some Americans will be alleviated. This will inevitably perpetuate this confusion.

8.3.4   Discussion

Citizens of the United States pride themselves on the nation's revolutionary origin and on its ideology of liberty. When compared with the other great product of eighteenth-century libertarianism – republican France – it is certainly true that the alteration of society in the 13 colonies was achieved with surprisingly little violence. Yet in many ways the United States and France are ideologically similar.

Perhaps this similarity is most marked in their linguistic ideologies. The creators and promoters of the ideologies of both saw the cultivation of the standard language, at the expense of other dialects and languages, as a central tenet of their nation building programme. In France, fear of the linguistic 'other' stemmed from the strain felt between the centre and the periphery during the seventeenth and eighteenth centuries, and particularly during the Revolution. In America, the long-term consequences of mass immigration were central. Both nations have been collectively guilty of linguistic intolerance; America, because of its stress on individual rights, has largely been able to ameliorate the effects of this ideology upon its citizens, however (a point made also by Spolsky (2004: chapter 7)). But the treatment of speakers of African American Vernacular English, at least until very recently, has not always demonstrated this tolerance, not primarily for racial reasons, but because of its peculiar status as a variety of English, culturally and linguistically divergent from the 'national language'.

8.4 Language, equality and ideology: the Soviet Union

Whilst the United States has seen itself on occasion as a 'city on a hill', a place of election where opportunity presented itself to people from all sources, remade in the nation's ideological (and linguistic) image, the founders of the Soviet Union were faced with a rather more complex situation. In many senses, a post-colonial framework prevailed: a dynasty,

—·— Tsarist Empire in 1904　▨ Soviet Union in 1940　▨ Soviet Union 1945

Map 5　The Soviet Union

which had ruled a multinational Empire, had been overthrown; in theory, national self-determination would follow. This did not happen in anything approaching a straightforward manner, however. Yet in other ways, the United States and the Soviet Union, despite their obvious ideological differences, were faced with a similar situation: the need to produce a new unified nation, emphasizing a break with the past. But the linguistic consequences, whether in the short or the long term, could not have been more different.

A recent historian of the early stages of the Russian Revolution (Figes 1996) has described the process as a 'people's tragedy'. In the main, I take this to refer to the dreadful human cost of the revolution and its aftermath: in starvation, civil war and the abuse of power by all sides, as well as the growing corruption and betrayal of the initial idealism, as the revolution was drowned in dictatorial bureaucracy. Language use, and ethnolinguistic identity, was an integral part of this process. Over a 50-year period, the incredible optimism of the various ethnic groups within the former Tsarist Empire, both for the recognition of their national and cultural aspirations, and for the development of their languages as vehicles of the apparently bright new future, were initially encouraged, but eventually betrayed. The seeds of this flowering, and betrayal, can be found in two sources: the history and nature of the Tsarist Empire in its final century, and the debates on the 'nationalities question' within the radical elements of the social democratic movements of Europe during the decades before the outbreak of the First World War.

8.4.1   'Russia' before the Revolution

For various reasons, both positive and negative, the Russian Empire was often portrayed by outsiders as monolithic. Whilst this made it easier for external observers to comprehend a state of such vast proportions and population, the desire on the part of the rulers of the Empire, no matter how constituted, to throw a cloak of security over the country, in a manner bordering paranoia, did not help to clarify the natures of 'Russia'. Yet the state itself, from at least its period of expansion in the sixteenth century, was always multi-ethnic, multi-cultural and, most importantly, multilingual, even if speakers of Russian made up an absolute majority. That the apparent homogeneity actually masked considerable diversity can be established by the speed with which the state unravelled into its constituent parts both in 1917–1922 (after which a new, ostensibly non-Russocentric, union was established) and again in 1990–1991.[2]

As a dynastic state, the Romanov Empire stumbled upon nationalism as an effective form of cohesion at a relatively late date. This is not surprising, given the particularly absolutist nature of the governmental structure of Russia. The emperor did not need to explain himself or his policies. Nevertheless, during the sixteenth and seventeenth centuries, the originally Muscovite state had expanded to include practically all other ethnic Russians. It had a centre which was deeply homogenous, therefore, a point which conservative nationalists of the nineteenth century were quick to seize upon (Thaden 1964). An ideology of 'holy Russia', with the people united in their adherence to orthodoxy, autocracy and the peasant ideal, was officially fostered. Although, as it turned out, the Russian people's attachment to the Romanov family's personal rule was over-estimated, many other parts of this programme were attractive to large parts of the population. The sense of mission, of being the 'third Rome', was not merely posturing on the part of the ruling classes. Even if Tsarist power collapsed, therefore, it was unlikely that the central parts of the previously existing state would not have adhered to each other, no matter how the government was constituted ideologically. This point was recognized at the time of the revolution by Meillet (1918), who compared the position of Russia favourably with what was beginning to happen in the Habsburg territories.

Within the other nationalities of the Empire some national and ethnic groupings were more likely to be able to constitute viable polities than others. Much of this ability stemmed from the histories and sense of cultural identity of the various groups. We might envisage the relationship between these groups and the Russian heartland as being one of concentric circles. In the centre were those who considered themselves to be ethnic Russians. In the circle immediately outside were, in the first place, groups who shared many cultural or linguistic similarities with the Russians.

As the Commonwealth of Poland and Lithuania collapsed, the expanding 'Russian' state, based upon Moscow, inherited many speakers of east Slav dialects which were sufficiently distinct from Russian to be considered systems in their own right: Ukrainian and Belarusian. Of the two, the former language/ethnic grouping probably had a stronger sense of its distinctiveness than had the latter, perhaps because of its greater number of speakers, and its physical distance from the Muscovite centre, as well as due to elements of its culture, such as the tradition of Cossack collective democracy. Most members of both groups were Orthodox in confessional tradition (although some were Uniate), which made their inclusion within the broad mass of the Empire easier to accomplish, and also rendered their nation-building activities much more difficult. By the end of the nineteenth century, the cities and towns of both regions were dominated by Russian speakers, whether immigrants or Russified locals,

Slav or Jewish. After the First World War, many members of these groups came under Polish or Czechoslovak rule. When reunited after the Second World War, their experience (sometimes even their written language) turned out to be significantly different from those who remained within the Soviet Union, a point touched upon in Armstrong (1963).

In the same circle might be placed other groups of people whose numbers and relatively recent introduction to nationalist ideas made their reliance on Russia acute. Although groups such as the Volga Germans and other smaller immigrant groups of western origin might be included within this group, the main area in which these groups were to be found was Siberia. A plethora of different peoples, embracing different cultures and speaking different languages, inhabited these vast territories. By the end of the nineteenth century, however, only one set of languages – those of the Mongols and their relatives – had regular written expression. There was a considerable Russian presence throughout the region.

In the next concentric circle were ethnic and national groups which often had a strong sense of their religious, ethnic, linguistic and historical identity, expressed in terms of a national homeland. The first of these were Muslim subjects of the Tsar, in particular from the territories east of the Caspian Sea (although also including Turkic peoples on the Volga and in the Crimea).

Turkistan – the term preferred for Central Asia in the nineteenth century – is a confusing concept. The area itself is vast, stretching from the Volga to the western regions of China, and, until very recently, was largely unknown to most Europeans. Nor is it fair to give too much emphasis to the Turkic nature of the region. Although most of the indigenous populations of the Tsarist territories in central Asia were speakers of a Turkic dialect, some, such as the Tadzhiks, were not. It is probably best to concentrate on the Moslem nature of the civilizations which Russians encountered and conquered in their push towards the east and south.

From the sixteenth century on, Russian powers had turned their interest increasingly to the steppe areas lying to the south of their native territories. In a reversal of the earlier spread of Turkic and Mongol peoples into the valleys of the Rivers Volga and Don (Yemelianova (2002)), and into the Crimean peninsula, Russian interests now spread into these regions and beyond, at precisely the same time as the Ottoman Empire was in decline, the trade routes which had made the cities of central Asia so prosperous were beginning to be undermined by the development of sea routes by Europeans and, by the eighteenth century, British interests in particular were expanding in India and Persia. In a process which is often termed the 'great game', Russia and Britain vied for influence over vast areas of

Asia in the late eighteenth and nineteenth centuries. In the end it was Russia which gained the most in terms of land, before their expansion finally petered out in the debateable territories of the western marches of the Chinese Empire (Meyer and Brysac 1999).

The cultures which the Russians encountered were by no means uniform, although most were Moslem. While there had been a number of powerful principalities, none of them corresponded exactly to one ethnic grouping, however. For instance, Samarqand and its hinterland was dominated numerically by Turkic-speaking Uzbeks; a significant population of Aryan-speaking Tadzhiks also lived in the city, and made up a considerable proportion of the professional classes, however. Across the region, a variety of lifestyles were followed, from specialized urban craftspeople, to semi-nomadic farmers and herders. To some extent, different ways of life may have represented different ethnic backgrounds and traditions.

A variety of literary languages were available. There was the possibility of the use of Arabic, the classical and sacred language of most inhabitants' religion. The Tadzhiks (and, to some extent, the other literate inhabitants) also used varieties of Persian. There was also a Turkic written language – Chagatay – which, whilst archaic, was still marginally comprehensible to most inhabitants. All of these standards were traditionally written in the Arabic script, sometimes as filtered through the Persian medium. There is also considerable evidence that the Turkic dialects were, to some extent, mutually intelligible with each other. It is unlikely that many of their speakers would have classified these dialects as being separate languages.

With the Russian take-over, most of these territories began to open for large-scale immigration from other parts of the Empire. Mostly ethnic Russians, these immigrants mainly formed two groups: peasants, and workers in developing industries. There was also a small commercial and official Russian bourgeoisie. Russian language, and Cyrillic script, had a considerable presence, therefore, although it is questionable how much actual bilingualism on the part of the Moslem inhabitants there was.

The other main group within this circle were the inhabitants of Trans-Caucasia, some of whom possessed languages which had a considerable written history. This is most notable with the Armenians, whose presence in the areas they inhabit is attested from very early times indeed, but is also true for the Georgians. Both of these peoples had developed standard (sometimes even classical) forms of their languages, which were written in unique scripts. Most had maintained their own forms of Christianity, thus further emphasizing their identity. Both communities had long traditions of resistance – and bitterness – towards external enemies. The other major ethnic element in the southern Caucasus were the Azeri people, who spoke a Turkic dialect which bore similarities both to the Turkistan dialects already discussed, and to Turkish. Like Turkish, the language could potentially be reduced to a Persian variant of Arabic script. All three ethnic groups were well represented in bordering ethnic territories, as well as in neighbouring states.

The many other languages of this region (with the exception of that of the Greek community spread around the littoral) may have had some marginal written existence in a variety of scripts; it is likely, however, that the few speakers of these languages who could read were literate in another language. Although the peoples of the Caucasian mountains were developing a sense of 'national' identity for themselves, this did not reach fruition until the Soviet period. It remains a bone of contention between the Muscovite centre and the Caucasian periphery until the present.

The circle model does not work so well for the next ethnic group to be analysed: the Jews. Because of their unwelcome (as well as unwilling) presence within the Empire, Jewish people could be seen as inhabiting a much less well-connected circle. At the same time, however, the fact that there was no Jewish homeland within the Tsarist territories makes their status as a nation problematical, as well as rendering their presence pervasive in the other circles.

When we think of the Jewish population of the Russian Empire, we tend to think of the Yiddish-speaking Ashkenazim of the Polish border-lands. But whilst these were by far the largest single population of people of Jewish faith, there were actually significant numbers of Jewish people who spoke different languages throughout the Empire; in particular in the Caucasus. Nevertheless, it is the Ashkenazim who will be given the chief focus, since they suffered most under various forms of anti-Semitism, and were eventually almost annihilated by the Nazi conquest of the area. It is also the development of their language – Yiddish – under the Soviet system which will be discussed in the following.

In the late middle ages and early modern periods, the evolving Commonwealth of Poland–Lithuania became a haven for people of Jewish faith, fleeing from persecution further west. These immigrants brought a form of German with them as their use language; they may also have found remnants of a Jewish population already in the area, since the Khazars, a Turkic people, had converted to Judaism some thousand years before. The Commonwealth was not free of anti-Semitism, but there was considerable tolerance demonstrated at a high level. Jewish people settled in a broad arc across what would eventually become eastern Poland and the Ukraine, in a variety of different occupations. The status of the Jewish population gradually declined as the effects both of the Counter-Reformation and of expanding Muscovite power (both expressly anti-Semitic) made themselves felt over the 'Pale of Settlement'.

The Ashkenazim participated in the main currents of Jewish life at that time, as discussed in Chapter 7. Some moved towards greater levels of Orthodoxy; others wished to participate more closely in the broader European culture. In this, however, they were often frustrated by the anti-Semitic policies of the Empire, designed to stop 'clever Jews' from taking too many 'comfortable' jobs from 'honest Christians'. The Jewish 'culture of the book' worked both as an advantage and disadvantage in these circumstances. Many emigrated, when they could: to western Europe, occasionally Palestine, often north America. Since emigration implied considerable financial resources, those involved were regularly among the most affluent and best educated of the population.

At the same time, the growing industrialization of the Empire was concentrated in those areas where there were considerable Jewish populations. Their relatively high levels of education, and history of craft work, led many Jewish people into these industries, as did the fact that their traditional life was under considerable stress from economic and social forces. Socialism, both of an all-Russian and a peculiarly Jewish cast, became particularly strong in this population. Growing prosperity led to the development of an urban bourgeoisie, acting as traders in the towns in these territories; Jewish people again played a considerable part in these developments. By 1917, Jews were the most urbanized of all the 'nationalities' of the Tsarist Empire. Of all the non-east Slav populations, they were also becoming the most Russified in language.

Beyond this circle were groups of people whose presence within the Empire was contingent, and also relatively recent. Many from these backgrounds had higher levels of national consciousness and literacy in their own languages than had Russians. When this was less developed, the peoples involved were less able to maintain their independence in the aftermath of the revolution. This was particularly the case in the Baltic territories.

This region was neither linguistically nor culturally homogenous: many of the residents spoke Finnic languages, others Baltic or Slavonic, whilst a significant minority in all territories spoke Germanic languages; many were Lutherans, some were Catholics, some Jewish, whilst a few were Orthodox. Like the Empire's Polish territories, they were relatively recent additions to Tsarist territory; unlike Poland, however, all of the ethnic groups involved (with the partial exception of Lithuania)[3] had, for most of their existence in an economically and politically integrated European community, been dominated by external powers. All of the provinces involved were linguistically mixed; when coupled to ethnic or religious associations, this made the development of nationalism extremely complex. Moreover, the areas south of the Gulf of Finland were dominated by a ruling class which, whilst rarely Russian in language, were extremely loyal to the Tsar. Much of this loyalty was self-interest, since the ruling class were often German (or occasionally Swedish) speakers, surrounded by a peasantry who spoke another language. The same was true of the townspeople of the area, who, no matter their ethnic origin, were often sundered from their surroundings in speech and culture. Although attempts at both linguistic codification, and a national romanticism based upon Scandinavian models, had been tried in all of these territories, by 1900 their results had been patchy.

A number of these territories became independent of the Russian centre in the period following 1917. Many of the regimes established were of a highly nationalist cast; language planning, particularly status planning, was high on their list of objectives. It is dubious whether Russian ever fully disappeared from use in the territories, however, since the presence of their large neighbour to the east could never be ignored. Their incorporation into the Soviet Union during the Second World War led to sometimes aggressive Russification in some domains; nevertheless, the languages (with the exception of Livonian, and a few much smaller language varieties) managed to hold their own.

With the other two groups from the western territories of the Empire – Poles and Finns – the chances for actual independence were considerably greater. To a large extent this was due to the size of the groups involved, their level of cultural and, in particular, linguistic development and, especially in the case of the Poles, the strong sense of a historical pedigree and destiny which had included periods of domination over large numbers of east Slavs. This last group also had many members living in the Hohenzollern and Habsburg territories, so that complete Russian domination was unlikely. Those nations or ethnic groups, such as the Poles or Finns which had the strongest traditions of their own identity, and relatively high levels of literacy in their national variety, as well as (often) their own 'Western' institutions, were those which were not included within the post Brest–Livotsk 'Russian' state, when actors, both linguistic and political, attempted to 'plan' the language situation under the new order.

8.4.2 Socialism and nationalism

As has already been suggested, the late nineteenth century was a period of considerable change for the Russian Empire. Whilst the majority remained tied to primary agriculture, and levels of literacy were low, there were the beginnings of an 'industrial revolution' (Thalheim 1971). The fact that the system was autocratic led to tensions within society, however, which crossed ethnic and linguistic frontiers, although they did not necessarily negate them. The intransigence of the system led to a particularly violent radicalization of sections of the intelligentsia, including those we might have expected to have been the natural allies of the government. A case in point is the family of Vladimir Illyich Ulyanov, later known as Lenin. Members of the minor country nobility, it might have been expected, given their surprisingly intellectual and outward-looking approach, that they would have been progressives, or at least liberals. The climate of the country did not allow for moderate change of this type, however. Vladimir's elder brother was executed for an act of terrorism; his own adult life was largely spent in either internal or external exile, before he returned to Russia towards the end of his life as the leader of a radical Marxist party, which eventually seized power and introduced a dictatorship, carried out in the name of a democratic proletariat which did not quite exist.

The nature of this radicalization led to eccentricities in its intellectual development. These had profound effects upon the development of ethnic, cultural and linguistic policies after the radicals gained control of the state. For a large part of the time, the despotic apparatus of the Empire, allied to the illiteracy of a great part of the potential proletariat, led to the policies of these radicals being mainly unknown within the Empire – except for a few months in 1905–1906. This meant that the dogmatism of their interpretation of a number of the teachings of radical ideologues (particularly Marx) was never tempered by the pragmatism of a 'normal' parliamentary system. The small exile communities in western Europe and elsewhere must often have felt that they were speaking to the void.

This was never seen more clearly than in the long-standing debates by the left (of Russia and elsewhere) on what a socialist party's attitudes to the concepts of nationality and nationalism should be. This discussion was particularly pressing, as we might expect, in the context of the multi-ethnic and multilingual territories controlled by the Tsar, in comparison with the relatively neat distribution of peoples and languages to be found in the west.[4]

There has always been a distinct strain of millenarianism running through the more radical forms of socialism. Come the socialist millennium, it would become plain that all of the problems of society (and, in particular, for our purposes, the tensions between ethnic and cultural groups and their language use) were products of the capitalist system. Whilst undoubted differences between peoples would remain, such as languages (and even this point was questioned by some), the universal solidarity felt between workers throughout the world would greatly outweigh this. This belief was enforced by the fact that most of the early socialist theoreticians were products of western European societies which were relatively homogenous in linguistic, if not necessarily cultural, terms. Furthermore, as inheritors of the most radical forms of Jacobinism, nineteenth-century European radicals were generally distrustful of minority populations, which were felt to be an affront to the idea of the equality (interpreted as homogeneity) of the population of the nation state.

This view of nationalism, perhaps even the concept of ethnic identity, as essentially a product of capitalist reactionary 'false consciousness', rapidly became a tenet of the revolutionary left, with a few notable exceptions, such as James Connolly, the Scottish-born Irish revolutionary. At its most militant, this view has been termed 'national nihilism': the active espousal of the end to all national and ethnic distinctions.

Yet whilst liberating in some senses, since it envisaged and encouraged an end to petty quarrels among people who had more in common with each other than they had with their respective ruling classes, this view had the great disadvantage that it could reinforce the existence of the status quo. Since national (rather than state) boundaries would become essentially meaningless under the new dispensation, there was no real need felt among most radicals for these state boundaries to be changed. Whilst this was unjust to the minority populations of western Europe, it was even more difficult to apply in the context of the dynastic empires of central and eastern Europe. This meant that radical organizations were caught in a cleft stick of their own making: how could they preserve internationalism, while at the same time apparently 'liberating' the oppressed peoples of these empires?

In the Romanov Empire, this discussion could be largely avoided, if not ignored, because there was no true representative organ for either the majority or minority populations; in the Habsburg lands, however, some degree of popular representation was established, which necessitated discussion of how the socialist movement in the Empire could avoid splits along national lines, whilst at the same time not appearing to be a cipher for the dominant German- and Magyar-speakers (themselves not the majority populations). These problems led to the creation of a new trend in Marxism, much condemned at the time by other leftists: Austro-Marxism.

To its opponents, Austro-Marxism represented a surrender to nationalism, which would eventually lead to national struggles, rather than the desired class struggle. In fact, this overstepped the mark considerably. What the view did espouse was the idea that, in a socialist Austria–Hungary, all citizens would have the right to define themselves according to national criteria, whether this be in their ethnic homeland, or elsewhere in the country, where their cultural and, in particular, linguistic rights would, wherever possible, be respected.

This view of multiple, overlapping, identities was anathema not just to the far left of 'national nihilists', but also to the leaders of strict hierarchical movements (which could be seen as dictatorial), associated with very dangerous political situations, such as the Bolshevik wing of the Russian Social Democrats. It would, of necessity, lessen the chance for the uniformity of ideology and purpose which they craved. It is one of the ironies of the history of socialism that Austro-Marxism was never attempted in the Habsburg lands; instead, a form of it was attempted by these very ideological opponents in what became the Soviet Union.

It is always difficult to reconstruct what the Bolshevik movement's views on 'the nationalities question' at any given time were, both because the internal Leninist dictatorship of the pre-Revolutionary party was never as effective as might have been desired by some, and also because many ideological positions were reinterpreted after the event, in an attempt either to curry favour, or merely to survive in an increasingly tyrannical atmosphere. What is certain is that, for a large part of his active life, Lenin himself veered towards the 'national nihilist' position, seeing large-state conglomerations as the best means to achieve socialism, and having little in the way of active sympathy towards the idea of minority rights. For political and strategic reasons, however, he gradually espoused the principle of 'self-determination' for all the peoples of the Russian Empire (although not necessarily of the right to secede from the Empire in its new, democratic, socialist form); this view was not shared by most of his fellow ideologues (and leaders) in the party. As a catch phrase whose interpretation differed according to time, place and user, 'self-determination of peoples' was enforced before 1917 as a marker of party discipline, however.

8.4.3   The linguistic results of 1917 and its aftermath

This is not the place to discuss in depth the chaos of the Russian revolution of 1917, the Bolshevik coup and the civil war. What is certain, however, is that, by the end of this period, Bolshevik views on the nationalities question had been altered. In the first place, it became apparent that 'national nihilism' was a chimera: in the period after 1917, both historic and non-historic nations were (re)constituted across the former Tsarist Empire. As the Bolsheviks regained control of most of these territories, they often found themselves the allies of nationalists; the Bolshevik centre was also often more sympathetic to 'national' demands than were the revolutionaries on the ground who, particularly in central Asia and the Caucasus, tended either to be ethnic Russians, or deeply Russified. Moreover, the idea of national self-determination had to be brought into line with a system which demanded uniformity of political view and action. Towards the end of his active life, Lenin himself became horrified by some of the activities of Bolsheviks on the ground in non-Russian areas, seeing in their deeds a form of neo-imperialism, masquerading as revolution. Many of these actions were perpetrated by forces close to Stalin, whose power-base, within party and state, derived from being Commissar for Nationalities.

The Soviet Union was always a compromise between centrists and special interests in the republics. Under Lenin, this was not so problematical; it might have been thought that the situation would have improved for speakers of minority languages when Joseph Stalin began to build up a following within the Soviet system. Stalin himself had been a Georgian nationalist in his youth. Indeed he had originally taken the name of the Georgian national hero – Koba – as his pseudonym. Yet his background in the underground Bolshevik movement within Russia lent itself to close collaboration with many national nihilists. Although, as, at least overtly, Lenin's most trusted follower, Stalin used the rhetoric of national self-determination, it is dubious whether, before or after the Bolshevik seizure of power, he actually believed in it.

With Lenin's death, many of the nationalities within the new Soviet state, or at least those who had some access to the Bolshevik *apparat*, hoped that his changed philosophy on national self-determination would be implemented, if not by Stalin, at least by his rivals, most notably Trotsky. But Trotsky also came from a national nihilist background. In the end, while Lenin's views could not be ignored, those who followed him, of whatever ideological slant, generally only paid lip service to the concept.

The primary linguistic objective for the Commissariat of National Affairs was to 'modernize' the languages of the less-developed nations, or ethnic groups, within the new state. At the same time, the Bolsheviks certainly perceived language as having an ideological purpose within the state. Inevitably, these ambitions would come into direct conflict with those among the ethnic groups themselves, and their sympathizers, whose desires were fed by a perceived need for modernization and education, or by the feeling that a true modern nation had to have its own means of communication. In the early days, it was relatively straightforward to accommodate both viewpoints, since neither had been fully developed. It would have seemed quite natural to most Marxists that, for the purposes of *agitprop*, as well as a basic achievement of justice, all oppressed peoples should have access to the 'means of production' in their own language. The most logical representation of that language (from their point of view) should therefore be developed.

Of course, none of the language planners involved in the process was free of ideological bias. This would be practically impossible under most, if not all, circumstances. For instance, as Fierman (1991) reports, in central Asia, those who took a generally Islamist viewpoint would have been largely sympathetic to a revised Arabic script for their 'national language'. Due to the fluctuations in power and influence within these territories during the 1920s, it was inevitable that this viewpoint would not be successful. This was particularly the case because the Soviet authorities, and many secularists in the territories in question, were alarmed at the prospect of pan-Islamist propaganda. What script to use, therefore?

In a country numerically dominated by speakers of Russian, it would seem logical for the Cyrillic script to be employed. But the Roman script in a developed form was preferred for many of the languages involved. There appears to have been a widespread prejudice against Cyrillic within the upper echelons of the Bolshevik movement. Many had spent a large part of their adult lives in exile in western Europe; it is very likely that many of them were more used to reading German, English or French than they were to reading Russian. Moreover, their ideological sympathies lay more closely with the industrial proletariats, and intelligentsia, of the countries where these languages were spoken than with the peasantry of their own country. Roman script implied progress; Cyrillic, on the other hand, implied autocracy. Of course, from a purely linguistic point of view, neither script represented these languages better.

A further reason for script reform was a spirit of cross-fertilization with the Kemalist reforms in Turkey. At first, these tendencies were supported by the central hierarchy, since revolutionary Turkey was one of the few allies the early Soviet Union had. As the ideological distinctions between the two new republics became increasingly apparent, the Soviet authorities became less keen on the association. This was especially the case in Azerbaijan, where the local language was sufficiently close to the Turkish of Turkey to render them mutually intelligible.

As has already been noted, Soviet Central Asia had had an archaic common language – Chagatay. Whilst there were a number of reasons why this language was unacceptable to Soviet language planners, not least the fact that it was particularly associated with Islamic tradition, there is some reason to suspect that the creation of a number of separate languages for the area, such as Kazakh or Turkmeni, was intended, at least by some, as a means of lessening common cause among the non-Russian inhabitants of the area, a point emphasized by Carmichael (2000), although Martin (2002) provides a considerably more positive interpretation of the process. On the other hand, there were a number of intellectuals involved in the process, especially those residing in the centre, whose typological activities were spurred by contemporary views on anthropology, particularly the concept that occupational activity was predicated upon ethnic background. Thus the herding, semi-nomadic, peoples of Turkic language were distinguished from the largely seden-tary, farming, peoples of Turkic language, the former being defined as Kazakhs, with, eventually, a distinct Ausbau variety, the latter being defined as Uzbeks, with the same provision. Some may even have been interested primarily in the means by which mass literacy could be achieved.

Elsewhere in the new Soviet Union, similar processes were at work. In both Ukraine and Belarus, or at least those parts which remained within the new state, language activists were encouraged to develop the local speech varieties as independent Ausbau varieties. Obviously, in the case of Ukrainian, this was a simpler task, since the local variety had had some literary use before the revolution. It was more difficult to create a national variety for Belarus. Furthermore, much of Belarus was incorpo-rated in the early 1920s into Poland. Awareness among the inhabitants of this territory that they had a separate nationality from Russia was also limited, and may not have been encouraged by the Bolshevik authorities.

Nevertheless, mass literacy programmes were at work. In most areas, the situation resembled a *tabula rasa*. In Siberia, for instance, Russian literacy levels were extremely low outside the towns. Interestingly, *graphization* took place in Roman script with the vast majority of these languages, despite this marginal Russian literacy. In those areas where the language spoken was Mongolian or a close relative, the traditional scripts were not encouraged. The partially logographic nature of traditional

Mongolian script might have rendered a mass literacy campaign difficult, because of the expense of developing a printing and typing technology for the script; moreover, the association of the script with a priestly caste, whose primary interest in developing it may have been to restrict literacy, would not have been attractive to the officially atheist Bolsheviks. In Armenia and Georgia, of course, alphabetic scripts already existed. Both were associated with a form of Christianity, but they could not be ignored. Instead, mass literacy programmes began to be instituted for these languages in their traditional scripts.

All of this sounds utopian. Great strides were made in the first ten years of Bolshevik rule in the development of teaching materials which would guarantee mass literacy. Ideologically, however, moves towards dictatorial centralization led many of the activities of the vernacular mass literacy programme, and of its actors, to become politically suspect. In the tyrannical atmosphere of Stalinist Moscow, the term *national deviationism* began to be used regularly of anyone whose loyalty was not entirely committed to this centralizing project. Russian nationalists within what was becoming, increasingly, a Stalinist party, may also have become uncomfortable with the extent to which minorities within the state were allowed to move away from traditional Russian hegemony. It must have been particularly distressing that many people from minority backgrounds were not able to use Russian in a fluent way. To many, it might have seemed discriminatory towards these minorities, since, inevitably, Russian became the language of the Union. At this point, it is worth recalling that Stalin himself was a renegade nationalist.

Because of the internationalist ideology of the Soviet Union, it would have been impossible to ignore the other nationalities of the state. The Communist International was, after all, attempting to associate the class struggle with the liberation struggle of all colonized peoples. It would be counter-productive if too much time were spent promoting Russian at the expense of the other languages of the Union. Nevertheless, it was felt that something had to be done.

With those languages whose newly graphized form had been Roman script, encouragement was increasingly given to Cyrillic script. By the end of the 1930s, almost all of the newly literate languages of central Asia were now written in what was approaching a common script for the whole of the Soviet Union. Of course, there were sound reasons why Cyrillic was favoured. The cost of producing, or, more likely, importing, Roman script typewriters and printers was one the state could ill afford. Moreover, the argument could be – and was – made that the fact that the majority language of the union was written in Cyrillic must surely encourage the use of the same script for other languages, particularly since, as we have seen, there were very few, if any, places within the Soviet Union where no Russian speakers or Russian-literates were to be found. It would have been economically prohibitive to maintain two printing systems in one place. Further, in a state which increasingly wished to control the overt expression of thought by its citizens, the fact that all communication was in the script of the majority would make production relatively easy to censor. This was particularly the case since, as a number of commentators, such as Estraikh (1999: chapter 6), have noted, there was considerable encouragement in the corpus-planning initiatives of the period for similar, often Russian-based, ideological catch-phrases to be used in all languages.

But the primary reasons for this shift in emphasis were ideological. For all of the talk of self-determination, linguistic, cultural and perhaps even governmental, the Soviet system's inherent centralism was becoming obsessively so under Stalin. It was increasingly evident, and was eventually promulgated as law, that Russian was the first language of the Union. In a state of linguistic equality, some languages were more equal than others. In using Cyrillic script from the very beginning of the literacy process, it was believed that the acquisition of Russian literacy would be easier and that, eventually, Russian would spread beyond its present position to become the primary language of use of all citizens. In a system whose centralization was rigidly systematic, in terms of education, promotion in employment and many other fields, it became inevitable that the expanding middle classes of functionaries in the various non-Russian republics would become increasingly Russified. As part of official state policy, this had a certain logic to it. A range of people in 'middle management' were produced, who owed their positions to the maintenance of the system and its Russification policies. It also acted as an encouragement for parents to increase the use of Russian in their homes. These tendencies became even more marked during the Second World War, the 'Great Patriotic War', when the Soviet government played up many non-communist elements of the state, inevitably encouraging Russian patriotism at the expense of the other nationalities.

In this sense, the Soviet Union was no different from many other multinational polities where there was a dominant ethnic-linguistic group. Nevertheless, the ideology of the state made it extremely difficult to accept that this was what was being done. From this point of view, it is worth considering two rather different sets of speech communities which were problematical in this new order.

The first set are those speakers of Slavonic languages who were not Russian speakers; in particular, the Ukrainians. In the early, idealistic, phase of the Soviet Union's development, encouragement was given to the development of a national norm for this variety, actively distanced from Russian. In the late 1920s, attempts to develop a national orthography almost reached fruition, only for the experiment to be conveniently forgotten in the terror which followed, particularly harsh in the free-peasant atmosphere of Ukraine (Hornjatkevyč 1993). An especially striking example of the way in which Stalinism rigidly controlled language planning was the fact that the employment of the letter г (used for /g/ in Russian) for the sound /h/, present in Ukrainian but not in Russian, and the development of an independent letter г for /g/, was actively suppressed, presumably because it would have rendered the transition from one language to another more difficult. At the same time, those Ukrainian language planners who had escaped the purges (not of the most nationalist cast in any event) were encouraged forcefully to develop a corpus which brought the language more in line with usage in Russian, downplaying the Polish elements in the language, and discouraging the use of native equivalents for Russian terms associated with the state, even when, as was often the case, these terms appeared morphophonemically 'uncomfortable' in a Ukrainian framework. Since these 'reforms' were only accepted among Soviet Ukrainians, those who lived in other polities (a sizeable number before the Second World War in states such as Poland and Czechoslovakia, never mind the large Ukrainian diaspora in north America) were gradually distanced from their linguistic kin within the Soviet Union, which may have been the centre's intention.

Perhaps surprisingly, there are a number of similarities between the giant Ukrainian (which, in any other state, would have been considered a world language) and Yiddish, spoken in a number of disparate dialects by people holding strikingly different views. As Estraikh (1999) reports, Yiddish before the Revolution had a relatively developed literature; most Jewish males were also at least marginally literate, in marked contrast to many other ethnic groups. Although Romanization was discussed in the 1920s, and was popular among the most secular members of the community, often the most sympathetic to the new order, this was never seriously considered. Like Armenian or Georgian, the tradition of a script associated with the language was too strong. Moreover, an undesired similarity to German, another Soviet language, would then have been emphasized. On the other hand, corpus planning for Soviet Yiddish was particularly intense.

To some extent, this corpus planning could be construed as being purist, since a great many words of Semitic origin, whether Hebrew or Aramaic, were excluded from official forms of the language. It has to be borne in mind, however, that Slavonic borrowings were not treated in this way, except during the very earliest period. It is very likely that the encouragement to divorce the language from its Semitic underpinning was part of the anti-religious programme. As with Ukrainian, achieving a cleavage between speakers of Yiddish in the Soviet Union, and the majority of speakers residing elsewhere, most notably in Poland and the United States, might also have been desirable to the centre and its planners.

In a sense, this is what practically guaranteed the failure of the reform. Those who were committed to its promulgation, and to the social system which it represented, were those who were most likely to shift towards Russian, since they were unlikely to be practising Jews. Those who were practising, particularly the Orthodox, very quickly came into conflict with the state, and were likely to consider the loss of the Semitic aspects of their native language as an abomination perpetrated by the godless. The desire to leave the Soviet Union, or, at the very least, not to conform more than necessary to its dictates, would have been particularly strong within this group.

Even without this cleavage, two developments would have made success for Soviet Yiddish unlikely. In the first place, Russian anti-Semitism, masquerading at times as 'Scientific Atheism', made the development of a Yiddish-speaking, stable, communist elite very unlikely. At times, the most assimilated Jews faced persecution under Stalin for no other reason than ethnicity. Given the levels of education present among Jewish people in comparison to the Soviet population as a whole, it is not surprising that this potential elite should have been among the most targeted during the purges, even if they were not victims of actual anti-Semitism. Moreover, the Nazi occupation of the western Soviet Union led to the attempted annihilation of all people of Jewish 'race' within their territory; sadly, it is very likely that the most assimilated and Russified Jews, who fled with the retreating Soviet forces, were more likely to survive, rather than the largely Orthodox, Yiddish-speaking, populations who remained.

By the beginning of the 1950s, Soviet Yiddish as a language programme was practically dead. Under similar circumstances, the language development of groups such as the Volga Germans and the Crimean Tatars was halted, and perhaps even actively reversed, during the 1930s and 1940s. The smaller nationalities of the Soviet Union, including those who were incorporated after the changes of frontiers during the 1940s, inhabited a linguistic universe not dissimilar to that found in Tsarist times, where Russian was omnipresent. The difference was that mass literacy was making their positions far more untenable.

8.4.4 Analysis

The history of language policy in the Soviet Union can be construed as a clash between two different groups of actors: language planners and political ideologues. According to this interpretation, language planning became symbolic of the conflict between those who believed in the free use of a native language in a planned form as an essential human right, and those who saw language as a means of spreading ideology. Mass literacy, according to this interpretation, was not so much an end as a means.

Another interpretation is possible. The conflict between centrifugal and centripetal forces, which all multinational polities face, was particularly acute with the Soviet Union because of the tension between the emancipating and egalitarian ideology which its leaders embraced, and the day-to-day reality of maintaining totalitarian control over a massive territory, inhabited by people who could be distinguished from each other in almost every imaginable way. In a literate country, some recognition of the multiplicity of languages spoken had to be made. This could never be allowed to imperil the control exerted by party and state, however, either by too powerful a language coming into competition with Russian, or by too great a movement away from the dominant language and its script. In a sense, the language tensions mirror the wider problems which eventually brought the Soviet experiment to a halt.

8.5 Smaller nations and lesser-used languages: Scotland

In the modern world, there is an ongoing tension between the perceived efficiencies of large-scale political conglomerations and the right to determination desired by even the smallest ethnic group. This tension is played out regularly in language; indeed, all of the examples given earlier present different aspects of the problems faced by language planners, political ideologues and ordinary people. I wish, in the last case-study of this chapter, to turn to a particularly complex example of this tension, where a relatively small nation, submerged for a considerable period in a much larger, and, at one point, very powerful polity, whose language is dominant in the world, is faced with the question of the extent to which it might wish to express its developing political autonomy in terms of its linguistic difference from its overarching polity. The nation in question is Scotland; the variety Scots. The knowledge that comes from being an insider perhaps balances the lack of distance that is also inevitable.

The present status of Scots within Scotland is difficult to describe. We have no accurate idea of how many speakers of the language there are, largely due to unwillingness by the Scottish Executive to include questions on the matter on the census (Murdoch 1995; Macafee 2000b). Much more to the point: most Scots speakers cannot read (never mind write) Scots with any ease. Why have language planning activities failed to reach fruition? What, if anything, can be done?

A recent accessible work on Scots by a prestigious author (Jones 2002) makes the point that there are, in the speech community of non-Gaelic Scotland today, not two linguistic systems, but rather a continuum between dialect and standard, not at all dissimilar to that found in other countries. This is only part of the story, however. What marks off Scotland is the fact that the commonly accepted standard was in origin utterly exocentric, and that an endocentric standard was coming into being some 400 years ago, as we saw in Chapter 5.

Jones' account also sidesteps the question of national identity. In a strange, by no means straightforward, way, Scots acts as a powerful marker of Scottishness, not just – as is the case in many areas where local dialects are associated with strong regional pride – in speech, but also in a long, albeit patchy, written heritage. At the very least, its employment can be seen as a rather impotent challenge to hegemonic forces; in some incalculable way, it can also be a means of 'imagining' the Scottish community.

In this sense Scotland has many advantages over its rivals as 'new' nations in linguistic terms: it has two national vernaculars, both symbols of national identity to insiders and outsiders alike. Gaelic is already a fully planned Ausbau variety. Scots, on the other hand, appears to have gone backwards in terms of use and prestige in the last 200 years, at precisely the same time as other dispossessed vernaculars of Europe and elsewhere developed into fully fledged languages. The last 20 years have demonstrated a considerable desire among the Scottish population for political autonomy; linguistic autonomy for Scots has not been so successfully absorbed, however.

But if that is the case, what has been done, what should be done, to guide the development of Scots in the national domain? If its credentials are to remain largely literary, is there any point in 'planning'? To what extent is language planning for Scots a process which will contribute to the health and integrity of the language?

As we saw in Chapter 5, unlike many lesser-used languages, Scots is haunted by an impressive literary pedigree, in a period in which it came close to standardization as any other European language of the time, and was established as the medium of government. It is also haunted by the history of the collapse of this status, and the creation of a sociolinguistic relationship between considerable literacy in English and the existence of divergent, largely unwritten, Scots dialects. By the end of the eighteenth century, any written Scots was produced in a melange of orthographical styles which lent themselves to seeing it as a corrupt English.

I use the word *haunted* consciously. The history of both the language and its activism has been played out in the shadow of these events. For instance, some activists in their planning for the future of Scots have decided to ignore the input of the 'decline' of the variety in status in the seventeenth and eighteenth centuries into the present state of Scots in its varieties. Indeed, some – most notably, Hugh MacDiarmid (Grieve 1926, as discussed by Milton 1986) – have taken particular umbrage with the fact of present dialectal diversity, seeing in it a form of deviation away from, and corruption of, the once and future standard. In a perverse way, this mimics the views often held by monodialectal users of any standard about speakers of other varieties – with the added twist of there being no standard available for writers to use.

The opposing view has also been prevalent in a wide range of language planning initiatives, and also very commonly in the writings of creative artists: the *year nothing* fallacy. Little or no attention is paid to any aspect of this 'glorious' past. With creative artists, this tendency shows itself in what literary critics term 'phonetic spelling'. If any corpus planning is involved, it is a belief in the accuracy of the speech of urban reality. Its main failing is that its supposedly phonetic status is based upon an adherence to the conventions (or at least tendencies) of English spelling, a point made in some of the analysis of urban Scottish writing in Hagan (2002).

When employed by language planners, the system involved is not normally Anglocentric; it may, however, seem Martian. Perhaps the most striking example of this is the spelling system of Stirling (1994), which is so enamoured of Scandinavian orthography that it does not recognize either the manifest differences in phonemic system between these languages and Scots or the willingness of a Scottish writing and reading public to embrace what to them would be an utterly foreign system, as shown in my use of his orthography in the following – famous – excerpt:

> Ii dut na whiils, bitt thu mii thiv;
> Whitt thenn? pär bisti, thu munn livv!
> A dämunn ikkurr inn a thräv
>   'S a sma riqquesst:
> Ii'll gett a blessin wä thi läv
>   Annd nivvurr miss't.

With this in mind, there is a third tendency which needs to be considered. If I was being unkind, I might term this the *kailyard* fallacy, referring to the literary movement of the late nineteenth and early twentieth centuries which harked back to an (imagined) Scottish rural utopia, where everyone knew their place in a rather conservative social structure (Knowles 1983; Millar 2004b), but it might be fairer to see it as the *post-Burns* tendency. From this point of view, Scots would be treated as a series of dialects to be used in a relatively ad hoc way – with the exception of a healthy dose of the lexis and structures employed by Burns and his immediate followers – to describe conventionally senti-mental or comic subjects often dealing with past events. This tendency is arguably the most widespread in the use of Scots, primarily because it is written Scots of this type to which most people are exposed at school and in the popular press. As a point of comparison, here is the same excerpt from Burns' 'To a Mouse' in the orthography in which it was originally printed:

> I doubt na, whyles, but thou may thieve ;
> What then ? poor beastie, thou maun live !
> A daimen icker in a thrave
>   'S a sma' request :
> I'll get a blessin wi' the lave,
> And never miss't !

This is Scots written to be as intelligible to speakers of English as possible. To a corpus planner, the most glaring problem with Scots written this way is the use of apostrophes in words such as *sma'* 'small' or *wi'* 'with'. From an economic point of view, this practice made sense: if English speakers were prompted to recognize that the words they were reading had English cognates which included more sounds, it would have been easier to interpret. From an ideological point of view it is highly damaging, however: it makes Scots look like a corruption of English. Because of the prestige of writers like Burns and Scott, this system still permeates Scottish life, as some of the findings in Fässler (1998) imply.

Any Scots language planner is faced either with an attempt to reconcile these mutually exclusive tendencies or with stepping outside the present debate and choosing a new route.

The second issue which any planner of Scots faces is the existence of a number of relatively strong parties within the small group of activists for or in Scots. Although these 'parties' are not adhered to strictly, and can be fluid in their allegiances, they are nonetheless well demarcated, and there can be considerable tensions between them. The single greatest 'party' split is that between what I term the *official* party and the *cultural* party.

The official party, in its most ambitious sense, is concerned with no less than the extension of Scots in its use to all domains of literary and non-literary activity which are presently inhabited by English. Although perhaps only its most optimistic members would desire the actual replacement of English by Scots in these domains, nevertheless there is a desire to fulfil, and extend, the criteria suggested by Kloss for the development of an Ausbau language. In the work of Allan (such as, for instance, his 1998 doctoral dissertation), this has become associated with a 'ceivil service Scots', the need for a dictionary, and a linguistic force behind it, which is prescriptive in terms of orthography, lexis and usage, and which would be enforced by the state as part of policy. An example of Allan's own orthography (Allan 1995) demonstrates an attempt at both internal consistency and systemic distinctiveness:

> A dout na, whyles, bit thou may theiv ;
> What then ? pair beastie, thou maun live !
> A daimen icker in a thrave
> > 'S a smaw request :
> A'll get a blessin wi the lave,
> > An never miss't !

To members of the cultural party, these developments are very much a case of putting the cart before the horse. Put most eloquently by Macafee (2000a), this view stresses the need to connect the language in the first place to the rich vernacular culture from which it springs. To many of the official party, such a view is anathema, since it could be taken as encouraging regional separatism, thereby weakening the movement as a whole. More worrying for the cultural viewpoint is the fact that, if applied rigidly, an interest in the folk life of an area may distance the movement from the very people who speak the local dialect, many of whom have little or no interest in their local culture. Far worse is the association which local culture may have with the past, particularly during a period of instability and change in local economic and occupational patterns. The motto of the Buchan Heritage Society is *Dinna tyne't*, 'Don't lose it', written beneath a line drawing of a horse drawing a plough. This is a laudable intention: the rich folk life associated with the old ways *should* be recorded, and an interest by children in particular *should* be encouraged. But the language itself must be independent of its apparent ties, or it will be dangerously compromised by that culture's moribundity. Nevertheless, in its best sense, the cultural imperative looks both forward and back.

There is a central problem with all of this. In the first place, the actors either have had to deal with the tendencies and counter-tendencies discussed here – which way lies heartache if not madness – or they have chosen to ignore them, claiming them to be examples of false consciousness, of deviation from a 'line'. Most of the actors, of course, accept the necessity for compromise in these matters; the problem comes from the question of how far any compromiser would be willing to go, and who should be included in any committee. Even if a committee is established, there is always the danger (and this has happened) either of external commitments meaning that the committee only meets a few times, or that significant elements within the movement sit on the committee, and either leave before the end, or refuse to endorse the findings, as McClure (1995b: 25–6) illustrates. In fact, at present, two different planning authorities are touting divergent spelling systems simultaneously.

Corpus planners for Scots are faced, therefore, with an extremely difficult situation. If a maximalist position is taken – in other words, that a Standard Scots would have an implied standard lexis *ab initio*, and an underlying phonemic pronunciation – they leave themselves open to the accusation of lack of realism (although it has to be said that all linguistic initiatives of this type have been accused of just such a failing: some *have* succeeded, nonetheless). Many activists for, and practitioners of, Scots would see any such proposals as dictatorial (I have seen much less radical suggestions treated as such). As ever, they will remain mere proposals if major organizations, both public and private, are not willing to promote and enforce them.

If a rather more minimalist position is taken, there is the danger that anything will pass for Scots. Whilst an argument could be made for such a position, this would certainly not suit many members of the official party, who would see this as an example of trimming towards colloquial English in a Scottish guise. Some members of the cultural party would also object; perhaps for exactly the same reason. The problem is that, as Macafee (1994) pointed out in her discussion of knowledge of specifically Scots lexis in the Glasgow area, and demonstrated elsewhere in Scotland by, for instance, Pollner (1985) and McGarrity (1998), the younger the informants, the less rich their knowledge of traditional vocabulary, and the less likely they are to recognize their speech as Scots. It is difficult to see how this could be solved by corpus planning alone.

This leads us on to status planning. If corpus planning is to be anything more than an intellectual exercise, it needs to be 'taken to the people'. Naturally, this is easier said than done, primarily because most Scots language planners are relatively far removed from the centres of power. It would be very easy to portray the Scottish Executive, the Scottish Office and the educational establishment, top to bottom, as enemies of the development of Scots; easy, but unfair, as McClure (1975) and Niven and Jackson (1998) demonstrate. The problem is not so much one of inimical feelings as it is of faulty prioritization and lack of experience. It is unfortunate that the present Scottish Executive is an inheritor of the British tradition. English has never had any official language planning (although, as we saw in Chapters 5 and 6, it has had plenty of the unofficial variety, often of a rather authoritarian nature). Given the sometimes shocking lack of knowledge (or interest) which British people have in matters outside the English-speaking world, it is not, perhaps, surprising that there is little understanding of the fact that the intervention of governmental and semi-governmental organizations in language use is the norm in many places. Whilst the Executive may make warm noises about Scots in its cultural strategy, it might genuinely not occur to many of its members that Scots would be in need of status planning in the same way as Gaelic is,[5] although, in the last year or so, Executive policy leaflets have been available in Scots, along with a number of immigrant languages, due to the work of a Cross Pairty Committee for Scots in the Parliament (Scots Pairlament Cross Pairty Group on the Scots Language 2003). Nevertheless, the lack of a strong idea of what Scots is probably leads to non-linguists shying away from too much discussion of the matter.

When it comes to education, it is a different matter. The educational authorities have put the study of Scottish language into the curriculum, at a variety of different levels, as a compulsory element. There is also considerable goodwill felt towards the language, and its varieties, by most teachers. The problem comes from a very understandable compartmentalization: the curriculum for the 5–14 age group, arguably the place where the fightback for Scots would be most important, is already stuffed with 'absolutely vital' matters which must be attended to. There is only so much teachers can do. We might argue about the validity of treating many children's mother tongue as a fairly low priority; this is not the decision of individual teachers, but rather part of the intellectual climate handed down by the educational authorities. Of course, the situation is not helped by there being a relatively limited – although often extremely impressive – set of teaching materials available; more importantly, the largely passive induction to literature in Scots is not always matched by a more proactive writing *in* Scots, largely due to vagueness over the necessity of corpus planning.

I was recently one of the leaders of a day's in-service course for teachers of 'English' on methods and means of teaching, and incorporating, Scots in the upper levels of High School. It was, in general, a highly positive experience, from which I learned a great deal. The great majority of the teachers with whom I spoke were interested in teaching about the local vernacular and encouraging its use in certain spheres. The only sour note was when I introduced the idea of a spelling norm for Scots: many of the teachers felt that this would be an authoritarian imposition upon a creative act (which tells us something of how they viewed the vernacular's position in communication). Many also believed strongly that the teaching of another system to children who struggled with English spelling would be counter-productive for the teaching of English. If these were the views of teachers who were sufficiently well-enough disposed towards Scots to attend a day's course on the language, it can be imagined what the opinions would be of those who were not so positive about it.

Finally, there is the matter of acquisition planning. Many people in Scotland have no more than a passive understanding of Scots (if that). Whilst any language planning initiative towards children would be relatively straightforward, any outreach towards adults would be difficult. Further, it is not only the matter of non-natives. Many Scots-speaking adults have had inculcated in them, from a very early age, that the language of literacy is English. This view could not be changed overnight. Indeed, more than one language planning initiative has foundered because of the unwillingness of native speakers to change a sociolinguistic situation in which they felt relatively secure.

8.5.1   Discussion

Why has Scots been less than successful in achieving full Ausbau status? In the first place, it has to be recognized that Scotland already possesses a potent linguistic symbol – Gaelic – which has, if we are being cynical, the advantage both of Abstand status and a geographical heartland which makes it relatively straightforward to be ignored by the great part of the population, except in highly formulaic and token circumstances. Status and acquisition planning for Scots would be much more expensive. This may be a cost which no government (or population) in Scotland would be willing (or able) to foot. This also points to the second reason for the lack of success for Scots language planning.

No matter how much of a symbol of national distinctiveness Scots is, there have been four centuries of decline in its prestige as a language to be used in what Kloss termed *Sachprosa*: non-literary prose. Some varieties passing through the standardization process may have too small or insignificant a literary corpus. As Joseph suggests, this may act to their disadvantage. This is not the case for Scots, however. On this occasion, there is too much literary activity, with too little non-literary. This warps the perception of the variety. Moreover, over a century of mass education in English has led many people to see not only that the path to advancement leads through Standard English, but also that Scots itself is merely a corrupt dialect of the standard. A view held by Scots speakers, as much as by those who do not speak the variety, this prejudice is extremely difficult to break through.

Finally, and most sadly, part of the fault lies with the language planners themselves: in their characters, and in their relationships with each other. Of course, language planning in any speech community is inevitably a heated process, given the range of decisions which any organization must take. The level of animosity and dissent produced within the very small community of activists in Scotland is remarkable, however. Moreover, in concentrating so much on corpus planning, often of a highly purist nature, most language planners have ignored the real and glaring need for Scots: status and acquisition planning. This may, of course, be because some planners have recognized the problems about status already mentioned, and prefer instead to 'perfect' their Scots, rather than embarking on what could be interpreted as a quixotic errand.

Yet Scotland remains, as an idea and a reality. Because of the slant of this book, it might sometimes be assumed that language is the sole means to construct a nationality. This is, of course, not the case. Some countries, such as Norway, and, to some extent, Wales, have a strong sense of their own cultural and linguistic identity as ethnic nations. Whilst there is an ethnic and linguistic sense to the expression of Scottish identity, Scotland comes much closer to the idea of a civic nation, where to belong is to a large extent expressed through residence and attachment. In the future, it might be possible to have a coherent language policy for the country, including Scots. More achievable, however, might be the establishment of *de jure* status for a particularly Scottish form of English.

At present, there is *de facto* recognition for Scottish Standard English, a variety which incorporates a considerable amount of Scots lexis, and some grammatical features, into a basically English framework. It would be quite possible for this to be developed in a more Scots direction, along the lines of Bokmål in comparison with Riksmaal in twentieth-century

Norway. Yet even this would take considerable status and acquisition planning beforehand; it would be very unlikely not to meet with considerable opposition.

8.6   Conclusion

The development of national consciousness often has a linguistic element; never more so than in the nationalist climate which has been dominant around the world since 1789. There are certainly other ways in which nationality can be expressed; none of them has the immediacy which language use has, however.

Yet the idea of a monolingual and monocultural population, united in its use of a much-revered national language, may be just that: an idea. All four of the case-studies examined in this chapter exhibit tendencies towards either multilingualism or the triumph of a hegemonic language. On almost all occasions, language planning has been shown both to be a product, and to some extent a victim, of political ideology, of whatever type. Language planning is a near-essential element in nation-building; so essential, in fact, that it is sometimes difficult to distinguish between the nation and its languages.

In the final chapter, some of the central points of the book will be reviewed, along with a discussion of the impact of the globalization process on the idea of the linguistic nation-state.

9
Conclusion

9.1 Language, nation and power

In theory, all varieties of language are equal. In essence, all human beings have the same ability to communicate all ideas, both abstract and concrete. Yet this is not our perception of the way the (linguistic) world works. We all assume that some varieties of language, more importantly, that some languages, possess greater economic and political resources than do others. The source of these inequalities is power: political, economic, cultural, historical and social power. This power can often be expressed in terms of national prestige.

From the very earliest written records, it can be assumed that the language variety of some individuals or groups was preferred over that of others; in those contemporary cultures which have been least influenced by the western model of 'progress', it is still true that the language of some members – often that of the 'elders' – will be preferred over all others, more often than not because of its identification with all that is 'true' or 'good' about the group. In an age in which mass literacy prevails over large parts of the world, in which some polities and regions wield greater economic and political power than do others, in which language is associated strongly with adherence to, and obligation towards, a particular polity or way of life, the consequences of these attitudes are inevitably much more wide-ranging.

Since the late middle ages, western Europe has been embarked upon an experiment whereby a nation (previously rather more like a corporation which controlled a territory according to its own rules) became identified with all of the people who lived within a polity's frontiers, no matter how that polity was formed. The 'citizens' of this nation were assumed to have more in common with each other in terms of culture and, most importantly, mutual obligation, even if, inevitably, it was impossible for any citizen ever to meet all the other citizens. This vision was extremely powerful, and, by the end of the nineteenth century, had become the view held by the citizens of all the nations most affected by the experiment. Since these nations were the most powerful at the time, they were also the most emulated (whether voluntarily or by force). What had been one option of viewing a territory became the norm, if not obligatory.

Central to the idea of an 'imagined nation', this new sense of mutual sharing and obligation, was language. Identification of a particular language (or language variety) with a particular nation became a central part of the nationalist project in many places – particularly Europe. The problem, inevitably, was that the question of *what* language, *what* language variety, was most representative of the nation would be asked. Since even today it is rare to find a nation where the citizenry share one mother tongue (and it is practically impossible to find a majority population, all speaking the same language, where there is no dialectal or sociolectal variation), tension between users of one language (variety) and another was (and is) inevitable.

Inherent in this is language planning. In an age of mass-literacy, and a large-scale capitalist print industry, standards of language uniformity inevitably develop. The processes of acculturation and elaboration, of Ausbau, were illustrated in Chapters 3–7. In circumstantial language standardizations (those which developed without the conscious input of language planning actors, even if the literary and didactic activities of the elite did affect language through their attitudes and usage), a particular variety of a language became synecdochic for that language. This variety was then developed by elites, again often by unconscious or semi-conscious usage and attitude, to make it the (perceived) equal in appropriateness and 'elegance' of languages whose speakers or writings (in the case of a classical language) possessed more (cultural or economic) power. In engineered language standardizations, much the same developments occurred, although the time involved was much briefer, the actions of language planning agents were much more conscious and the dangers for the language variety itself, should the planning be less than successful, were concomitantly greater.

The creation of a standard, national, variety of a language is undoubtedly a means by which a nation imagines itself; in intangible ways it can give the nation, so constituted and associated, considerable power, both internally, and on the international stage. Its effects on other language varieties, or languages, spoken within the boundaries of the 'nation' can be disastrous, however.

Part of this problem can be associated with the difficulties, exemplified in Chapter 3, over what we mean by a language or a dialect. In western Europe, during this crucial period, this was particularly acute with language varieties which were borderline Abstand with the 'national' variety, but which were obvious relatives, examples of which being Occitan, Low German and Scots. Scots is, as we saw in Chapter 5, an especially poignant example of the process, since its near-standardized 'national' variety of the early modern period failed in its competition with its exonormic relative, Standard English. To see why, it is profitable to compare Scots with the development of Modern Norwegian (of whatever variety) in Chapter 7, in relation to Danish. Perhaps for geographical reasons, Norway was able to maintain its geographical identity and integrity in a way that Scotland never could. The unification process between English and Scots (and also, although this was always less successful and more contingent, England and Scotland) was due to a very large extent to changes in power structures both in the island of Britain itself (the accession of a King of Scots to the throne of England and the associated movement towards the richer and more attractive south, whether ideologically or physically, of intellectual and governmental elites), and in Europe as a whole (the association of the majority populations – in particular their elites – of both England and Scotland with the Protestant camp). Norwegian's 'declaration of independence', however, came during a period of disassociation both with the previous hegemonic force/imperial power Denmark, and the new power Sweden, at the same time as the idea of nationalism was becoming increasingly fashionable – indeed, dominant – in that part of Europe. For these 'kin tongues' the future looked (and looks) increasingly bleak, unless they can be associated with a nationalism (or even regionalism) which also has considerable cultural and economic power underlying it.

For fully Abstand varieties, also spoken within the national territory, the situation was generally equally bleak, if not more so, primarily because, if the minority speaking the Abstand variety had significant levels of economic power, they could be perceived as a threat to the majority community's hegemony (or, put a different way, their vision of themselves as *the* nation). A good example of this, within a European framework, is the fate of the Magyar-speaking minority of Transylvania, after the transfer of that territory to Romania, as discussed in Chapter 2. When the Abstand-speaking minority did not have access to economic power, their fate was often to be ignored, or to be actively encouraged, sometimes forcibly, to conform to the norm, activities which have regularly been attempted against speakers of Basque, in both Spain and France.

This final situation could have particularly significant – not to say violent – results when the Abstand-speaking population were associated with what to most speakers of the hegemonic language would have seemed as an alien, perhaps even an inimical, ideology or belief-system. Particularly challenging were those situations where the 'minority' was actually a majority in its own 'national' territory, not recognized by the hegemonic nation. As we saw in Chapter 7, the situation of speakers of the Irish language in the early modern period is especially apposite. The overwhelming majority of Irish speakers were adherents to the Catholic tradition, when the majority of English people had become Protestants; the cultural traditions of Ireland, ignoring the religious situation entirely, did not suit English ideas of mercantile capitalist progress; many Irish speakers viewed the Protestant succession to the throne as an imposition, maintaining their loyalty to the legitimate, Catholic, claimants; the very presence of an 'alien' language in an English dominion was inimical to the idea, beginning to spread at this time, of a homogenous nation. Deprived by war and exile of their native elites, their economy associated with subsistence agriculture (in particular the sole cultivation of a crop which bore the deadly possibility of failure), Irish speakers were the first – perhaps the only – people of western Europe to have suffered imperialism associated with an apparently 'progressive' ideology entirely alien to them, part of whose ideological precepts was associated with acquisition of, and adherence to, a particular language.

These problems were exported to the rest of the world, as part of the western European model of societal development. In those areas where European settlers never overwhelmed local population, either in numbers or in cultural force, there was an added problem: the local languages had generally not been developed in the same ways the hegemonic languages had. Moreover, the new territories, as they became states, as (overt) European (and European offshoot) imperialism retreated, were often faced with the problem of creating 'nations' from disparate sources. In Africa in particular, new sovereign territories came into being whose populations had practically nothing in common with each other in cultural terms – never mind linguistic. The elites of these new nations had to make a range of choices over language policy, any of which might have effects for both good and ill for their countries. If they chose the nationist solution of employing the language(s) of the former imperialists in order to avoid ethnolinguistic conflict, not only was the cause of nationalism not served (in other words, it was difficult to distinguish between any number of particular nations which had been ruled by another nation), there was also the danger that the use of a language, known only by a small group, almost all of whom would be members of the elite, would create a situation not dissimilar to that under the former imperialists (as well as to the agrarian literate societies which preceded the modern nations of Europe), with a small caste of influentials mediating information to a divorced majority.

If the nationalist route of choosing a national vernacular (or vernaculars) as the national language (or languages) was taken, there was a considerable danger that ethnolinguistic tensions would develop, particularly, perhaps, when a number of almost equally matched groups, whether in terms of power or population, was present. The bitter civil war fought in Nigeria in the late 1960s is an example of what can happen when nationalist impulses in cultural and linguistic terms are given free rein by some, or all, of the population. This delicate balance – initiated in the rather more receptive environment of western Europe – has been played out repeatedly throughout the world in the last 200 years. For good and ill, language is a central element in the construction of a nation and its identity.

9.2   Language, nation and power: the future

As we saw in Chapter 7, the Irish republican party, Sinn Féin, saw itself as standing for the creation of an Ireland of autonomous, Irish-speaking communities, where the best parts of the Irish past (as analysed and interpreted by them) would be replicated in the future, through the direct action of the Irish people itself. This desire, although seldom so overtly expressed, was also present in a variety of nationalist/liberation movements around the world, from Zionism, to the Self-Help movement in India, to the Liberation Theology of Latin America in the 1980s. Not all of these movements could have a fully blown linguistic element (as we saw in Chapter 2, this would have been disastrous for India, for instance); it is interesting to note, however, that it was those nationalist/liberation movements which had the strongest association of language and autonomous development that were most successful, even if, for instance, the self-help ideology of the Zionist kibbutz system was soon downplayed by mainstream Israeli politicians.

Will movements of this type be able to make such a connection between language, ethnic culture and economic autonomy in the years to come? Will the intrinsic connection between nation and language be such a significant feature of world power politics in the future? The short answer is 'no'. For better *and* for worse, there are few polities whose domestic economic system is not interwoven with the world macro-economic system, or which will not be so in the very near future. As we have seen in a number of the case-studies discussed in this book, people will always move to find work, or better chances for bettering their position. In most parts of the world, such a movement has almost inevitably meant the acquisition of skills in another language or languages. We are likely to see more and more of this process taking place as globalization increases. More striking, however, is a point made in Phillipson (2003). In the future (indeed, in the present in large parts of western and central Europe) many people may 'migrate' from one culture, one language community, to another when they enter their place of employment, even when they spend the rest of their lives 'at home'. What are the consequences of this set of developments?

In the first place, the hegemonic languages of European imperialism may succumb (at least in terms of their influence external to their native areas) to the greater hegemonic force of World English, supported by the presence of the United States as the only superpower, militarily and economically. As I write this, even the United States' ideological enemies are regularly forced to use the American language. In less dangerous arenas, it would be quixotic to attempt to conduct trade outside your language community in anything other than English. It is this reality which has fuelled the rearguard action by Francophonie within its own boundaries to maintain the use of French in cultural and business domains. An especially striking example of this is in the 'research' domain suggested by Kloss, discussed in Chapters 3 and 4, where the French government in particular has used both 'carrot' and 'stick' to encourage France-based academics to use French when publishing research, particularly in the natural sciences, where the 'victory' of English has been near-total. Yet even in Francophonie, the importance of teaching English as a foreign language to children has had to be fully recognized.

Yet I, for one, am suspicious at the extent to which globalization will mean linguistic homogenization. As Europe began to unite in the 1980s and 1990s, it became increasingly apparent that, along with a rather monolithic governmental structure, the ongoing changes in the conception of the nation state as sovereign were also allowing some of the smaller, previously submerged, nations of Europe to re-emerge, often along with their languages. Of course it would be a foolhardy person indeed who would expect that even Scots, quite a major language in terms of population for Europe, would ever achieve the status of English, French or German; this would, I would suggest, be even less likely for Walloon (spoken in Belgium and Luxembourg), Samogetic (spoken in the southern Baltic region) or Friulian (spoken in Italy and Slovenia), to name but three of the lesser-used languages of Europe. Nor would the overwhelming majority of any of these language communities ever question the importance to the population of learning a major language. But the use of the 'home' language in 'home' domains – including print and other media – has actually been made easier by the globalized technology which might have been expected to eclipse it. In the end, the success, or lack thereof, of any such initiative does rest, to a large extent, on the will of the language community involved. It also demands that the language planning agents involved plan intelligently, not neglecting status and acquisition planning, as well as knowing which battles to pick. A good example of this can be found with Luxembourgish. At least at present, status planning for the language has accepted the external role of French within the community, as well as its status as carrier of culture (although not, now, the *sole* carrier of culture).

Moreover, as was noted in Chapter 2, increased freedom of movement has meant that you will find people speaking a variety of languages of recent immigration in almost any city of the globalized world. Although it is very likely that these speakers, or their descendants, will eventually be assimilated into the majority linguistic culture, they will always, it can be predicted, be replaced by new immigrants, speaking their own languages.

Yet I may be painting too rosy a picture here: even the poorest area in Europe (or in European-initiated areas, such as north America) still has more access to the exercise of economic (although not necessarily political) power. Many people in the world today will, as Skutnaab-Kangas (2000) suggests, become victims of 'linguistic genocide'. It could therefore be argued that the ideological equation of language and nation along European lines has had profoundly positive and negative effects for the development of both languages and their speakers' economic position in the world. In a sense, the presence of English as *the* language of globalization has only been made possible by the previous nationalist language planning and language policy initiatives. The equation of language and nation may not always survive; the equation of language with *power* inevitably will.

Notes

1 An Introduction: *Diglossia* and its Aftermath

1. Shou-yi (1961) describes an ongoing process in the history of Chinese letters whereby the need for comprehensibility was always in conflict with the desire to mimic and match the language of the classics of Chinese governmental and social philosophy. At times, such as during the introduction of Buddhist ideas into the empire (1961: chapter 24), there was a vernacular impulse to speak 'directly to the people', analogous to undercurrents in Christian tradition; like Christianity, this impulse often foundered upon a desire to match the dignified register of their opponents.

2 Nation and Language

1. The present royal family are not terribly ancient; nor are many of the apparently ancient rituals associated with them. Appearance is all in these circumstances.
2. The following is based primarily on material from Barta *et al.* (1975).
3. This situation is rendered more complex by the fact that a development of Dutch – Afrikaans – has become the native language of many people in the territory, including many who do not have any Dutch ancestors. Afrikaans could be more readily compared to the creoles spoken widely in areas of former and continuing imperialism.
4. The following is based primarily on material in Davies (2001).

3 Language and Dialect

1. Many scholars would take issue with a blanket acceptance of Ferguson's conception of pidgin genesis. That does not in any way invalidate the categorization, however.
2. It can be assumed, although it is never explicitly stated, that there is a hierarchy of use, since he does not employ some symbols when others have been employed in his formulae.
3. Ferguson does not actually discuss the abbreviation *i*; from context, and from Stewart's work, we can assume that it means 'international', however.
4. Discussion of the nature of language was at the heart of the life's work of Kloss. Because he wrote mainly in German, this work is less well known in the English-speaking world than it should be. Because of the problem of comprehension, most references in the following will be to his 1967 article.
5. There have been a number of attempts at providing versions of these originally German terms in a range of other languages (most notably those of Muljačić 1981, 1986, 1989; Goebl 1989). There is a considerable amount to be said for retaining the original German usages, however, as long as they are understood as metaphors for an underlying concept. Further developments of considerable merit from some of Kloss' ideas are to be found in Haarmann 1986 and Trudgill 2002.

6. Naturally, recent developments have made the last example particularly problematical. A better example of this phenomenon might be sought in the relationship between the two standard forms of modern Armenian current in the Soviet era. One form of Armenian was preferred in the émigré communities which came about as a result of the 'ethnic cleansing' of Anatolia in the early years of the twentieth century in particular; there is some evidence that its western features may have suited these communities better. The other variety of Armenian was prevalent in the Armenian Soviet Socialist Republic, and may have represented the eastern dialects of the language spoken there rather better (Cowe 1992). Given the lack of communication between the communities, the divergences between them were solidified quickly.

7. Kloss and Haarmann also suggest (1984: 21) the term *How come? languages* (German *Wieso-sprachen*) for this phenomenon.

8. '... zwar weniger ausgebaut ist als eine Ausbausprache, aber mehr als ein Normaldialekt' (my translation).

9. 'Ein Normaldialekt ist in Deutschland im wesentlichen beschränkt im schriftlichen Gebrauch auf Belletristik und im Rundfunk auf Unterhaltung (Humor und leichtere Bellelettristik); er ist mehr oder weniger ausgeschlossen von (z.B.) Presse, Schule, Kirche, Film, politischen Körperschaften mit Ausnahmen allenfalls der Kommunalparlamente' (my translation).

10.

Anwendungsbereich	Anwendung eines Ausbaudialekts ('Halbsprache') möglich	Fast nur Anwendung einer Ausbausprache (Vollsprache) denkbar
1. Kirche	Predigten, zumal Abendpredigten, und Kasualien	Sonntagmorgenpredigt; Liturgie
2. Parlament	Diskussionen, zumal in Ausschlüssen und in Kommunalparlamenten	vorbereite Ansprachen; Berichte von Regierungsvertretern
3. Rundfunk (außer den auch den Normaldialekt offenstehenden Unterhaltungssendungen)	gehobene Mda.-Dichtung einschl. Hörspielen; einfacher Nachrichtendienst; volkstümlich belehrende Vorträge, z.B für Bauern	wissenschaftliche Belehrung
4. Literatur (außerhalb der auch dem Normaldialekt zugänglichen Bereiche von Humor und Lyrik)	Gehobene Belletristik (einschließlich Romanen und ernsthaften Schauspielen). Vereinzelte volkstümliche Sachprosa, z.B. Broschüren zur Heimatkunde oder Mundartliteratur	der größere Teil der Belletristik; fast das ganze Sachschriftum
5. Presse	vereinzelte Zeitschriften oder Zeitschriften-Rubriken nichthumoristischen, zumal literarischen, biographischen oder religiösen Inhalts	große Mehrheit der Zeitschriften, alle Zeitungen
6. Schule	Fibeln und andere Schulbücher für Schulanfänger	das Gros der SchulbuchLiteratur
7. Film	leichte Unterhaltungsfilme, zumal Lustspiele	das Gros der Produktion, zumal der anspruchsvollen Filme

6   Language Planning: Process

1. The second edition of the *Oxford English Dictionary* (Simpson and Weiner 1989: s.v. *envision*) provides some British background to *envision*, dating its first appearance to Lytton Strachey (an Englishman) in 1921. Its use in the rest of the twentieth century – at least according to this source – was patchy, but still international. It would be interesting to see material on this usage from the 1990s.
2. Similar comments might be made about the first Language Congress for Turkish, as described by Landau (1993). Ostensibly a rather dry academic congress on the history of the Turkish language, participants regularly stressed the non-Muslim and ancient nature of the language. No doubt these views were expressed to shore up the language reforms of the Kemalist regime by stressing continuity in the face of actual considerable (and radical) change. This topic will be discussed in greater detail in Chapter 7.
3. In America, as we will see, it was the opinion-forming nature of this new lower Middle Class elite which attempted to enforce linguistic norms. In England, given different constitutional and political conditions, the development, whilst analogous, was not quite the same.
4. A point also emphasized by Norway's pre-War fascist movement, the *Nasjonal Samling*, where the uniformed wing of the party, which also served as the bodyguard of the *fører*, Quisling, were named the *hird*, the name given to the bodyguard of the ancient Norse kings (Dahl 1999).

7   Language Planning: Testing the Models

1. The following analysis derives material from Bach (1970) and Wells (1985).
2. This territory had the strange advantage from a purist point of view of coming to standard High German as a relative outsider, since so many of its inhabitants, from the highest nobility down, spoke Low German as their mother tongue, but had a peculiarly developed sense of the appropriateness of High German inculcated by the Church (Wells 1985: 310).
3. Perhaps inevitably, this party structure has also come into being with the descendant of Landsmaal, *Nynorsk*. There are Landsmaal ultras, who will not accept any changes to Aasen's project. Often they refer to their ultra-nynorsk as *Høgnorsk* 'high, elevated Norwegian'. They are extremely scathing towards other official varieties of Norwegian, which they often term *unorsk*, 'unNorwegian', or *ikkje-norsk*, 'not Norwegian'; *Bokmål* and *Riksmaal* are often referred to not as *dansk-norsk*, 'Dano-Norwegian', a term which is now somewhat out of date, but is certainly neither insulting nor controversial, but rather as *norsk-dansk*, suggesting that these varieties are 'mere' Danish with a Norwegian patina. The Høgnorsk party is much outweighed by the moderates; like all extremists their minority status is probably taken as proof of their 'correctness' and ideological purity in relation to others, however.
4. As Mango (1999) points out, Mustafa Kemal himself could barely call himself Ottoman: his father was a very minor official; as both enemies and friends remarked, he was linguistically Turkish but may not have been an ethnic Turk. This was not uncommon, however. Many of the greatest Ottoman leaders, such as Muhammad Ali, the reformer of Egypt in the early nineteenth century,

were ethnic Albanians (as were, it should be noted, a number of early Greek nationalists). An Albanian or Slav (perhaps even Greek) background cannot be ruled out for Kemal, particularly since his family background was in the then main city of Macedonia, Salonika (now the Greek city of Thessaloniki). What is important, however, is that he admired Anatolian peasant life and, in later life, when settled in Ankara (chosen as capital for strategic reasons, but doubt-less ideologically preferable to a believer in 'pure Turkishness' in favour of cosmopolitan Istanbul), became a keen farmer himself. Nevertheless, it would be profitable to compare him with the avid reformers and proselytizers of Afrikaans in late nineteenth-century South Africa discussed above, who were often French rather than Dutch in origin. Like them, Kemal did not have an emotional stake in the preservation of a High culture and language (Dutch or Ottoman).

5. The 'sun-language theory' (*Günes-Dil Teorisi*) to which Atatürk subscribed towards the end of his life is too eccentric to be described here. Yet, as Lewis (1999) suggests, its claim to trace all languages to a common Turkish source may have been an attempt on Atatürk's part to rein in the excesses of neologism by 'proving' the Turkish source of all borrowings.

6. Much of the preceding has been based upon the discussions in Kutscher (1982: chapter 8) and Sáenz-Badillos (1993: chapter 8).

7. Much of the data in the following is based on the findings of Levine (1990), Fishman (1991) and Bourhis (2001).

8. That is not to say that some Irish Parliamentary Party politicians were not sympathetic to the revival of the Irish language in a Home-Rule Ireland, as discussed by Ó Huallacháin (1994), pp. 49–51.

9. This semiotic linguistic nationalism is maintained in the names of the two successor parties to the Sinn Féin of the revolutionary period, Fianna Fáil and Fine Gael, which are still the most popular political groups in the present Irish Republic, as well as in the name of the Irish Parliament – the *Dáil* – and the Prime Minister – *taoiseach* – among others. It should be noted that these terms are used exclusively, even by non-Irish commentators. No matter the state of spoken Irish in the country, there is no doubt that the victory of the expression of national separation through language has been near total.

8   Language and Nation-building

1. Interestingly, this confusion is often used by supporters of English as the official language to pillory their opponents. I am sure it is the case that many such supporters have no desire other than the achievement of *de jure* recognition for English; it is nevertheless true that many of those who contribute to the websites of the supporting organizations, as well as the slant on some of the news stories they cover, appear to have a decided anti-immigrant language flavour.

2. Much of the following information has been derived from the work of the contributors to Smith (1990).

3. Lithuania is a peculiar case: although the union between Poland and the Grand Duchy of Lithuania was carried out by an ethnic Lithuanian, the power base of the territory shifted inexorably either towards Poland proper, or towards Polonized natives of Baltic or east Slav ethnicity. This explains why the Vilnius

area has been so argued about, if not fought over, over the last hundred years, as Zielińska (2002) discusses.

4. The following draws heavily upon the analysis of Pipes (1964) and Smith (1999) in particular.

5. Scots and Gaelic are both recognized as lesser-used languages by the Council of Europe *European Charter for Regional or Minority Languages* (ETS 148), which, in the case of Scots, was ratified by the United Kingdom in March 2001. Unfortunately, whilst Gaelic is accorded support based upon Part III of the charter, which means that member states where the language is spoken are obliged to give it considerable support in terms of education, media and government itself, Scots is accorded support based only upon Part II, which means, essentially, that the language's existence is recognized, but without much more than encouragement to member states to give its speakers some support. Ironically, the Good Friday Agreement of 1998 has meant that the Scots dialects of Ulster, both in Northern Ireland and the present Republic, are accorded much greater recognition by both the United Kingdom government and the Northern Irish Assembly than are the dialects of Scots spoken in its 'homeland'.

Bibliography

Abd-el-Jawad, R.S. Hassan, 1992. 'Is Arabic a pluricentric language?'. In Clyne, Michael (ed.), *Pluricentric Languages. Differing Norms in Different Nations* (Berlin and New York: Mouton de Gruyter, 1992) 261–303.

Adams, J.N., *Bilingualism and the Latin Language* (Cambridge: Cambridge University Press, 2003).

Allan, Alasdair, 'Scots Spellin: Ettlin efter the Quantum Lowp', *English World-Wide* 16 (1995) 61–103.

——, New Founs fae Auld Larachs. Leid-plannin for Scots (Unpublished PhD dissertation, University of Aberdeen, 1998).

Anderson, Benedict, *Imagined Communities. Reflections on the Origin and Spread of Nationalism*. 2nd edn (London and New York: Verso, 1991).

——, *The Spectre of Comparisons. Nationalism, Southeast Asia and the World* (London: Verso, 1998).

Andersson, Lars-Gunnar and Peter Trudgill, *Bad Language* (London: Penguin, 1992).

d'Ardenne, S.R.T.O. (ed.), *Þe Liflade ant te passiun of Seinte Iuliene* (London: Oxford University Press, 1961).

Armstrong, John A., *Ukrainian Nationalism*. 2nd edn (New York: Columbia University Press, 1963).

Ascherson, Neal, *Black Sea: The Birthplace of Civilisation and Barbarism* (London: Random House, 1996).

Bach, Adolf, *Geschichte der deutschen Sprache* (Heidelberg: Quelle & Meyer, 1970).

Bailey, Guy, 'The Relationship between African American Vernacular English and White Vernaculars in the American South: A Sociocultural History and Some Phonological Evidence'. In Lanehart, Sonja L. (ed.), *Sociocultural and Historical Contexts of African American English* (Amsterdam: John Benjamins, 2001) 53–92.

Balibar, Renée, *L'institution du français. Essai sur le colinguisme des carolingiens à la république* (Paris: Presses Universitaires de France, 1985).

bar-Adon, Aaron, *The Rise and Decline of a Dialect. A Study in the Revival of Modern Hebrew* (The Hague, Paris and New York: Mouton, 1975).

Barber, Charles, *The English Language: a Historical Introduction* (Cambridge: Cambridge University Press, 1993).

Barron, Dennis, *The English-Only Question. An Official Language for Americans?* (New Haven and London: Yale University Press, 1990).

Barta, István, Iván T. Berend, Péter Hanák, Miklós Lackó, László Makkai, Zsuzsa L. Nagy and György Ránki, *A History of Hungary* (London and Wellingborough: Collet's, 1975).

Bartlett, Robert, *The Making of Europe: Conquest, Colonization and Cultural Change 950–1350* (London: Allen Lane, 1993).

Bauer, Otto, *Die Nationalitätenfrage und die Sozialdemokratie* (Vienna: Europaverlag, 1924).

Baugh, Albert C. and Thomas Cable, *A History of the English Language*. 4th edn (London: Routledge, 1993).

212   *Bibliography*

Baugh, John, *Beyond Ebonics. Linguistic Pride and Racial Prejudice* (New York and Oxford: Oxford University Press, 2000).

Beal, Joan C., *English Pronunciation in the Eighteenth Century: Thomas Spence's Grand Repository of the English Language* (Oxford: Clarendon Press, 1999).

Bennett, David H., *The Party of Fear. From Nativist Movements to the New Right in American History* (Chapel Hill, NC: The University of North Carolina Press, 1988).

ben Yehuda, Eliezer, *A Complete Dictionary of Ancient and Modern Hebrew; Prolegomena.* Popular edition (Jerusalem: ben-Yehuda Hozaa-La'Or Le zecher Eliezer ben-Yehuda, 1948).

Berg, Guy, *'Mir wëlle bleiwe, wat mir sin': Soziolinguistische und sprachtypologische Betrachtungen zur luxemburgischen Mehrsprachigkeit* (Tübingen: Niemeyer, 1993).

Berlin, Ira, *Many Thousands Gone. The First Two Centuries of Slavery in North America* (Cambridge, MA: Harvard University Press, 1998).

Bernstein, Basil, 'Social Class, Language and Socialization'. In Giglioli, Pier Paolo (ed.), *Language and Social Context* (Harmondsworth: Penguin, 1972) 157–78.

Blackall, Eric A., *The Emergence of German as a Literary Language 1700–1775* (Cambridge: Cambridge University Press, 1959).

Bonfiglio, Thomas Paul, *Race and the Rise of Standard American* (Berlin and New York: Mouton de Gruyter, 2002).

Bourdieu, Pierre, *Language and Symbolic Power.* Edited and Introduced by John B. Thompson; translated by Gino Raymond and Matthew Adamson (Cambridge: Polity Press, 1991).

Bourhis, R.H., 'Reversing Language Shift in Quebec'. In Fishman, Joshua A. (ed.), *Can Threatened Languages be Saved?* (Clevedon: Multilingual Matters, 1991).

Braunmüller, Kurt, *De nordiske språk.* 2nd edn, translated by John Ole Askedal (Oslo: Novus forlag, 1998).

Browning, Robert, *Medieval and Modern Greek.* 2nd edn (Cambridge: Cambridge University Press, 1983).

Buck, Carl Darling, *The Greek Dialects* (Chicago, IL: University of Chicago Press, 1955).

Bucken-Knapp, Gregg, *Elites, Language, and the Politics of Identity: The Norwegian Case in Comparative Perspective* (Albany, NY: State University of New York Press, 2003).

Cahill, Thomas, *How the Irish Saved Civilisation: The Untold Story of Ireland's Heroic Role from The Fall of Rome to The Rise of Medieval Europe* (London: Hodder and Stoughton, 1995).

Cameron, Deborah, *Verbal Hygiene* (London and New York: Routledge, 1995).

Carmichael, Cathie, 'Coming to Terms with the Past: Language and Nationalism in Russia and its Neighbours'. In Barbour, Stephen and Cathie Carmichael (eds), *Language and Nationalism in Europe* (Oxford: Oxford University Press, 2000) 264–79.

Clark, Urszula, *War Words. Language, History and the Disciplining of English* (Oxford: Elsevier Science, 2001).

Cooper, Robert L., *Language Planning and Social Change* (Cambridge: Cambridge University Press, 1989).

Cowe, S. Peter, 'Amēn teł hay kay: Armenian as a pluricentric language'. In Clyne, Michael (ed.), *Pluricentric Languages. Differing Norms in Different Nations* (Berlin and New York: Mouton de Gruyter, 1992) 325–45.

Crowley, Tony, *The Politics of Discourse: The Standard Language Question in British Cultural Debates* (London: Macmillan, 1989).

——, *Language in History. Theories and Texts* (London: Routledge, 1996).

——, 'Curiouser and curiouser: Falling Standards in The Standard English Debate'. In Bex, Tony and R.J. Watts (eds), *Standard English. The Widening Debate* (London and New York: Routledge, 1999) 271–82.

Crowley, Tony (ed.), *The Politics of Language in Ireland 1366–1922* (London: Routledge, 2000).

Dahl, Hans Fredrik, *Quisling: A Study in Treachery*. Translated by Anne-Marie Stanton-Ife (Cambridge: Cambridge University Press, 1999).

Davies, Norman, *Heart of Europe: the Past in Poland's Present*. 2nd edn (Oxford: Oxford University Press, 2001).

Davies, Norman and Roger Moorhouse, *Microcosm: Portrait of a Central European City* (London: Jonathan Cape, 2002).

Davis, Norman, 'A Paston Hand', *Review of English Studies* NS 3 (1952) 209–21.

——, 'The language of the Pastons', *Proceedings of the British Academy* 40 (1954) 119–44.

Del Valle, Sandra, *Language Rights and the Law in the United States. Finding Our Voices* (Clevedon: Multilingual Matters, 2003).

Deumert, Ana and Wim Vandenbussche (eds), *Germanic Standardizations: Past to Present* (Amsterdam and Philadelphia, PA: Benjamins, 2003).

Devitt, A.J., *Standardizing Written English: Diffusion in the Case of Scotland 1520–1659* (Cambridge: Cambridge University Press, 1989).

Dillard, J.L., *Toward a Social History of American English* (Berlin and New York: Mouton, 1985).

——, *A history of American English* (Harlow: Longman, 1992).

Dobson, E.J., 'Early Modern Standard English', *Transactions of the Philological Society* 53 (1955) 25–54.

——, *English Pronunciation 1500–1700*. 2 vols, 2nd edn (Oxford: Oxford University Press, 1968).

Donaldson, William, *Popular literature in Victorian Scotland: Language, Fiction and The Press* (Aberdeen: Aberdeen University Press, 1986).

Dorian, Nancy C., *Language Death: The Life Cycle of a Scottish Gaelic Dialect* (Philadelphia, PA: University of Pennsylvania Press, 1981).

Du Nay, Alain, André Du Nay and Arpad Kosztin, *Transylvania and the Rumanians. Transylvania: Fiction and Reality; the Daco-Roman Legend* (Hamilton, Ontario: Matthias Corvinus Publishing, 1997).

Durkacz, Victor Edward, *The Decline of the Celtic Languages* (Edinburgh: John Donald, 1983).

Ehrlich, Konrad (ed.), *Sprache in Faschismus* (Frankfurt am Main: Suhrkamp, 1989).

Estraikh, Gennady, *Soviet Yiddish. Language Planning and Linguistic Development* (Oxford: Clarendon Press, 1999).

Eyongetah Mbuagbaw, Tambi, Robert Brain and Robin H. Palmer, *A History of The Cameroon*. 2nd edn (Harlow: Longman, 1987).

Fasold, Ralph, *The Sociolinguistics of Society* (Oxford: Blackwell, 1987).

Fässler, Isabel, The evolution of written Scots and the perception of spelling standardisation in the North-East of Scotland (Unpublished MA dissertation, University of Lausanne, 1998).

Fellman, Jack, *The Revival of a Classical Tongue: Eliezer Ben Yehuda and The Modern Hebrew Language* (The Hague: Mouton, 1973).

Ferguson, Charles A., 'Diglossia'. In Giglioli, Pier Paolo (ed.), *Language and Social Context* (Harmondsworth: Penguin, 1972) 232–51; also *Word* 15 (1959) 325–40.

Ferguson, Charles A., 'National Sociolinguistic Profile Formulas'. In Bright, William (ed.), *Sociolinguistic. Proceedings of the UCLA Sociolinguistics Conference, 1964* (The Hague and Paris, Mouton, 1966) 309–24.

——, 'Language Development'. In Fishman, J., C. Ferguson and J. Das Gupta (eds), *Language Problems of Developing Nations* (New York: Wiley, 1968).

Fierman, William, *Language Planning and National Development: the Uzbek Experience* (Berlin and New York: Mouton de Gruyter, 1991).

Figes, Orlando, *A People's Tragedy: The Russian Revolution, 1891–1924* (London: Jonathan Cape, 1996).

Fischer, David Hackett, *Albion's Seed: Four British Folkways in America* (New York: Oxford University Press, 1989).

Fisher, John H., *The Emergence of Standard English* (Lexington: University Press of Kentucky, 1996).

——, 'British and American, Continuity and Divergence'. In Algeo, J. (ed.), *The Cambridge History of the English Language*. Vol. VI. *English in North America* (Cambridge: Cambridge University Press, 2001) 59–85.

Fishman, Joshua A., 'Bilingualism with and without Diglossia', *Journal of Social Issues* 32 (1967) 29–38.

——, 'Nationality–Nationism and Nation–Nationism'. In Fishman, J., C. Ferguson and J. Das Gupta (eds), *Language Problems of Developing Nations* (New York: Wiley, 1968) 39–52.

——, *Language and Nationalism* (Rowley, MA: Newbury House, 1973).

——, *Reversing Language Shift* (Clevedon: Multilingual Matters, 1991).

Fishman, Joshua A. (ed.), *Readings in the Sociology of Language* (The Hague and Paris: Mouton, 1968).

——, *Can Threatened Languages be Saved?* (Clevedon: Multilingual Matters, 2001).

Fishman, Joshua A., Michael H. Gertner, Esther G. Lowy and William G. Milán, *The Rise and Fall of the Ethnic Revival: Perspectives on Language and Ethnicity* (Berlin, New York and Amsterdam: Mouton, 1985).

Forster, Peter G., *The Esperanto Movement* (The Hague, Paris and New York: Mouton, 1982).

de Fréin, Seán, *The Great Silence* (Dublin: Foilseacháin Náisúnta Teoranta, 1965).

Friedman, Victor A., 'The first philological conference for the establishment of the Macedonian alphabet and the Macedonian literary language: Its precedents and consequences'. In Fishman, J. (ed.), *The Earliest Stage of Language Planning. The First Congress Phenomenon* (Berlin and New York: Mouton de Gruyter, 1993) 159–80.

Gal, Susan, *Language Shift: Social Determinants of Linguistic Change in Bilingual Austria* (New York: Academic Press, 1979).

Gellner, Ernest, *Nations and Nationalism* (Oxford: Blackwell, 1983).

Gilles, Peter, 'Virtual Convergence and Dialect Levelling in Luxembourgish', *Folia Linguistica* 32 (1998) 69–82.

Glenny, Misha, *The Balkans 1804–1999. Nationalism, War and the Great Powers* (London: Granta Books, 1999).

Gneuss, Helmut, 'The Origin of Standard Old English and Æthelwold's School at Winchester', *Anglo-Saxon England* 1 (1972) 62–83.

Goebl, Hans, 'Quelques remarques relatives aux concepts *Abstand* et *Ausbau* de Heinz Kloss'. In Ammon, Ulrich (ed.), *Status and Function of Languages and Language Varieties* (Berlin and New York: Walter de Gruyter, 1989) 277–90.

Golea, Traian, *Transylvania and Hungarian Revisionism: A Discussion of Present-day Developments*. 2nd edn (Miami Beach: Romanian Historical Studies, 1988).

Görlach, Manfred, *Introduction to Early Modern English* (Cambridge: Cambridge University Press, 1991).

——, 'Regional and Social Variation'. In Lass, Roger (ed.), *The Cambridge History of the English Language*. Vol. III *1476–1776* (Cambridge: Cambridge University Press, 1999) 459–538.

Greenberg, Robert D., *Language and Identity in the Balkans. Serbo-Croatian and Its Disintegration* (Oxford: Oxford University Press, 2004).

Greenfield, Liah, *Nationalism. Five Roads to Modernity* (Cambridge, MA: Harvard University Press, 1992).

Grieder, Jerome B., *Intellectuals and The State in Modern China* (New York: The Free Press, 1981).

Grieve, C.M., *Contemporary Scottish Studies. First Series* (London: Leonard Parsons, 1926).

Groenke, Ulrich, 'How "archaic" is Modern Icelandic?' In Firchow, E.S. *et al.* (eds), *Studies by Einar Haugen: Presented on the Occasion of His 65th Birthday, April 19, 1971* (The Hague: Mouton, 1972) 253–60.

Haarmann, Harald, *Language in Ethnicity: A View of Basic Ecological Relations* (Berlin and New York: Mouton de Gruyter, 1986).

Hagan, Anette I., *Urban Scots Dialect Writing* (Oxford: Peter Lang, 2002).

Hartog, François, *The Mirror of Herodotus: The Representation of The Other in The Writing of History*. Translated by Janet Lloyd (Berkeley: University of California Press, 1988).

Haugen, Einar, *Language Conflict and Language Planning. The Case of Modern Norwegian* (Cambridge, MA: Harvard University Press, 1966).

——, 'Dialect, Language, Nation'. In Firchow, E.S., K. Grimstad, N. Hasselmo and W.A. O'Neil (eds), *Studies by Einar Haugen: Presented on the Occasion of His 65th Birthday, April 19, 1971* (The Hague: Mouton, 1966) 496–509.

——, *The Scandinavian Languages. An Introduction to their History* (London: Faber and Faber, 1976).

——, 'The Implementation of Corpus Planning: Theory and Practice'. In Cobarrubias, J. and J.A. Fishman (eds), *Progress in Language Planning: International Perspectives* (Berlin and New York: Mouton de Gruyter, 1983) 269–89.

Hochschild, Adam, *King Leopold's Ghost: A Story of Greed, Terror, and Heroism in Colonial Africa* (Boston: Houghton Mifflin, 1998).

Hock, Hans Heinrich and Brian D. Joseph, *Language History, Language Change and Language Relationship. An introduction to Historical and Comparative Linguistics* (Berlin and New York: Mouton de Gruyter, 1996).

Hoensch, Jörg, *A History of Modern Hungary: 1867–1994*. 2nd edn, translated by Kim Traynor (London and New York: Longman, 1996).

Holliday, Lloyd, 'The First Language Congress for Afrikaans'. In Fishman, J.A. (ed.), *The Earliest Stage of Language Planning. The 'First Congress' Phenomenon* (Berlin and New York: Mouton de Gruyter, 1993) 11–30.

Holm, John, *Pidgins and Creoles*. 2 vols (Cambridge: Cambridge University Press, 1988–1989).

Honey, John, *Does Accent Matter?* (London: Faber, 1989).

——, *Language is Power: The Story of Standard English and its Enemies* (London: Faber, 1997).

Hornjatkevyč, Andrij, 'The 1928 Ukrainian orthography'. In Fishman, J.A. (ed.), *The Earliest Stage of Language Planning. The 'First Congress' Phenomenon* (Berlin and New York: Mouton de Gruyter, 1993) 293–304.

Hsü, Immanuel C.Y., *The Rise of Modern China.* 6th edn (New York and Oxford: Oxford University Press, 2000).

Ó Huallacháin, Colmán, *The Irish and Irish – A Sociolinguistic Analysis of the Relationship Between a People and Their Language.* Edited by Rónán Ó Huallacháin and Patrick Conlan (Dublin: Irish Franciscan Provincial Office, 1994).

Hutton, Christopher, *Linguistics and the Third Reich* (London: Routledge, 1999).

Izikowitz, Karl G., 'Neighbours in Laos'. In Barth, F. (ed.), *Ethnic Groups and Boundaries. The Social Organization of Cultural Difference* (Bergen and Oslo: Universitets forlaget, 1969) 135–48.

Jack, Ronald D.S., 'The Language of Literary Materials: Origins to 1700'. In Jones, C. (ed.), *The Edinburgh History of the Scots Language* (Edinburgh: Edinburgh University Press, 1997) 213–63.

Jaffe, Alexandra, *Ideologies in Action. Language Politics on Corsica* (Berlin and New York: Mouton de Gruyter, 1999).

Jahr, Ernst Håkon, 'Norwegian'. In, Deumert, A. and W. Vandenbussche (eds), *Germanic Standardizations Past to Present* (Amsterdam and Philadelphia: Benjamins, 2003) 331–53.

Jahr, Ernst Håkon (ed.), *Nordisk og nedertysk. Språkkontakt og språkutvikling i Norden i seinmellomalderen* (Oslo: Novus forlag, 1995).

Janicki, Karol and Adam Jaworski, 'Language purism and propaganda: The First Congress for Polish'. In Fishman, J.A. (ed.), *The Earliest Stage of Language Planning. The First Congress Phenomenon* (Berlin and New York: Mouton de Gruyter, 1993) 219–32.

Jernudd, Bjørn, 'Language planning as a type of language treatment'. In Rubin, J. and R. Shuy (eds), *Language Planning: Current Issues and Research* (Washington, DC: Georgetown University Press, 1973) 11–23.

Jones, Charles, *The English Language in Scotland: An Introduction to Scots* (East Linton: Tuckwell, 2002).

Joseph, John Earl, *Eloquence and Power. The Rise of Language Standards and Standard Languages* (London: Frances Pinter, 1987).

Kelly, Adrian, *Compulsory Irish: Language and Education in Ireland 1870s-1970s* (Dublin: Irish Academic Press, 2002).

Kelly, Susan, 'Anglo-Saxon lay society and the written word'. In McKitterick, R. (ed.), *The Uses of Literacy in Early Medieval Europe* (Cambridge: Cambridge University Press, 1990) 36–62.

Kerswill, Paul, *Dialects Converging: Rural Speech in Urban Norway* (Oxford: Clarendon Press, 1994).

Khubchandani, Lachmon, 'Language Ideology and Language Development', *Linguistics* 193 (1977) 33–52.

Kloss, Heinz, ' "Abstand Languages" and "Ausbau Languages" ', *Anthropological Linguistics* 9 (1967) 29–41.

——, *Research Possibilities on Group Bilingualism: a Report* (Quebec: International Centre for Research on Bilingualism, 1969).

——, 'Abstandsprachen und Ausbausprachen'. In Göschel, J. *et al.* (eds), *Zur Theorie des Dialekts* (Wiesbaden: Frank Steiner Verlag, 1976) 301–22.

——, *Die Entwicklung neuer germanischer Kultursprachen seit 1800.* 2nd edn (Düsseldorf: Schwann, 1978).

——, 'Interlingual Communication: Danger and Chance for The Smaller Tongues', *Scottish Studies* (Frankfurt) 4 (1984) 73–7.

Kloss, Heinz and Harald Haarmann, 'The Languages of Europe and of Soviet Asia'. In Kloss, Heinz and G.D. McConnell (eds), *The Linguistic Composition of the World*. Volume 5: *Europe and the USSR* (Québec: Les Presses de l'Université Laval, 1984) 11–62.

Kniezsa, Veronika, 'The Origins of Scots Orthography'. In Jones, C. (ed.), *The Edinburgh History of the Scots Language* (Edinburgh: Edinburgh University Press, 1997) 24–46.

Knowles, Thomas D., *Ideology, Art and Commerce: Aspects of Literary Sociology in the Late Victorian Scottish Kailyard* (Göteborg: Acta Universitatis Gothoburgensis, 1983).

Koenig, Edna L., Emmanuel Chia and John Povey, *A Sociolinguistic Profile of Urban Centers in Cameroon* (Los Angeles: Crossroad Press, 1983).

Kovács, Mária M., *Liberal Professions and Illiberal Politics: Hungary from the Habsburgs to the Holocaust* (Washington, DC, New York and Oxford: Woodrow Wilson Center Press and Oxford University Press, 1994).

Krapp, George Philip, *The English Language in America*. 2 vols (New York: Century, 1925).

Kratochvíl, Paul, *The Chinese Language Today: Features of An Emerging Standard* (London: Hutchinson, 1968).

Kutscher, Eduard Yechezkel, *A History of the Hebrew Language*. Edited by Raphael Kutscher (Leiden: E.J. Brill, 1982).

Labov, William, 'The Logic of Nonstandard English'. In Alatis, J. (ed.) *Georgetown Monograph Series in Languages and Linguistics 22* (Washington, DC: Georgetown University Press, 1969) 1–44.

Lacqueur, Walter, *A History of Zionism* (New York: Schocken Books, 1976).

Laffan, Michael, *The Resurrection of Ireland: the Sinn Féin Party, 1916–1923* (Cambridge: Cambridge University Press, 1999).

Lambert, Peter, 'Paving the "Peculiar Path": German Nationalism and Historiography since Ranke'. In Cubitt, G. (ed.), *Imagining Nations* (Manchester: Manchester University Press, 1998) 92–109.

Landau, Jacob M., 'The First Turkish Language Congress'. In Fishman, J.A. (ed.), *The Earliest Stage of Language Planning. The 'First Congress' Phenomenon* (Berlin and New York: Mouton de Gruyter, 1993) 271–92.

Langer, Nils, *Linguistic Purism in Action. How Auxiliary Tun Was Stigmatized in Early New High German* (Berlin: Walter de Gruyter, 2001).

Levine, Marc V., *The Reconquest of Montreal. Language Change and Social Change in a Bilingual City* (Philadelphia, PA: Temple University Press, 1990).

Lewis, David Levering, *The Race to Fashoda: European Colonialism and African Resistance in The Scramble for Africa* (London: Bloomsbury, 1988).

Lewis, Geoffrey, *The Turkish Language Reform. A Catastrophic Success* (Oxford: Oxford University Press, 1999).

Linn, Andrew Robert, *Constructing the Grammars of a Language. Ivar Aasen and Nineteenth Century Norwegian Linguistics* (Münster: Nodus Publikationen, 1997).

Lippi-Green, Rosina, *English with An Accent: Language, Ideology, and Discrimination in the United States* (London: Routledge, 1997).

Lodge, R. Anthony, *French, from Dialect to Standard* (London: Routledge, 1993).

Macafee, C.I., *Traditional Dialect in the Modern World: A Glasgow Case Study* (Frankfurt am Main: Peter Lang, 1994).

Macafee, C.I., 'Older Scots Lexis'. In Jones, C. (ed.), *The Edinburgh History of the Scots Language* (Edinburgh: Edinburgh University Press, 1997) 182–212.

——, 'Lea the Lead Alane', *Lallans* 57 (2000a) 56–65.

——, 'The Demography of Scots: The Lessons of The Census Campaign', *Scottish Language* 19 (2000b) 1–44.

——, 'A History of Scots to 1700'. In *A Dictionary of the Older Scottish Tongue* 12 (Oxford: Oxford University Press, 2002) xxi–clvi.

McClure, J. Derrick, 'Scots: its range of uses'. In Aitken, A.J. and T. McArthur (eds) *Languages of Scotland* (Edinburgh: Edinburgh University Press, 1979) 26–48.

——, 'The synthesisers of Scots'. In McClure, J.D. (ed.), *Scots and Its Literature* (Amsterdam: John Benjamins, 1995a) 190–99.

——, 'The Concept of Standard Scots'. In McClure, J.D. (ed.), *Scots and Its Literature* (Amsterdam: John Benjamins, 1995b).

McClure, J. Derrick (ed.), *The Scots Language in Education* (Aberdeen: Aberdeen College of Education and the Association for Scottish Literary Studies, 1975).

McGarrity, Briege, A Sociolinguistic Study of Attitudes Towards and Proficiency in The Doric Dialect in Aberdeen (Unpublished MPhil dissertation, University of Aberdeen, 1998).

Magocsi, Paul Robert (ed.), *A New Slavic Language Is Born: The Rusyn Literary Language of Slovakia* (Boulder: East European Monographs, 1996).

Mamak, Alexander F., *Colour, Culture and Conflict: A Study of Pluralism in Fiji* (Rushcutters Bay, N.S.W.: Pergamon Press Australia, 1978).

Mango, Andrew, *Atatürk* (London: John Murray, 1999).

Markus, Manfred, ' "The men present" vs "the present case": Word-order Rules Concerning The Position of the English Adjective', *Anglia* 115 (1997) 487–506.

Martin, Terry, *The Affirmative Action Empire: Nations and Nationalism in the Soviet Union 1923–1939* (Ithaca, NY: Cornell University Press, 2002).

Mayo, Peter, 'Belorussian'. In Comrie, B. and G.G. Corbett (eds), *The Slavonic Languages* (London and New York, Routledge, 1993) 887–947.

Mazrui, Ali A. and Alamin M. Mazrui, *Swahili State and Society. The Political Economy of An African Language* (London: James Currey, 1995).

Meillet, Antoine, 'La Situation Linguistique en Russie et en Autriche–Hongrie'. *Scientia (Rivista di Scienza)*, Serie 2, 23 (1918) 209–16.

——, *Les langues dans l'Europe nouvelle*. 2nd edn (Paris: Payot, 1928).

Meurman-Solin, Anneli, *Variation and Change in Early Scottish Prose: Studies Based on the Helsinki Corpus of Older Scots* (Helsinki: Suomalainen Tiedeakatemia, 1993).

——, 'Differentiation and Standardisation in Early Scots'. In Jones, C. (ed.), *The Edinburgh History of the Scots Language* (Edinburgh: Edinburgh University Press, 1997) 3–23.

——, 'On the Conditioning of Geographical and Social Distance in Language Variation and Change in Renaissance Scots'. In Kastovsky, D. and A. Mettinger (eds), *The History of English in a Social Context. A Contribution to Historical Sociolinguistics* (Berlin and New York: Mouton de Gruyter, 2000) 227–55.

Meyer, Karl and Shareen Brysac, *Tournament of Shadows. The Great Game and the Race for Empire in Asia* (London: Little, Brown and Company, 1999).

Millar, Robert McColl, 'Covert and Overt Language Attitudes to the Scots Tongue Expressed in the *Statistical accounts of Scotland*'. In Kastovsky, D. and A. Mettinger (eds), *The History of English in a Social Context. A Contribution* to *Historical Sociolinguistics* (Berlin and New York: Mouton de Gruyter, 2000) 169–98.

——, 'Language, Genre, and Register: Factors in The Use of Simple Demonstrative Forms in the South-West Midlands of the Thirteenth Century'. In Allen, R. *et al.* (eds), *Lazamon Contexts, Language and Interpretation* (London: King's College London Centre for Late Antique & Medieval Studies, 2002) 227–39.

——, ' "Blind attachment to inveterate customs." Language Use, Language Attitude and the Rhetoric of Improvement in the First *Statistical Account*'. In Dossena, M. and C. Jones (eds), *Insights into Late Modern English* (Bern: Peter Lang, 2003) 311–30.

——, 'Linguistic History on the Margins of the Germanic-speaking World: Some Preliminary Thoughts'. In McClure, J.D. (ed.), *Doonsin' Emerauds: New Scrieves anent Scots and Gaelic/New Studies in Scots and Gaelic* (Belfast: Cló Ollscoil na Banríona, 2004a) 3–17.

——, 'Kailyard, Conservatism and Scots in the *Statistical Accounts of Scotland*'. In Kay, C.J. *et al.* (eds), *New Perspectives on English Historical Linguistics* (Amsterdam: John Benjamins, 2004b) 163–76.

Milton, Colin, 'Hugh MacDiarmid and North-East Scots'. *Scottish Language* 5 (1986) 39–47.

Moleas, Wendy, *The Development of the Greek Language* (Bristol: Bristol Classical Press, 1989).

Montgomery, Michael, 'Exploring the Roots of Appalachian English', *English World-Wide* 10 (1989) 227–78.

——, 'The Scotch-Irish Element in Appalachian English: How Broad? How Deep?' In Wood, C. and T. Blethen (eds), *Ulster and North America: Transatlantic Perspectives on the Scotch Irish* (Juscoloosa: University of Alabama Press, 1997) 189–212.

——, 'In the Appalachians They Speak like Shakespeare'. In Bauer, L. and P. Trudgill (eds), *Myths in Linguistics* (Harmondsworth: Penguin, 1998) 66–76.

——, 'British and Irish Antecedents'. In Algeo, J. (ed.), *The Cambridge History of the English Language* Vol. VI *English in North America* (Cambridge: Cambridge University Press, 2001) 85–153.

Moskowitch, Isabel, 'The Adjective in English: the "French type" and Its Place in The History of the Language', *Folia Linguistica Historica* 23 (2002) 59–71.

Mufwene, Salikoko S., 'Pidgins, Creoles, Typology and Markedness'. In Byrne, F. and T. Huebner (eds), *Development and Structures of Creole Languages: Essays in Honour of Derek Bickerton* (Amsterdam: John Benjamins, 1991) 123–43.

——, 'What is African American English?' In Lanehart, S.L. (eds), *Sociocultural and Historical Contexts of African American English* (Amsterdam: John Benjamins, 2001) 21–51.

——, 'African-American English'. In Algeo, J. (ed.), *The Cambridge History of the English Language*. Vol. VI *English in North America* (Cambridge: Cambridge University Press, 2001) 291–324.

Mugglestone, Lynda, *Talking Proper: The Rise of Accent as Social Symbol* (Oxford: Clarendon Press, 1995).

Mugglestone, Lynda (ed.), *Lexicography and the OED: Pioneers in The Untrodden Forest* (Oxford: Oxford University Press, 2000).

Muljačić, Žarko, 'Il termine *lingue distanziate apparentemente dialettalizzate* e la sua rilevanza per la sociolinguistica romana', *Studia Romanica et Anglica Zagrabiensia* 26 (1981) 85–102.

Muljačić, Žarko, 'L'Enseignement de Heinz Kloss (Modifications, Implications, Perspectives)', *Langages* (Paris) 21 (1986) 53–63.
——, 'Über den Begriff *Dachsprache*'. In Ammon, U. (ed.), *Status and Function of Languages and Language Varieties* (Berlin and New York: Walter de Gruyter, 1989) 256–75.
Murdoch, Steve, *Language Politics in Scotland* (Aberdeen: Aiberdeen Universitie Scots Leid Quorum, 1995).
Murray, K.M. Elisabeth, *Caught in the Web of Words* (New Haven, CT: Yale University Press, 1977).
Neustupny, J.V., 'Basic Types of Treatment of Language Problems', *Linguistic Communications* 1 (1970) 77–98.
Niedzielski, Nancy A. and Dennis R. Preston, *Folk Linguistics* (Berlin and New York: Mouton de Gruyter, 2003).
Niven, Liz and Robin Jackson (eds.), *The Scots Language: Its Place in Education*. (Dumfries: Watergaw, 1998).
Ochs, Elinor, 'A Sliding Sense of Obligatoriness: The Polystructure of Malagasy Oratory', *Language in Society* 2 (1973) 225–43.
Oergel, Maike, 'The Redeeming Teuton: Nineteenth Century Notions of the Germanic in England and Germany'. In Cubitt, G. (ed.), *Imagining Nations* (Manchester: Manchester University Press, 1998) 75–91.
Pâclişanu, Zenobius, *Hungary's Struggle to Annihilate its National Minorities. Based on Secret Hungarian Documents*. Translated by Dora Kennedy (Miami Beach: Romanian Historical Studies, 1985 (1941)).
Palmer, Leonard R., *The Greek Language* (London: Faber and Faber, 1980).
Park, Nahm-Sheik, 'Language Purism in Korea Today'. In Jernudd, B. and M.J. Shapiro (eds), *The Politics of Language Purism* (Berlin and New York: Mouton de Gruyter, 1989) 113–39.
Parkin, David, 'Language, Government and The Play on Purity and Impurity. Arabic, Swahili and The Vernaculars in Kenya'. In Fardon, R. and G. Furniss (eds), *African Languages, Development and the State* (London: Routledge, 1994) 227–45.
Parry, Mair, 'Sardinian'. In Price, G. (ed.), *Encyclopaedia of the Languages of Europe* (Oxford: Blackwell, 1998) 273–5.
Pašeta, Senia, *Before the Revolution: Nationalism, Social Change and Ireland's Catholic Elite, 1879–1922* (Cork: Cork University Press, 1999).
Pfalzgraf, Falco, 'Sprachschutzvereine und Rechtsextremismus', *German Life and Letters* 1 (2003) 102–16.
Phillipson, Robert, *English-Only Europe? Challenging Language Policy* (London: Routledge, 2003).
Pipes, Richard, *The Formation of the Soviet Union: Communism and Nationalism 1917–1923* (Cambridge, MA: Harvard University Press, 1964).
Pollner, Clausdirk, 'Old words in a Young Town', *Scottish Language* 4 (1985) 5–15.
Pope, M.K., *From Latin to Modern French*. 2nd edn (Manchester: Manchester University Press, 1952).
Preston, Dennis R., 'Where the Worst English Is Spoken'. In Schneider, E.W. (ed.), *Focus on the USA* (Amsterdam and Philadelphia: John Benjamins, 1996) 297–360.
Pulgram, A., 'Spoken and written Latin', *Language* 26 (1950) 458–66.

Quatrième Congrès International de Linguistes (eds), *Actes du Quatrième Congrès International de Linguistes* (Copenhagen: Einar Munksgaard, 1938).

Ó Riagáin, P., 'Irish Language Production and Reproduction 1981–1996'. In Fishman, J.A. (ed.), *Can Threatened Languages be Saved?* (Clevedon: Multilingual Matters, 2001) 195–214.

Rindler Schjerve, Rosita (ed.), *Diglossia and Power. Language Policies and Practice in the 19th Century Habsburg Empire* (Berlin and New York: Mouton de Gruyter, 2003).

Rubin, Joan, 'Evaluation and language planning'. In Rubin, J. and B.H. Jernudd (eds), *Can Language Be Planned?* (Honolulu: University Press of Hawaii, 1971) 217–52.

Sáenz-Badillos, Angel, *A History of the Hebrew Language.* Translated by John Elwode (Cambridge: Cambridge University Press, 1993).

Sahlins, Peter, *Boundaries: the making of France and Spain in the Pyrenees* (Berkeley: University of California Press, 1989).

Samuels, M.L., 'Some Applications of Middle English Dialectology'. In Laing, M. (ed.), *Middle English Dialectology. Essays on Some Principles and Problems* (Aberdeen: Aberdeen University Press, 1989) 64–80.

Saulson, Scott B. (ed.), *Institutionalized Language Planning. Documents and Analysis of the Revival of Hebrew* (The Hague: Mouton, 1978).

Schiffman, Harold F., *Linguistic Culture and Language Policy* (London: Routledge, 1996).

Scots Pairlament Cross Pairty Group on the Scots Language, *Scots. A Statement of Principles. A Road Forrit for the Scots Language in a Multilingual Scotland* (Edinburgh: Scots Pairlament Cross Pairty Group on the Scots Language, 2003).

Ševčik, D., 'Český jazkový purismus z hlediska funkční teorie spisovného jazyka', *Sborník prací Filosofické fakulty Brnnské university, Řady jazykov dné* 22–23 (1974–1975) 49–58.

Shaw, Stanford J. and Ezel Kural Shaw, *History of the Ottoman Empire and Modern Turkey.* 2 vols (Cambridge: Cambridge University Press, 1977).

Shevelov, George Y., 'Ukrainian'. In Comrie, B. and G.G. Corbett, (eds), *The Slavonic Languages* (London and New York: Routledge, 1993) 947–98.

Shou-yi, Ch'ën, *Chinese Literature. A Historical Introduction* (New York: The Roland Press Company, 1961).

Simpson, David, *The Politics of American English, 1776–1850* (New York and Oxford: Oxford University Press, 1986).

Simpson, J.A. and E.S.C. Weiner (eds.), *The Oxford English Dictionary.* 2nd edn (Oxford: Clarendon Press, 1989).

Skutnaab-Kangas, Tove, *Linguistic Genocide in Education – or Worldwide Diversity and Human Rights* (Mahwah, NJ: Lawrence Erlbaum Associates, 2000).

Smith, Anthony D., *Theories of Nationalism* (London: Duckworth, 1971).

Smith, Graham, *The Baltic States: the National Self-determination of Estonia, Latvia and Lithuania* (New York: St. Martin's Press, 1994).

Smith, Graham (ed.), *The Nationalities Question in the Soviet Union* (Harlow: Longman, 1990).

Smith, Jeremy, *The Bolsheviks and the National Question, 1917–23* (Basingstoke: Macmillan Press, 1999).

Smith, Jeremy J., *An Historical Study of English: Function, Form and Change* (London: Routledge, 1996).

Smith, Richard J., *China's Cultural Heritage: The Qing Dynasty, 1644–1912*. 2nd edn (Boulder, CO: Westview Press, 1994).

Sommerfelt, Alf, 'Conditions de la formation d'une langue commune'. In Quatrième Congrès International de Linguistes (eds), *Actes du Quatrième Congrès International de Linguistes* (Copenhagen: Einar Munksgaard, 1938) 42–8.

Spolsky, Bernard, *Language Policy* (Cambridge: Cambridge University Press, 2004).

Stanley, E.G., 'Lazamon's Antiquarian Sentiments', *Medium Ævum* 38 (1969) 23–37.

——, 'Karl Luick's "Man schrieb wie man sprach" and English Historical Philology'. In Kastovsky, D. and G. Bauer (eds), *Luick Revisited* (Tübingen: Naar, 1988) 311–34.

Stein, Dieter and Ingrid Tieken-Boon van Ostade (eds), *Towards a Standard English 1600–1800* (Berlin and New York: Mouton de Gruyter, 1994).

Stewart, William A., 'An Outline of Linguistic Typology for Describing Multilingualism'. In Rice, F.A. (ed.), *Study of the Role of Second Languages in Asia, Africa, and Latin America* (Washington, DC: Center for Applied Linguistics of the Modern Language Association of America, 1962) 15–25.

——, 'A Sociolinguistic Typology For Describing National Multilingualism'. In Fishman, J.A. (ed.), *Readings in the Sociology of Language* (The Hague and Paris: Mouton, 1968) 531–44.

Stirling, Angus, 'On a Standardised Spelling for Scots', *Scottish Language* 13 (1994) 88–93.

Suleiman, Yasir, *The Arabic Language and National Identity* (Edinburgh: Edinburgh University Press, 2003).

Thaden, Edward C., *Conservative Nationalism in Nineteenth-Century Russia* (Seattle: University of Washington Press, 1964).

Thalheim, Karl C., 'Russia's Economic Development'. In Katkov, G. *et al.* (eds), *Russia Enters the Twentieth Century* (London: Temple Smith, 1971) 85–110.

Thomas, George, *Linguistic Purism* (London and New York: Longman, 1991).

Thomason, Sarah Grey and Terrence Kaufman, *Language Contact, Creolization, and Genetic Linguistics* (Berkeley, CA: University of California Press, 1988).

Thomson, George, *The Greek Language* (Cambridge: W. Heffer & Sons, 1960).

Trudgill, Peter, *On Dialect* (Oxford: Basil Blackwell, 1983).

——, 'Contact and isolation in linguistic change'. In Breivik, L.E. and E.H. Jahr (eds), *Language Change. Contributions to the Study of its Causes* (Berlin and New York: Mouton de Gruyter, 1989) 227–37.

——, 'Greece and European Turkey: From Religious to Linguistic Identity'. In Barbour, S. and C. Carmichael (eds), *Language and Nationalism in Europe* (Oxford: Oxford University Press, 2000) 240–63.

——, *Sociolinguistic Variation and Change* (Edinburgh: Edinburgh University Press, 2002).

——, *New-Dialect Formation: The Inevitability of Colonial Englishes* (Edinburgh: Edinburgh University Press, 2004).

Ureland, Sture (ed.), *Sprachkontakt in der Hanse. Aspekte des Sprachausgleichs im Ostsee- und Nordseeraum* (Tübingen: Max Niemeyer Verlag, 1987).

Veltman, Calvin, *Language Shift in the United States* (Berlin, New York and Amsterdam: Mouton, 1983).

Vital, David, *The Origins of Zionism* (Oxford: Clarendon Press, 1975).

Weber, Daniel Erich, *Sprach- und Mundartpflege in der deutschsprachigen Schweiz: Sprachnorm und Sprachdidaktik im zweisprachformigen Staat* (Frauenfeld: Huber, 1984).

Weinreich, Max, *A History of the Yiddish Language*. Translated by Shlomo Noble with the assistance of Joshua A. Fishman (Chicago and London: University of Chicago Press, 1973).

Wells, C.J., *German: A Linguistic History to 1945* (Oxford: Clarendon Press, 1985).

Wheatcroft, Andrew, *The Habsburgs: Embodying Empire* (London: Viking, 1995a).

——, *The Ottomans: Dissolving Images* (Harmondsworth: Penguin, 1995b).

Williams, A. and P. Kerswill, 'Dialect Levelling: Change and Continuity in Milton Keynes, Reading and Hull'. In Foulkes, P. and G. Docherty (eds), *Urban Voices* (Oxford: Oxford University Press, 1999) 141–62.

Willinsky, John, *Empire of Words: The Reign of the OED* (Princeton: Princeton University Press, 1994).

Winder, R. Bayly, *Saudi Arabia in the Nineteenth Century* (London: Macmillan, 1965).

Wolf, Hans-Georg, *English in Cameroon* (Berlin and New York: Mouton De Gruyter, 2001).

Wolfram, Walt, Carolyn Temple Adger and Donna Christian, *Dialects in Schools and Communities* (Mahwah, NJ: Lawrence Erlbaum Associates, 1999).

Woolard, Kathryn A., 'Voting Rights, Liberal Voters and the Official English Movement: An Analysis of Campaign Rhetoric in San Francisco's Proposition "O" '. In Adams, K.L. and D.T. Brink (eds), *Perspectives on Official English. The Campaign for English as the Official Language of the USA* (Berlin and New York: Mouton du Gruyter, 1990) 125–37.

Wormser, Richard, *The Rise and Fall of Jim Crow* (New York: St. Martin's Press, 2003).

Wright, Sue, *Language Policy and Language Planning. From Nationalism to Globalisation* (Palgrave Macmillan: Basingstoke, 2004).

Yemelianova, Galina M., *Russia and Islam: A Historical Survey* (Basingstoke: Palgrave, 2002).

Zielińska, Anna, 'The Sociolinguistic Situation of the Polish Language of the Slavic–Lithuanian Borderlands (the Region of the Present-day countries: Byelorussia, Lithuania and Latvia)', *Folia Linguistica* 36 (2002) 359–80.

Index